Key Contemporary Social Theorists

Key Contemporary Social Theorists

Edited by

Anthony Elliott and Larry Ray

Blackwell
Publishing

© 2003 by Blackwell Publishers Ltd
a Blackwell Publishing company

350 Main Street, Malden, MA 02148-5018, USA
108 Cowley Road, Oxford OX4 1JF, UK
550 Swanston Street, Carlton, Victoria 3053, Australia
Kurfürstendamm 57, 10707 Berlin, Germany

First published 2003 by Blackwell Publishers Ltd

Library of Congress Cataloging-in-Publication Data

Key contemporary social theorists / edited by Anthony Elliott and Larry Ray.
    p. cm.
Includes bibliographical references and index.
    ISBN 0–631–21971–4 (alk. paper) — ISBN 0–631–21972–2 (alk. paper)
    1. Social sciences—Philosophy.   2. Sociologists.   I. Elliott, Anthony.
II. Ray, Larry.
    H61 .K473 2002
    300′.1—dc21

                                                            2001007499

A catalogue record for this title is available from the British Library.

Set in 10.5 on 12 pt. Imprint
by Ace Filmsetting Ltd, Frome, Somerset
Printed and bound in the United Kingdom
by MPG Books Ltd, Bodmin, Cornwall

For further information on
Blackwell Publishers, visit our website:
http://www.blackwellpublishing.com

Contents

Contributors

Zygmunt Bauman is Emeritus Professor of Sociology at the Universities of Leeds and Warsaw

Ted Benton is Professor of Sociology at the University of Essex.

Roy Boyne is Professor of Sociology at the University of Durham.

Rex Butler is Senior Lecturer in Art History at the University of Queensland.

Howard Caygill is Professor of Cultural History at Goldsmiths College, University of London.

Claire Colebrook is at the University of Edinburgh.

Paul Colomy is Professor of Sociology at the University of Denver.

Gerard Delanty is Professor of Sociology at the University of Liverpool.

John S. Dryzek is Professor of Political Science at the Australian National University.

Anthony Elliott is Professor of Social and Political Theory at the University of the West of England, where he is Director of the Centre for Critical Theory.

Matthew Festenstein is Lecturer in Politics at the University of Sheffield.

Stephen Frosh is Professor of Psychology at Birkbeck College, University of London.

Phillip Hansen is Professor of Political Science at the University of Regina, Saskatchewan.

Kevin Hart is Professor of English and Comparative Literature at Monash University, Melbourne.

Annamarie Jagose is Senior Lecturer in English and Cultural Studies at the University of Melbourne.

Michael Kenny is Reader in Politics at the University of Sheffield.

Robert van Krieken is Senior Lecturer at the Department of Social Work, Social Policy and Sociology in the University of Sydney.

John Lechte is Associate Professor in Sociology at Macquarie University, Sydney.

Kwok Wei Leng is Consultant at the National Centre for Gender and Cultural Diversity, Swinburne University of Technology, and Fellow of the Ashworth Centre for Social Theory, University of Melbourne.

Joost van Loon is at Nottingham Trent University.

Kevin McDonald is Senior Lecturer in Sociology at the University of Melbourne.

Scott McQuire is Senior Lecturer in the Media and Communication Program at the University of Melbourne.

Diana Tietjens Meyers is at the University of Connecticut, Storrs.

Don Miller is Associate Professor and Head of Anthropology at Monash University, Melbourne.

Andrew Milner is Professor and Director of the Centre for Comparative Literature and Cultural Studies at Monash University, Melbourne.

Bart Moore-Gilbert is Reader in Postcolonial Studies and English at Goldsmiths' College, University of London.

Maggie O'Neill is Reader in Sociology at Staffordshire University.

William Outhwaite is Professor of Sociology at the University of Sussex.

Larry Ray is Professor of Sociology at the University of Kent.

Dieter Rucht is Professor of Sociology at the Social Science Research Center, Berlin.

Barry Smart is Professor of Sociology at the School of Social and Historical Studies at the University of Portsmouth.

Kay Torney Souter is Senior Lecturer at the School of Communication, Arts and Critical Enquiry at La Trobe University.

Nick Stevenson is Senior Lecturer in Sociology and Social Policy at the School of Sociology and Social Policy at the University of Nottingham.

Jem Thomas is Associate Dean, Faculty of Economics and Social Science, at the University of the West of England.

Ian Varcoe is Lecturer in Sociology at the University of Leeds.

Malcolm Waters is Professor of Sociology at the University of Tasmania.

David West is Senior Lecturer in Political Theory at the Australian National University.

James Williams is Lecturer in Philosophy at the University of Dundee.

Yves Winkin is Professeur des Universités (Sciences de la Communication) at the École Normale Supérieure Lettres et Sciences humaines, Lyon.

Introduction

Anthony Elliott and Larry Ray

Over the past twenty years, social theory has undergone dramatic changes. There has been a widespread sense of disillusionment with classical forms of social thought (Marxist, Durkheimian, Weberian), and a significant proliferation in new conceptual approaches. This diversification has ranged from a re-examination and revitalization of older traditions of thought, such as the remarkable resurgence of Marxist cultural theory, largely under the impact of a major revival of radical political activity in the post-communist period, to the elaboration of novel standpoints, including cultural studies, postfeminism and queer theory (notably Sedgwick). Traditions of thought previously ignored or marginalized have been retrieved or rediscovered, oftentimes reinterpreted and transfigured in the process. So it was that the "return to Freud" advanced by Jacques Lacan sought to recontextualize the unconscious codes which govern intersubjectivity around interpretive processes of culture and communication. A similarly impressive reinterpretation of classical texts has been evident in hermeneutics, as developed especially in the writings of Ricoeur and Gadamer. And in the face of the explosion of interest in structuralism and poststructuralism across Europe, the 1990s witnessed the rise of postmodernism, in which core poststructural tropes – decentered subjectivity, difference, otherness, undecidability, and ambivalence – were applied writ large to postmodern culture and other forms of identity politics.

This rapid expansion in competing versions of social theory has in turn been conditioned by broad-ranging changes in social relations and modern institutions. For example, the analysis of postmodern or cosmopolitan culture as a core concern of social theory can be viewed as the complex overdetermined effect of the power and process of globalization, transnational finance and capital movements, as well as global civil society. Indeed, a vast range of social developments and political transformations – including new information technologies, the hypertechnologization of war, the proliferation of globalized risk (ecological problems, pandemics, etc.) – have been critical to both disciplinary specialization and interdisciplinary studies within the academic humanities and social sciences. As a result social theory, while thrown into disarray in terms of the established canon, has been equally reinvigorated or reinvented; indeed, contemporary social theory has underpinned academic output in fields as diverse as gender studies, cultural studies, film studies, psychoanalytic studies, communications and media studies, postcolonialism, and queer theory.

One of the most significant political transformations reshaping the social sciences and social theory has been the global impact of the collapse of Soviet communism. According to many, at least in the initial aftermath of the disintegration of the Soviet bloc countries during 1989, socialism was dead as a model for an alternative social order. This was said to be true at both the level of practice (as a system of economic management, socialism was entirely discredited) and that of theory (Marx's arguments concerning the transcendence of capitalism by socialism were fundamentally flawed). Alongside this was the crisis in Western social democracy and the post-World War II welfare settlement, theorized in different ways by Stuart Hall and Claus Offe, among others. We are now faced, as for instance Offe and Alain Touraine have argued in various ways, with the fragmentation of many postwar structures and their associated identities. The two processes were mutually supportive in that the demise of social democracy combined with the new global neoliberal hegemony to set the terms of prevailing analysis and options in the post-communist world. Even so, contentions about the "end of history" and the final nail in Marx's intellectual coffin proved to be premature and ideological. For while many Marxist social theorists acknowledged both the determinism and scientism that pervades Marx's writings, it is the case that the critical and utopian strands that characterized his approach to social scientific understanding remain of key importance to the development of social theory.

Critical theory, associated here particularly with Theodor Adorno, Max Horkheimer, Walter Benjamin, Herbert Marcuse, and latterly Jürgen Habermas, has had a crucial role in these developments. Revived in the late 1960s as prophets of counter-cultural politics and the Grand Refusal, they were gradually integrated into the canon of social theory in the following decades. Critical theory in turn had drawn upon a powerful array of thinkers within the canon of social theory, including Marx, Nietzsche, Weber, and Freud, who were melded into a self-consciously uneasy association. Weber's work was deployed in this and many other subsequent developments. Eschewing Weber's resignation regarding rationalization, the "iron cage" of rationality and bureaucracy, critical theory recovered a utopian moment of potential redemption that could be located in transcendent forms of art and philosophy. Nonetheless, Weber was deployed in critical theory's novel and devastating critiques of bureaucratic domination, scientific and technical reason, and authoritarianism. Though not without contemporary feminist critics, Adorno, Horkheimer, and Marcuse anticipated many contemporary themes including the interconnections between patriarchy, psychodynamics, ecological destruction, the body, colonialism, and scientific reason, which had been treated as largely unproblematic by orthodox Marxism. Critical theory represented a decisive departure from orthodox Marxism. Modern cultural and productive conditions, with their new "subtle apparatuses" (as Horkheimer put it) protected capitalism against revolutionary consciousness, which meant that the traditional addressee of Marxism, the proletariat, was no longer a meaningful subject. Critical theory thus had a crucial role in shifting the terrain of Western Marxism into the areas of cultural critique and psychoanalysis in ways that were later to become central to contemporary social theory.

A diversity of figures in the last fifteen or twenty years has been involved in rethinking the broader political dimensions of Marx's social theory – including Raymond Williams, Fredric Jameson, Slavoj Žižek, and many others. One central element of such reformulation or questioning of the Marxist tradition has involved an attempt to enlarge the conception of the economic ramifications of capitalism itself, so that the historical, political, psychological, ideological, and philosophical resonances of the dynamic role of the free market might become more available to critical self-reflection and thus transformation. Certainly, Habermas's formulation of communications theory is an especially impressive attempt to reconnect the energizing critical component of Marxism to the challenges posed by globalizing social forces. Another element has involved a thorough-going investigation into the mystifying sociocultural forms through which late or advanced capitalism expands ruthlessly across global political space, penetrating deeply into the fabric of daily life and the emotional core of interpersonal relationships. The principal figure here is Jameson, who in a breathtaking articulation within a transfigured Marxist discourse deconstructs postmodernism as part and parcel of the cultural logic of the global market. A related analysis has been developed by Žižek, who ties structural Marxism and Lacanian psychoanalysis together in a reflective configuration to examine the symbolic forms of post-contemporary culture as well as the reified, ahistorical frame of global politics.

Most of the substantive debates in social theory of the past few decades have in some sense concerned the relation between self and society. Of course, the influence of Freud looms large here. For Freud, the relationship between self and society is one of conflict, tension, and ambivalence, not only as the result of impinging oppressive social forces, but because sexual contradiction and emotional dislocation are fundamental to the interpenetration of the individual and society. The subtle and subversive power of the repressed unconscious in day-to-day social life is one of Freud's principal themes, from *The Interpretation of Dreams* to *Civilization and its Discontents*. It is fair to say that Freud's account of the trade-off between repressed desire and cultural order has long influenced the terms of debate in social, cultural, and political theory – from the writings of the German critical theorist Herbert Marcuse to the analysis of self-identity developed by the British sociologist Anthony Giddens.

A new chapter was opened in the dialogue between social theory and psychoanalysis when the French psychoanalyst Jacques Lacan declared, infamously, that "the unconscious is structured like a language." Until some twenty years ago the main line of conceptual orientation in psychoanalytically inspired social thought was drive theory, in which the tension between psyche and culture was carved as a battle of competing organic forces – self-preservation vs. pleasure, Eros vs. the death drive. Rereading Freud through the linguistic turn in social philosophy, Lacan dramatically changed all this, the upshot of his argument being that the structure of language constitutes the repressed unconscious, with the speaking subject cast as derivative of those metonymic substitutions around which desire forever circulates. The Lacanian tradition, in Europe and the USA, quickly established itself as the preeminent version of Freud in social-theoretical debate and cultural analysis. Somewhat ironically, given that Lacan's self-appointed task was to systematically ground the tenets of Freudianism in a "scientific" mathematical logic, social theorists initially turned to Lacan's Freud to rectify the impasses of a dominant rationalistic theory of the human subject. In more explicitly political terms, it was the attempt to build a bridge to Marxism that led social theorists to Lacan's ideas, principally as represented in the writings of Louis Althusser, yet similar lines of thought were also evident in the works of Jameson, Hall, Žižek, and many others.

The popularity of Lacan in social theory was nowhere more evident than in feminism. During the late 1970s and early 1980s, feminist theoreticians borrowed heavily from Lacan to examine the psychic consequences of capitalist patriarchy, and indeed the uniquely pessimistic phallicism that pervaded French Freudianism reproduced itself in Anglo-American studies of all things sexual – from fetishism to gender bending. However, the political fatalism of structural psychoanalysis –

particularly the dead ends of Lacan's linguistic phallocentrism – eventually exhausted his most seemingly devoted supporters, which bred in its wake the conceptual development of neo-Lacanianism or post-Lacanianism. While broadly sympathetic to the conceptual edifice of Lacanianism, this brand of feminist social thought is also "anti-Lacanian" in that it dethrones the view that woman can only be defined as the mirror opposite of masculine subjectivity. In the writings of the French feminist Luce Irigaray one finds, for instance, an explicit attempt to give the slip to phallic law by symbolizing and refiguring the multiple and plural dimensions of female sexuality. In a related, though analytically distinct manner, Julia Kristeva also tracks the emotional impact of the feminine in the constitution of the self, which she theorizes as unfolding during the pre-Oedipal "semiotic" space of mother–infant interaction.

A similar suspicion of symbolic determination and linguistic phallocentrism can be found in feminist object-relations theory. Rejecting the Freudian and Lacanian conceptualization of Oedipal and symbolic productions of gender, feminist object-relations theorists refocus psychoanalysis upon pre-Oedipal emotional communication, with particular attention given to the mother–infant bond. The American social theorist Nancy Chodorow, more than any other feminist, has been a central figure here. In Chodorow's feminist sociology, the small infant's interactions with the pre-Oedipal mother are treated as crucial to the formation of gender in the drafting of selfhood and sexual identity. Chodorow's claim that exclusive female mothering is pivotal to the reproduction of male-dominant gender relations has been hugely influential in feminist social theory, even if subsequent studies in gender relations have sought to modify or extend the parameters of her original thesis. Somewhat like Chodorow, Jessica Benjamin has also directed attention to both pre-Oedipal and post-Oedipal relational configurations in the constitution of gendered identity. Benjamin's work is extremely subtle, focusing analytical attention on the complex forms of sexuality and gender as experienced by men and women.

The attempt to theorize beyond conventional categories and divisions informs much other contemporary social theory too. Beck's theory of the "risk society" has sought to undermine more traditional notions of class, ethnic, and gender divisions and has opened up a new terrain of theorizing. Bhabha's concepts of ambivalence, hybridity, mimicry, and the "third space" have challenged conventional understandings of colonial relations, and have made him one of the most influential theoreticians of diasporic culture. Deleuze's attempt to think "life" freed from any specific point of view or actual being is a radical assault on philosophies that attempt to ground themselves in fixed foundations. The undermining of foundations and the development of new forms of subversion was central too in Derrida's critique of presence, difference, writing, and logocentrism.

However, with the collapse of earlier certainties, newly emerging lines of cleavage have appeared. There is considerable dispute as to the significance of recent social changes as there is around theories that seek to radically undermine post-Enlightenment forms of thinking. While Bauman wished to celebrate postmodernity as modernity becoming conscious of itself and aware of its own limits, others see various dangers in these developments, notably of relativism. Contemporary social theory thus inevitably exhibits tensions and controversies. Against postmodernist theory there has been a sustained return to more classical forms of modernist sociological theory. The incorporation of Weberian themes in social theory, which was central in critical theory, took a different and anti-utopian direction in the development of evolutionary functional theories of social differentiation. In Talcott Parsons, Jeffrey Alexander, Niklas Luhmann, and Habermas (despite very significant differences between them) social differentiation and increasing complexity are seen as the over-arching features of modern societies. One consequence of this analysis is to limit the possibilities for radical political action to those areas of social organization where change is consistent with managing complex and multiple layers of social interaction. Institutional differentiation of society into spheres of economy, state, community and personality, public and private realms, interactions between which are steered by media such as money and power, are viewed as evolutionary achievements. Any project of social reconstruction that entails, in Luhmann's terms, de-differentiation, collapsing boundaries between these subsystems, is doomed either to failure or regression or both. Indeed, for Habermas, postmodern philosophy and politics risk abandoning the intellectual and institutional achievements of modernity – notably democratic polity, universalism, civil society, and rights-based republican legality.

Theories of social differentiation highlight a number of contemporary social changes crucial to understanding the potential for critical political practice. This poses the key question of what basic rights free and equal citizens must mutually accord one another if they want to regulate their common life legitimately. There are several issues here. First, is pluralism a world of complex institutions, practices, norms, and values, which give human experience its identifiable character? In bearing with others, as Arendt puts it, we accept principles of plurality and the "otherness" of others. One consequence of this is that social integration becomes increasingly formal and procedural, since we share in common fewer and fewer substantive norms and beliefs. Another approach to this is offered by Bryan S. Turner, who attempts to ground a theory of human rights in an ontological vulnerability that ultimately binds us all together. Secondly, there is the process of "disenchantment of the world," in which appeal to mystical and magical forces recedes from modern worldviews. Most public institutions can no longer derive legitimacy from an appeal to spiritual or supernatural forces or beliefs and in everyday life we are compelled to provide good reasons, rather than supernatural invocations, for ethical choices. This is a controversial claim since there are always potentials for the resurgence of myth, but virtually all contemporary theorists regard the world as knowable, rather than mysterious, albeit via radically different methods of inquiry. Thirdly, there is the process of globalization and formation of transnational identities. Unprecedented population mobility in the later twentieth century, combined with worldwide and often instantaneous flows of cultural images, finance, and media, elevated these processes onto a global scale. One consequence of this, as Bhabha has highlighted through the concept of its hybrid "third space," has been to generate new forms of cultural hybridity and transnational identities. Globalization is more generally credited by Giddens with a radical distanciation of time and space, as social interactions are stretched across time and space in ways that render problematic traditional understandings of "society" as a territorially bounded space.

These processes have in turn been bound up with long-term shifts in self and society. First, social integration is dependent on the development of mechanisms for negotiating difference, which become increasingly based in legal procedures and rights. But, secondly, this is not a simple or automatic process. The extension of rights and entitlements based on universalistic principles (the struggles for suffrage and for civil rights) became one of the hardest fought political battles of the twentieth century. Again, there is no ontologically privileged subject of history, whose particular emancipation entails the emancipation of all. Rather, there are multiple practices and sites of conflict, especially those defined by the collapse of welfare and the intrusion of global processes into locales. In this process, social movements were crucial agents around which new conceptions of rights and entitlements were formed and institutionalized. Thirdly, blind obedience to external authority has been weakened by all of these changes mentioned above, and an increasing onus is placed on individual self-regulation and responsibility for the ordering and regulating of bodies and emotions. The disciplining and policing of motives and intentions acquire a more central place in systems of control. Fourthly, Norbert Elias claimed there is a "civilizing process," which is part of a profound change in public sensibilities. Repugnance towards physical violence increased with advancing thresholds of shame and embarrassment surrounding the body: thus acts once performed publicly, such as defecation and sexual intercourse, became intensely private. Elias noted how the growth of increasingly mannered social interaction, roughly from the seventeenth and eighteenth centuries, was accompanied by increased public intolerance of violence. Most people now regard carnivals of violence, such as public executions or the torture of animals, as deeply repugnant. This view is broadly consistent with Michel Foucault's depiction of the transition between the public spectacle of torture and the enclosed disciplinary practices of the carceral institution.

This brings us to the question, implicit in the above, but not posed directly: what is social theory for? There are of course many answers to this. For Comte, the purpose of sociology (which was always theoretical) was "savoir pour prévoir, prévoir pour pouvoir." For Marx, theory was to be the "head" to the "body" of the revolutionary proletariat. But classical sociologists, especially Weber and Simmel, also tended to have a clear sense of the paradoxes and ambiguities of modernity, which they attempted to capture within their theoretical framework. During the mid-twentieth century, positivistic conceptions of theory, as susceptible to verification through empirical research, became dominant, such that the abstrusely theoretical system-builder Talcott Parsons intended his work to be subject to empirical testing. This view of theory has now mostly receded, to be replaced by a more traditional notion of theories as organizing frameworks of sensitizing concepts. Another aspect of social theory (made more explicit in some than others) is that they do not merely generalize complex and nuanced social trends and processes within a systematic conceptual framework, but contain within them a vision of a good society. Even Luhmann's highly technocratic vision of society made up of self-closing autopoetic systems is quite prescriptive about what forms of political and social action can (and should) be contemplated and those which should not. Habermasian social theory is probably the most explicitly linked to a vision of a good (if ultimately unattainable) society of free and equal speaking citizens. But these implicit or explicit codas raise the issue not just of empirical but of ethical validity. Again, different theories have different ways of addressing this – from Habermas's explicit grounding of validity claims within a theory of speech acts to Richard Rorty's anti-foundationalism and then postmodern relativism. The answers given to these issues by the theorists in this volume will differ considerably. But they all invite the reader to engage with the central social, cultural, ethical, and political processes of the contemporary period.

1 | Theodor Adorno

Maggie O'Neill

Ideas
Authoritarian personality □ Culture industry □ Kulturkritik □
Negative dialectics □ Non-identity thinking □ Unintentional truth

Major books
The Authoritarian Personality (1950)
Prisms (1967)
Dialectic of Enlightenment (with Horkheimer) (1972)
The Jargon of Authenticity (1973)
Negative Dialectics (1973)
Minima Moralia (1974)
The Positivist Dispute in German Sociology (1976)
Against Epistemology (1982)
Aesthetic Theory (1984 and 1997)
Quasi una fantasia (1994)

Influences
Benjamin (Walter) □ Freud □ Hegel □ Kant □ Lukács □ Marx
□ Nietzsche

Biographical Details

Theodor Adorno (1903–69) was an outstanding social and cultural theorist, a member of the Frankfurt School, and Professor of Sociology and
Philosophy at the University of Frankfurt. His work is notoriously difficult to understand. Adorno refused to simplify his ideas into the con-
versational form of everyday language and "demanded of the listener
not mere contemplation but praxis" (Jay 1984: 11). Forced to flee Germany in 1934, and spending three and a half years at Merton College,

Oxford, Adorno officially joined the Institute for Social Research in New York in 1938. Here Adorno applied Freud's work to his analysis of the Holocaust which led to his involvement in *The Authoritarian Personality*, one of a multi-volume series of Studies in Prejudice. In *The Authoritarian Personality* Adorno et al. draw links between antisemitism and totalitarian thinking, arguing against analysis which looks for explanations only at the level of the psyche and arguing for analysis which also explores the social reality.

In 1949 Horkheimer, Pollock, and Adorno decided to return to Germany and rebuild the Institute for Social Research in Frankfurt. The Institute officially reopened in 1951 and in 1953 Adorno became Director of the Institute for Social Research.

One cannot deal adequately with the theoretical contributions of Adorno without reference to his friend, the critical theorist Walter Benjamin, since the lives and work of the two were inextricably connected. The letters of Walter Benjamin (1994) illustrate this. Indeed, the origins of negative dialectics are found in Benjamin's influence, especially his early work and the "intellectual dialogue" between Benjamin and Adorno (see Adorno 1995; see also Buck-Morss 1977: 64 and Nicholsen 1997).

Adorno was a philosopher, musicologist, and a sociologist. His life's work revolved around three key interrelated concepts: negative dialectics or non-identity thinking; *kulturkritik*; and the unintentional truth contained in certain works of art and their relation to philosophy and aesthetics. These three central ideas involve a focus upon the negative interrelationship between subjectivity and the social world; the growing commodification of culture; the loss of hope in history as progress; and the transformative potential of art and aesthetics.

Adorno looked not to the proletariat, or history, or technical production to facilitate change to a better world, or to be a cipher of hope. Instead he looked to art, what he called auratic art or autonomous art (art that unintentionally re-presents the truth of society) to find the sedimented "truths" of the social world. Adorno's work deals head on with the pessimism and utter hopelessness of challenging and changing what he called administered society marked by sexual and social oppression, and instrumental reason. Instrumental reason is defined as technological reason which dominates nature, and social reason that leads to the domination of other human beings. The drive for equivalence rooted in the exchange principle reduces the world and subjects to thing-like equivalences. This constitutes identity thinking. The non-identical become "commensurable and identical" (Adorno 1973a: 146).

Key Theoretical Contributions

Negative dialectics

Adorno took dialectics beyond Hegel and Marx to argue that there was no identity between subject and object; no teleological thinking (the proletariat were not going to usher in revolution); theory should not be subordinated to political goals (there could be no theory/practice relationship); and history is not synonymous with progress (as emphasized by Enlightenment thinkers). In *Negative Dialectics* Adorno argues against the drive for equivalence rooted in the exchange principle and for the non-identity between subject and object. The concept was not adequate to the object. He argued that concepts hide the "truth" of their origins and it was up to the subject (also an object) to access the "truth," but this proved to be very difficult because of reification – a version of identity thinking and ideology.

Reification was not conceptualized simply as a fact of consciousness (at the level of the psyche). It is a social category that refers to the way consciousness is determined but does not originate in consciousness. Psyche and society are two halves of the same whole. Adorno uses Freud to explore the contradictions of consciousness while maintaining the necessary tensions between subject and object/psyche and society. Ideology is rooted in the social and the structures of society without denying the tension between subject and object. Adorno establishes priority of the object and mediation of the subject/object. Change can only be brought about socially by changing society. Art and critical theory provide this change-causing gesture. It is the way unlike things appear as like and the mode of thinking that considers them as equal which constitute reification as a social phenomenon and as a process of thinking (see Rose 1978: ch. 3). For Adorno, our very subjectivity is being "liquidated," threatened by the sheer power of reification and identity thinking.

Negative dialectics is presented as an anti-system in reaction to the prevalent norms and values of society; for these norms and values serve to legitimize a society that does not correspond to them. Concepts as ordinarily used mask the truth – they have become lies. Here the influence of Nietzsche and Lukács is clearly evident. There can be no correspondence between concept and object. Negative dialectics looks to Marxism as method and dialectical thinking as the core of that method. Negative dialectics is the critical analysis of society and aimed for the negation of the negation.

Adorno discussed the non-identity between subject and object (and concept and object) in his critiques of phenomenology (Adorno 1982, 1973a), empiricism and positivism (Adorno et al. 1976), instrumentalism, and the teleological thinking of Hegel and Marx (Adorno 1973b, 1996, 1997; Adorno and Horkheimer 1995). Historicism, empiricism, instrumentalism, and positivism as examples of identity thinking serve to sanction and affirm the status quo.

Non-identity thinking confronts the partial truth of an object with the potential truth. Critical theory advances the interests of the truth by identifying the false through the form of the constellation – an argument is not built up in the usual stages but is assembled in a series of parts in the form of a constellation. Our social world is constituted by the false, and negative dialectics confronts the "false condition" of things through non-identity thinking. The role of the critical theorist was/is to look for the critical oppositional, to engage in non-identity thinking and to hold up a mirror to society.

Kulturkritik

"The culture industry perpetually cheats its consumers of what it perpetually promises" (Adorno and Horkheimer 1995: 139). The development of identity thinking, instrumental reason, the administered society, *and* the culture industry were for Adorno synonymous. He described the culture industry as the entertainment business. The culture industry helped to maintain the hold of reification over our thinking processes by demanding little effort on behalf of "consumers," prescribing our reactions, and thus helping to underpin capitalism and the rise of instrumental reason. (See "Cultural criticism and society" in Adorno 1995; "The culture industry: enlightenment as mass deception" in Adorno and Horkheimer 1995; Adorno 1991).

In his work on the culture industry Adorno stresses the need for dialectical criticism to replace "cultural criticism." For given the relationship between culture, the culture industry, and reification, cultural criticism serves only to reinforce the status quo. Cultural critics are described in "Cultural criticism and society" (Adorno 1995) as being first of all "reporters," orienting people to intellectual products; they then became experts and judges of taste and style "degraded to propagandists or censors ... The prerogatives of information and position permit them to express their opinion as if it were objectivity. But it is solely the objectivity of the ruling mind. They help to weave the veil" (ibid: 20). Instead there is a need for immanent dialectical criticism and the notion of culture itself to be negated. The problem here is that the kind of politics that emerges from dialectical criticism can show no commitment to transformation through politics at the level of action. For Adorno, committed art such as Brecht's *Mother Courage* merely demands a change of attitude in a system dominated by the entertainment business, where suffering can simply be consumed/enjoyed and its horror removed. "When genocide becomes part of the cultural heritage in themes of committed literature, it becomes easier to play along with the culture that gave birth to murder" (Adorno 1980: 189). Adorno famously said that there can be no poetry after Auschwitz.

Adorno is critical of social realism: for him, no message should be posited onto a work of art; rather, art should be allowed through form to re-present the sedimented stuff of society in unintentional ways. For Adorno, the notion of a message in art, even when politically radical, already contains an accommodation to the world. It is only by trying to say the unsayable, the outside of language, the mimetic, the sensual, the non-conceptual, that we can approach a "politics" which undercuts identity thinking, which refuses to engage in identity thinking, but rather criss-crosses binary thinking and remains unappropriated. The task of the artist and critic is to reveal the unintentional truths of the social world, to uncover the meaning of objects and to preserve independent thinking. Non-identity thinking or negative dialectics through *kulturkritik* performs this task. For Shierry Weber Nicholsen, Adorno offers a "non-discursive rationality" as an alternative to "a dominating, systematizing rationality that is the counterpart of an administered world" (Nicholsen 1997: 3).

The role of art and unintentional truth

In his search for the critical oppositional through non-identity thinking, Adorno stood clearly on the side of the innovative artist, and what he calls "auratic art." For him, theory and art could not be subordinated to political goals. He was intensely critical of Walter Benjamin's support of Brecht's work (see the essay "On commitment" in Adorno 1980). Art is a refuge for mimetic behavior and the artwork is a cipher of the social. Adorno compares artworks to picture puzzles or rebuses and what is contained in artworks is the sedimented content of society. The philosopher or critic could access these truths through critical reflection, through interpretive philosophy.

The social forces of production and the social relations of production enter all artworks and the crisis of modernism (ideology as reification) is represented in the increasingly affirmative nature of art. Adorno's concept of *Entkunstung* (desubstantialization) represents this. This is the loss of art's capacity to act as a medium of the truth. The crisis of art is its integration into life (art viewed as a thing among things, or as psychologism for the viewer or psychology for the producer) and results in the commodification of art. Resisting accommodation, against the "ontology of false conditions," auratic art remains the last vestige of hope in a damaged world. Auratic art invokes "frisson" or "shudder." In the realm of unfreedom freedom can find its re-presentation only fleetingly, unintentionally, as "coming and going" in the unresolved contradictions between mimesis (sensuousness/playfulness/spirit which animates artworks) and constructive rationality (means of production, relations of production, demands of the material and art sphere) in certain artworks. Adorno uses Picasso's *Guernica*, the music of Schoenberg, and the literary work of Beckett and Kafka as examples to express the enigmatic character of artworks. Their work illustrates the role of art as illusion, as ciphers of hope in a world dominated by the growth of capitalism, consumerism, and instrumental rationality, and for subjects damaged and blinded by the conditions of unfreedom and the power of reification. The socially critical dimensions of auratic artworks are those that hurt "where in their expression, historically determined, the untruth of the social situation comes to light. It is actually this against which the rage of art reacts" (Adorno 1997: 237).

Major Criticisms

The work of Theodor Adorno is perceived by some as elitist, as overly pessimistic, and "the more one plunges into *kulturkritik*, the less one is able to retrieve a decent theory of the historical process" (Merquior 1986). Karl Popper accused him of "talking trivialities in high sounding language" (Jay 1984: 12). Other major criticisms include reference to the fact that Adorno treated cultural consumers as passive dopes, and a methodological problem that led to stasis or paralysis in that theory is not linked to practice. Such claims need to be examined within the context of the knowledge/ideology axis that informs Adorno's work and an understanding of the role and importance given to reification and the administered society.

The charge of pessimism and elitism ignores the depth and complexity of Adorno's painstaking micrology, and misses the profound usefulness of his theoretical works to contemporary sociocultural theory. For Crook (1994), Adorno's work on authoritarian irrationalism raises unsettling questions about contemporary culture. He also draws comparisons between Adorno and Baudrillard, for example the interrelationship between panic production and authoritarianism; the way nostalgia and pastiche reinforce "cognitive reassurances in the face of loss of reality" (ibid: 28). Martin Jay reminds us that Adorno anticipated deconstructionism and that he died virtually the very year deconstruction was born with the publication of Derrida's *L'Écriture et la différance*.

Braidotti compares Adorno and the German tradition with Baudrillard and the French tradition, particularly with reference to the disenchantment and reenchantment of the world. Indeed Adorno has proved useful to feminists because he illuminated the contradictory nature of sexual and social oppression (see J. Benjamin 1993; Braidotti 1994; Nicholsen 1997; Battersby 1998; O'Neill 1999). For Nicholsen (1997), the importance of Adorno's usefulness for us today is his focus on the role of the subject and subjective experience, particularly the imaginary and imagination. In the words of Buck-Morss (1977: 186): "His was a negative anthropology; and its knowledge was to keep criticism alive." Robert Witkin (1998: 200) states: "No one has done more to persuade us of the moral dimension of all cultural construction and of the sociality that is the basis of anything truly creative and liberative."

For Adorno, the effects of instrumental reason, real domination, and the importance given to use-value *vis-à-vis* exchange-value in social relations, and the subsequent disenchantment of the world, depict almost total domination. The only hope lay in art and interpretive philosophy as critical theory. The usefulness of Adorno's *oeuvre* is that his work gives voice to the critical, moral, creative potential of non-identity thinking, *kulturkritik*, and the social role of art in dialectical tension with the role of subjective experience, within the context of a social world marked by identity thinking and instrumental reason.

Bibliography

Adorno, T. W. (1973a) *The Jargon of Authenticity*, trans. Knut Tarnowski and Frederic Will. London: Routledge and Kegan Paul
Adorno, T. W. (1973b) *Negative Dialectics*, trans. E. B. Ashton. London: Routledge and Kegan Paul.
Adorno, T. W. (1996) [1974] *Minima Moralia: Reflections from a Damaged Life*, trans. E. F. N. Jephcott. London: Verso.
Adorno, T. W. (1980) "Commitment" in *Aesthetics and Politics*, trans. and ed. Ronald Taylor. London: Verso.
Adorno, T. W. (1982) *Against Epistemology: A Metacritique*, trans. Willis Domingo. Oxford: Blackwell.
Adorno, T. W. (1984) *Aesthetic Theory*, ed. Gretel Adorno and Rolf Tiedemann, trans. Christian Lendhart. London: Routledge.
Adorno, T. W. (1991) *The Culture Industry: Selected Essays on Mass Culture*, ed. and intro. J. M. Bernstein. London: Routledge.
Adorno, T. W. (1994) *Quasi una fantasia*, trans. Rodney Livingstone. London:

Verso.

Adorno, T. W. (1995) [1967] *Prisms*, trans. Samuel and Shierry Weber. Cambridge, MA: MIT Press.

Adorno, T. W. (1997) *Aesthetic Theory*, ed. Gretel Adorno and Rolf Tiedemann, trans. Robert Hullot-Kentor. Minneapolis: University of Minnesota Press.

Adorno, T. W. and Horkheimer, M. (1995) [1972] *Dialectic of Enlightenment*, trans. John Cumming. London: Verso.

Adorno, T. W., Frenkel-Brunswick, E., Levinson, D., and Sandford, N. (1950) *The Authoritarian Personality*. New York: Harper and Rowe.

Adorno, T. W. et al. (1976) *The Positivist Dispute in German Sociology*, trans. Glyn Adey and David Frisby. London: Harper and Row.

Battersby, C. (1998) *The Phenomenal Woman: Feminist Metaphysics and the Patterns of Identity*. Cambridge: Polity Press.

Benjamin, J. (1993) *The Bonds of Love: Psychoanalysis, Feminism and the Problem of Domination*. London: Virago.

Benjamin, W. (1994) *The Correspondence of Walter Benjamin 1910–1940*, ed. Gershom Scholem and Theodor Adorno, trans. Manfred Jacobson and Evelyn Jacobson. Chicago: University of Chicago Press.

Braidotti, R. (1994) *Nomadic Subjects*. New York: Columbia University Press.

Bronner, S. E. (1994) *Of Critical Theory and Its Theorists*. Oxford: Blackwell.

Buck-Morss, S. (1977) *The Origin of Negative Dialectics: Theodor W. Adorno, Walter Benjamin and the Frankfurt Institute*. Brighton: Harvester Press.

Crook, S. (1994) *Adorno: The Stars Down to Earth and Other Essays on the Irrational in Culture*. London: Routledge.

Held, D. (1980) *Introduction to Critical Theory: Horkheimer to Habermas*. Berkeley: University of California Press.

Jay, M. (1984) *Adorno*. London: Fontana.

Jay, M. (1993) *Force Fields: Between Intellectual History and Cultural Critique*. New York: Routledge.

Lunn, E. (1985) *Marxism and Modernism: An Historical Study of Lukács, Brecht, Benjamin, and Adorno*. London: Verso.

Merquior, J. G. (1986) *Western Marxism*. London: Paladin.

Nicholsen, S. W. (1997) *Exact Imagination/Late Work: On Adorno's Aesthetics*. Cambridge, MA: MIT Press.

O'Neill, M. (ed.) (1999) *Adorno, Culture and Feminism*. London: Sage.

Rose, G. (1978) *The Melancholoy Science: An Introduction to the Thought of Theodor W. Adorno*. New York: Routledge.

Tester, K. (1995) *The Inhuman Condition*. New York: Routledge.

Witkin, R. (1998) *Adorno on Music*. Cambridge: Polity Press.

2 | Jeffrey C. Alexander

Paul Colomy

Ideas
Multidimensionality □ Micro–macro link □ Differentiation □
Cultural sociology □ Civil society

Major books
Theoretical Logic in Sociology (1982–3)
Action and Its Environments (1988)
Fin-de-Siècle Social Theory (1995)
Neofunctionalism and After (1998)
Evil and Good: A Cultural Sociology (2001)
The Possibilities of Justice (forthcoming)

Influences
Bellah □ Durkheim □ Geertz □ Habermas □ Parsons □ Weber

Biographical Details

Jeffrey C. Alexander (b. 1947) is one of America's preeminent social theorists. *Theoretical Logic in Sociology* (1982–3), his first major publication, was heralded as "the most important effort in theoretical synthesis of its generation," and even its severest critics acknowledged its intellectual sophistication. *Theoretical Logic* also revived interest in Talcott Parsons's sociology, no small feat given the blistering attacks directed at Parsons in the 1960s and 1970s. But Alexander always criticized Parsons as much as he praised him, and *Neofunctionalism* (Alexander 1985) (and several subsequent volumes) signaled his intent to reconstruct the Parsonian tradition. Alexander's neofunctionalism elaborated a postpositivist conception of social science, linked macro and micro levels of analysis, and reconceptualized core elements of functionalist sociology. Moving beyond a reconstruction of Parsons (and so beyond neofunctionalism), Alexander's most recent work (e.g., *Evil and Good: A Cultural Sociology* (2001) and *The Possibilities of Justice* (forthcoming)) develops a strong theory of culture and an equally powerful analysis of civil society. This overview discusses Alexander's evolving thought in terms of two genres: general theory and research programs.

Key Theoretical Contributions

General theory

Waging an aggressive campaign in defense of general theory, Alexander steers a middle course between radical relativism (especially in its postmodern form) and traditional positivism. Unlike the former, he articulates a nuanced case in support of decentered reason and the universalizing thrust of social theory. In contrast to the latter, he reproves the reduction of theory to fact, insisting (as Parsons had some four decades earlier) that concepts cannot be formulated nor evidence marshaled absent a general theoretical context of relevance and plausibility.

This postpositivist epistemology is joined to an ecumenical impulse that aspires to transcend the interminable debates between rival perspectives by moving to higher analytic ground. Multidimensionality is the best-known expression of this synthesizing ambition. Depicting social science as a continuum stretching from the abstract to the concrete, Alexander asserts that presuppositions are its most general and decisive element, while action and order comprise the key presuppositions. Historically, sociologists have addressed action by selecting either rational approaches that characterize action as an instrumental adaptation to material conditions or non-rational perspectives that claim action can be fully understood only by reference to internal dispositions (e.g., intentions) that mediate the relationship between actors and their (external) environments. They have addressed the problem of order by adopting either individualist theories that portray order as the product of individual negotiations and choice, or collectivist paradigms that explain order by adducing emergent properties of social organization itself (e.g., class structures).

Dominating (and constricting) the sociological imagination for over a century, these one-sided characterizations of action and order have produced one sterile polemic after another. Multidimensionality is a presuppositional synthesis aimed at breaking through this analytic impasse. Multidimensionality actually involves two distinct syntheses, the first (and stronger) of which holds that action is shaped by rational adaptations to external conditions *and* by actors' subjective commitments and perceptions. The weaker synthesis recommends a collectivistic stance to order while also acknowledging that individualistic theories, with their elucidation of the contingent dimensions of action, supply useful empirical insights into how social structures are (re)produced and transformed. In a multidimensional framework, then, the rational and non-rational determinants of action are given roughly equal analytic weight, while a collectivistic conception of order is preferred, though individualistic theories' accounts of empirical processes are recognized as crucial to a comprehensive understanding of social life.

Multidimensionality is not a simple classificatory scheme devised to sift and sort theories into contrived categories. Instead, its primary purpose is evaluative and prescriptive. Convinced that social science is a two-tiered process, propelled as much by theoretical logic as by empirical evidence, Alexander contends that sociological theory and research should be assessed not only by reference to facts but also in terms of their presuppositional commitments. Through dozens of critical readings (see, for example, Alexander 1982, 1987, 1995), Alexander indicates how classic and contemporary formulations (essayed by Marx, Weber, Mead, Habermas, Coleman, and many others) falling short of multidimensionality are rent by internal inconsistencies, residual categories, conflated levels of analysis, and empirical anomalies. These readings are not clunky, mechanical applications of an arid analytic grid to the material under scrutiny; rather, they are subtle, artful, and thick (in Geertz's sense), reflecting considerable erudition and remarkable acuity about the conceptual core of social thought. A faithful summary of these penetrating appraisals is not possible here, but Alexander's essential contention is this: one-sided presuppositional commitments invariably engender theoretical dilemmas and empirical shortcomings. These weaknesses prompt ad hoc revisions and refinements, but so long as the framework's presuppositions fall short of multidimensionality there are fundamental debilities that no amount of tinkering and fine-tuning can remedy. Ultimately, there is only one viable solution to such limitations: sociological theory and research must be reconstructed along multidimensional lines.

If presuppositions are the deep structure of social theory, ideology is its animating force. Sociological traditions attract adherents not only by the suasive power of their presuppositional logic or the empirical rigor of their scientific explanations, but also by providing resonant, evaluative characterizations of the contemporary world and its defining moments and struggles (e.g., the insurgent movements of the 1960s or the collapse of communist regimes in the 1980s). Alexander maintains that ideology in this moral, interpretive sense is integral to social science, and his critical readings reflect a discerning sensitivity to the ideological implications of several paradigmatic statements. Thus, complementing Alexander's objections to Bourdieu's one-dimensional presuppositions is an indictment of the brilliant French theorist's penchant for relativizing the differences between dictatorship and democracy and denying the very possibility of an inclusive, just society. Acknowledging the ideological dimensions of his own theorizing, Alexander attributes part of the appeal of multidimensionality and the middle-range concepts of differentiation, inclusion, and civil society elaborated in his research programs to their resonance with humane liberalism and social democracy, discourses he believes must be resuscitated in the current post-postmodern era (McLennan 1998: 77--8).

Alexander has also attempted to bridge the gap between macro and micro theorizing (e.g., Alexander 1988a). The centerpiece of this synthesizing project is an ambitious reformulation of Parsons's unit act, which had examined action in terms of means, ends, norms, and conditions; Parsons also referred to effort but gave it much less attention than the other elements. Alexander accords effort – the unexamined black box in Parsons's scheme – a more central position, describing it as the contingent element of action, and the motor that drives the combination of the other elements. Each leading micro perspective (e.g., rational choice theory, ethnomethodology) illuminates crucial aspects of effort, aids our understanding of ends and means, and contributes to the micro explanation of norms and conditions. From a multidimensional perspective, these micro traditions also clarify the interpretive and strategic dimensions of action. These dimensions imbue action with a contingent quality that carves a space between actors and their environments, a space that enables them to chart new lines of conduct. Action cannot be completely understood solely as the product of interpretation and strategization, however. The macro contexts in which agents' efforts are contemplated and carried out establish powerful limits on contingent action, and Alexander revises Parsons's tripartite model of culture, society, and personality to conceptualize the pertinent environments of action. Highlighting the dynamic interrelationship between action and environment, Alexander concludes that contingent action occurs within macro environments that inform and constrain it, while action shapes these environments, either reproducing or recreating them.

Research programs

Alexander has made innovative contributions to three areas of research: social change, cultural sociology, and civil society. His studies of social change reconstruct Durkheim's and Parsons's classic model of structural differentiation (e.g., Alexander 1990). He advances a more comprehensive and variegated conception of differentiation, supplementing Durkheim's and Parsons's identification of a "master trend" of increasing institutional differentiation with examinations of patterned departures (e.g., unequal, uneven, and incomplete differentiation) from that postulated trend and discussions of how dedifferentiation (manifest in such crucial developments as the Counter Reformation) has shaped modern world history. Alexander also amends the standard neoevolutionary explanations of differentiation, arguing that accounts depicting growing structural differentiation as an adaptation to environmental exigencies should be supplemented with more in-depth, historically informed investigations of how specific episodes of institutional change actually occur. In this vein, Alexander draws on S. N. Eisenstadt's pioneering work to underline the role that innovative institutional entrepreneurs and such dynamics as resource mobilization, coalition formation, and group competition and conflict have on the course of differentiation. Finally, Alexander offers a broader conception of the consequences of differentiation. Increased efficiency and reintegration may, as Durkheim and Parsons predicted, result from growing differentiation, but these outcomes are not the only possibilities. Highly differentiated societies also generate considerable anxiety, abundant social pathologies, new forms of conflict within and between differentiated institutions, and an escalation in the amount of inter- and intra-institutional contention (though the scope of this conflict is rarely generalized to the entire social order).

Cultural sociology is a principal focus of Alexander's current work. Characterizing culture as a partially autonomous dimension of social life, he rejects various sociologies of culture that reduce symbol systems to mere epiphenomenal reflections of more substantial structures and interests. He also rebukes Parsons's tendency to equate culture with values, an equation that effectively omits analysis of the purely symbolic phenomena (e.g., ritual, sacralization, myth) that a genuinely cultural sociology must address directly.

Bringing together elements of several traditions (e.g., structuralism, hermeneutics, semiotics, Durkheim's "religious sociology," and symbolic anthropology), Alexander characterizes culture as a structure composed of symbolic sets, contending that these interrelated symbols constitute a non-material structure that patterns action as surely as more visible material conditions. These ideational structures organize concepts and objects into symbolic patterns and convert them into signs, while complex cultural logics of analogy and metaphor, feeding on difference, enable extended codes to be elaborated from simple binary structures. The (partial) autonomy of culture is assured because meaning is derived not from the concrete referent signified by the symbol but from the interrelations of symbols. While culture structures reality cognitively, it also performs crucial evaluative tasks. Sacred symbols supply images of purity and oblige those committed to them to protect their referents from harm. Profane symbols embody this harm, providing images of pollution and danger, and identifying groups and actions that must be defended against. As the existence of profane symbols intimates, cultural systems are no less preoccupied with the "negative" than they are with the "positive:" the bad, evil, and undesirable are central components of all cultural systems and are symbolized every bit as elaborately as the good, right, and desirable. For Alexander, the conflict between good and bad functions inside culture as an internal dynamic; contention and negation are culturally coded and expected; repression, exclusion, and domination are vital elements of symbol systems; and pollution and purification are key ritual processes evident even in ostensibly secular societies.

Alexander employs his cultural sociology to shed new light on phenomena that have been conceptualized in an overly materialist and rationalistic way. In *Evil and Good: A Cultural Sociology* (2001) he objects to depictions of technology and the risk society as scientific, rationalized products imbued with objective force, noting that technology is also a social representation, one endowed with eschatological status and functioning as a vehicle for salvation and damnation in contemporary life. His discussion of computers and his analysis of civil society uncover the symbolic logic, binary oppositions, sacred and profane codings, and narrative forms shaping the discourse (and contention) about these objects. Social theory itself can be read culturally, and Alexander revisits Parsons's modernization paradigm, revealing its semantic codes, narrative structures, and culturally charged hopes and fears.

Alexander is also investigating the emergence and transformation of civil society. Describing the civil sphere as an arena analytically and empirically differentiated from other institutions (e.g., the state and market), he gives particular attention to the solidary aspects of the modern civil realm. Civil solidarity revolves around a distinctive type of universalizing community, an inclusive "we-ness," that comes gradually to be defined and enforced. Whereas Parsons believed that an ever-expanding inclusiveness was hardwired into the modern societal community and represented the fundamental, secular tendency of the contemporary world, Alexander understands the expansion of a universalizing community in a much more contingent way. The growth of the civil realm is far from inevitable, and moments of expansion are frequently followed by periods of particularistic retrenchment. The ebb and flow of civil solidarity are due, in part, to the interrelations between civil and non-civil spheres. These boundary relations assume three ideal-typical forms: destructive intrusions identify the outputs or products generated by other institutions that undermine the very possibility of inclusive, democratic social life; civil repairs emerge in response to these threats, with the institutions and actors of the civil sphere attempting to remedy the distortions spawned by other subsystems; facilitating inputs refer to the goods and social forms produced by other institutions that promote a more civil life.

Alexander amplifies his model of civil society, contingent conception of inclusion, and systemic analysis of boundary relations by examining the discursive struggles fought by social movements championing a more egalitarian society. The prospects of these movements depend largely on their ability to "translate" practical, concrete problems into the generalized discourse of civil society. Successful translations invoke the democratic, universalizing metalanguage of the civil realm to connect adherents' particular concerns to the symbolic center of civil society and its utopian themes. In *The Possibilities of Justice* (forthcoming), Alexander presents a provocative reinterpretation of the (American) civil rights movement, emphasizing its ability to translate the exclusion of African Americans into a profane transgression against the sacred core of American civil society. He reconceptualizes multiculturalism in a similar way, portraying it as a discursive project aimed at redefining the very terms of inclusion, and characterizing it as a form of incorporation decidedly superior, sociologically and morally, to assimilation and "hyphenization" (the other principal modes of incorporation).

Major Criticisms

The relationship Alexander posits between general theory and empirical research is not entirely clear. His postpositivism characterizes social science as a two-directional continuum, with practitioners moving back and forth across partially autonomous levels that stretch from abstract presuppositions to concrete empirical evidence. Claiming that the two-directional continuum is, in practice, a one-way street, critics charge that Alexander has merely turned conventional positivism on its head: rather than reducing theory to fact he treats statements about facts as mere reflections of underlying presuppositional commitments. Critics also complain that Alexander's general theorizing has not yet produced empirically oriented, multidimensional explanations of social structures and processes that are obviously superior to existing one-dimensional explanations.

Alexander's cultural sociology and his conception of civil society are infused with an idealism that appears to retreat from multidimensionality. His insistence on examining symbolic codes and ritual dynamics in their own terms represents not merely an argument against reducing culture to material conditions, but seems to preclude analysis of the ways in which culture is shaped by other subsystems. Likewise, his treatment of civil society focuses almost exclusively on discursive structures and struggles, giving relatively little attention to how more material dimensions of social life foster or impede inclusion.

Bibliography

Alexander, J. C. (1982–3) *Theoretical Logic in Sociology*, 4 vols. Berkeley: University of California Press.

Alexander, J. C. (ed.) (1985) *Neofunctionalism*. Beverly Hills: Sage.

Alexander, J. C. (1987) *Twenty Lectures: Sociological Theory Since World War Two*. New York: Columbia University Press.

Alexander, J. C. (1988a) *Action and Its Environments*. New York: Columbia University Press.

Alexander, J. C. (ed.) (1988b) *Durkheimian Sociology: Cultural Studies*. Cambridge: Cambridge University Press.

Alexander, J. C. (co-ed. with P. Colomy) (1990) *Differentiation Theory and Social Change: Historical and Comparative Perspectives*. New York: Columbia University Press.

Alexander, J. C. (1995) *Fin-de-Siècle Social Theory: Relativism, Reduction, and the Problem of Reason*. London: Verso.

Alexander, J. C. (1998a) *Neofunctionalism and After*. Oxford: Blackwell.

Alexander, J. C. (ed.) (1998b) *Real Civil Societies: Dilemmas of Institutionalization*. London: Sage.

Alexander, J. C. (2001) *Evil and Good: A Cultural Sociology*. Cambridge: Cambridge University Press.

Alexander, J. C. (forthcoming) *The Possibilities of Justice: Civil Society and Its Contradictions*.

McLennan, G. (1998) "Fin de Sociologie? The Dilemmas of Multidimensional Social Theory." *New Left Review*, 230: 58–90.

3 | Louis Althusser

Ted Benton

Ideas
Epistemological break □ Problematic □ Symptomatic reading □
Structural causality □ Social formations as "overdetermined
structures-in-dominance" □ Ideology as "imaginary relation to real
conditions of existence" □ Interpellation □ Conjuncture

Major books
For Marx (1965)
Reading Capital (1967)
Lenin and Philosophy and Other Essays (1971)

Influences
Bachelard and Canguilhem (historical epistemology) □ Lenin □
Mao Zedong □ Marx □ Psychoanalysis □ Saussure and Lacan
(structuralism)

Biographical Details

Louis Althusser (1918–90) was above all a philosopher of political engagement. Still more than is usually the case, his thought cannot be understood independently of successive historical, political, and theoretical
"conjunctures" through which he lived and wrote, and to the shaping of
which his own work made its distinctive contribution. My account of
his ideas therefore centers on those conjunctures, and the character of
Althusser's engagement with them.

He was born in Algeria, moving, with his parents, to France in 1930.
By his own account, his childhood was an unhappy one, characterized
by an inner torment which, perhaps, accounts for his later recurrent
depressions and final madness and personal tragedy. He was brought

up as a Catholic, but (on his account) influenced by the example of a fellow prisoner of war, was converted to communism, and joined the French Communist Party soon after the war. However, from the start he was an independent-minded intellectual, and came into repeated conflict with the Party leadership, from whom he was increasingly estranged.

His most distinctive and provocative writings were the outcome of seminars and lectures held at the École Normale Supérieure, in Paris, between 1960 and 1970. The political setting was shaped by two major events in the international communist movement. The first was the death of Stalin, and Khrushchev's 1956 denunciation of Stalin's crimes. This promised (but failed to deliver) a more open and tolerant Party and society. However, the official acknowledgment, from within, of the evils of Stalin's dictatorship did open the way for dissident voices on the left, both within and outside the Party, to call into question the official, Soviet version of the Marxian heritage. The second event was the growing division between the Soviet Union and China, and the associated influence of "Maoism," and Marxist currents of thought emerging from Third World revolutionary struggles. In France during the 1960s, especially, small Maoist groups emerged as a critical force to the left of the French Communist Party. The adoption of themes from their "imaginary" construction of the Cultural Revolution in China, and the revolutionary events of Paris, 1968, also had their effects on Althusser's thought, provoking a series of self-critical writing in which much of his earlier work is repudiated.

But if these features of the political conjuncture both enabled and demanded new ways of taking forward the legacy of Marxism, it was necessary for those who took this task upon themselves to find means of thought which lay *outside* that legacy. At the same time, and especially for those who, notwithstanding their dissident status, wished to remain inside the Communist Party, the exercise had to be conducted as though it were one, not of borrowing from outside, but, rather, of unearthing the "true" Marx from decades of interment in ideological distortion and misreading. In this task of critical renewal of the Marxist heritage, there were two broad and deeply antagonistic approaches. One, including major independent figures on the left, notably Sartre and Merleau-Ponty, as well as Communist Party "insiders" such as Garaudy and Seve, discovered in the early writings of Marx a philosophical view of history animated by ethical humanism. Reinforced by current philosophies of existentialism (Sartre) and phenomenology (Merleau-Ponty), these early works gave central place to self-conscious human agency in the creation of the future communist good life, and provided powerful grounds for the critique of the Soviet state-centralist regime. The French Communist leadership took up this theme, declaring Marxism to be the humanism of our time.

Key Theoretical Contributions

Althusser and his circle of students and collaborators vigorously contested the interpretation of Marxism as a "humanism." Instead, they presented an alternative reading of Marx's works, a reading informed (to an extent not always acknowledged by Althusser at the time) by contemporary non-Marxist intellectual currents then influential in Paris. Two of these are of utmost importance for any understanding of Althusser's most influential ideas. The first is structuralism. The structural linguistics of Ferdinand de Saussure is of primary importance, with its emphasis on language as an autonomous social fact, distinct from the agency and intentions of language users, which by its structure both conditions and limits the possibilities of speech. Despite recurrent criticisms of structuralists such as Lévi-Strauss who, according to Althusser, generalize the methods of structural linguistics beyond their proper domain, Althusser himself was greatly impressed by the structuralist reading of psychoanalysis achieved by Jacques Lacan. Althusser's critical debt to the structuralists' arguments is unmistakable in his "antihumanist" reworking of Marx.

The second non-Marxist intellectual resource deployed by Althusser was a distinctive French tradition for thinking about the history and nature of science: "historical epistemology." This is associated with the work of Koyre, Bachelard, and Canguilhem. Unlike the dominant English- and German-speaking philosophical approaches to science, which are concerned with the search for timeless criteria of scientific status, the French tradition was concerned with discontinuities in the history of the sciences, with the historical conditions of emergence, or "irruption" of new scientific disciplines, and with their subsequent internal transformations and transactions with surrounding ideologies. This tradition was also the prime source for Foucault's "archeology" of knowledge, and, by a more indirect route, for Thomas Kuhn's (1962) *Structure of Scientific Revolutions*, which transformed the terms of the English-speaking debate in the philosophy of science.

Althusser and his associates used the ideas of the historical epistemologists as a way of analyzing and periodizing the sequence of Marx's writings. They took two key concepts from historical epistemology. The first was the concept of "problematic," according to which texts were to be understood as effects of an underlying matrix of concepts which enabled the posing and answering of a certain range of questions, but at the

same time foreclosed others. The prescientific problematics shaping discourse in a field of inquiry were designated "ideological," so that the
emergence of a scientific problematic entailed the overthrow or displacement of these preexisting conceptual networks. This process was characterized by the second concept taken by Althusser from historical
epistemology: the concept of "epistemological break." Applied to Marx's
writings, this led to a periodization in which an epistemological break
was located *after* the composition of the *Economic and Philosophical
Manuscripts* of 1844 – the most compelling of the sources for the reading
of Marx as a philosophical humanist. But since many passages in Marx's
later writings also seem to echo the humanism of his youth, it had to be
recognized that the new, scientific problematic of "historical materialism" did not arrive fully-formed overnight. There was a more-or-less
extended transitional period, and even later, texts were often shaped by
the coexistence of scientific and ideological problematics. In defending
their argument for the epistemological break in the face of such textual
evidence, the Althusserians developed a practice of "symptomatic reading" (analogous to a psychoanalytic "reading" of slips of the tongue and
lapses of memory) through which inconsistencies and lacunae in the "surface" of a text could be traced to its underlying problematic or
problematics. The essays collected together in *For Marx* (1969) are primarily devoted to establishing this reading of Marx's work, with a subsequent collection, *Reading Capital* (various editions) offering more
elaborated accounts of key concepts and methods of the scientific problematic of historical materialism, grounded in the new way of reading
the "mature" writings of Marx, most especially *Capital*. This collection
included, along with Althusser's own essays, an extended elaboration of
the "basic concepts of historical materialism" by Althusser's then-close
collaborator, Balibar.

In some ways these works are much clearer about what Marxism as a
science of history is *not* than they are about what it *is*. But it is certainly
arguable that in this negative achievement alone, detaching Marx's
thought from then-prevalent readings, Althusser and his associates
opened up new and exciting possibilities for the reworking of the whole
Marxian heritage. Some of this work of critical reconstruction was attempted along with the deconstruction, and is best introduced by way of
an account of the negative task.

So what did the new reading show Marxism *not* to be? Althusser identified three main interconnected features of the problematic of the early
Marx which had entered into the mainstream of contemporary Marxist
orthodoxy: economism, historicism, and humanism. The mature Marx
was committed to none of these. On the question of "economism"
Althusser was in line with a long struggle on the part of twentieth-cen-

tury "Western Marxists," most notably Antonio Gramsci, to resist economic determinist readings of Marx, and to find ways of theorizing the specificity of cultural, political, and subjective processes. Althusser acknowledged Marx's emphasis on the causal weight of the economic structure, but insisted upon the "relative autonomy" of the "superstructures." An alternative way had to be found to theorize the structural complexity of whole societies, or "social formations." The notions of "structural causality," and of society as an "overdetermined structure in dominance," were introduced to address this problem: cultural and political struggles and processes were recognized as having their own specific character and role in the maintenance or transformation of societies, but still in ways shaped by the greater causal weight of economic processes and relations.

In orthodox readings of Marx, historical societies could be thought of as a series, in which each successive form arises out of contradictions in its predecessor, and constitutes an advance over it, towards a preestablished end state: the realization of human potential, the future communist society. So, the various "precapitalist" modes of production ("primitive" communist, ancient, and feudal modes) are so many "progressive" epochs, leading to capitalism and, eventually, through class struggle on the basis of economic contradictions, to socialism and communism as the culmination of historical development. This sort of account of history as a directional process of "development" towards a pre-given end state was, of course, very widespread beyond specifically Marxist circles, and it remains influential in the discourses of "modernization" and "development" (also, arguably and paradoxically, in the idea of "postmodernism"). Althusser labels such teleological ways of understanding historical processes "historicism," and argues that, far from subscribing to such a historical "metanarrative," Marx's great originality consisted in his abandonment of it. On Althusser's account, Marx, and later Lenin, theorized revolutionary transitions as "exceptional events," as "conjunctures," brought about by the contingent coming together of numerous contradictions inhabiting the complex structures of a social formation. The future is an open space of possibilities, with no predetermined dynamic *necessarily* leading to the overthrow of capitalism.

The third "ism" which, for Althusser, Marxism was not, was "humanism." Part of the scandal caused by Althusser's "anti-humanism" was simply a misunderstanding. It may help to distinguish three possible senses of "humanism." Moral humanism is the view that human individuals and their well-being are the primary or sole objects of moral concern. Althusser did not reject humanism in this sense, but was often misunderstood as doing so because of confusion with other senses of "humanism" to which he *was* opposed. One of these was the idea, a version of "historicism," that historical development is to be understood as a process of progressive "self-realization" of the human species. This is rejected as a consequence of the rejection of historicism. Another sense was humanism as belief in the power of individual creative human agency in forming and transforming human societies – sometimes called "voluntarism," and implicit in neoclassical economics, "rational choice" social and political theories, and in much "commonsense" individualism. Althusser was opposed to humanism in this sense, too, on account of his emphasis on the causal powers of social and economic structures in shaping the conditions for action.

Soon after the publication of *Reading Capital*, however, the combined impact of the Chinese Cultural Revolution and the upheavals of May 1968 evoked a self-critical response from Althusser. He had gone too far in the direction of the structuralists, and was also guilty of what he called "theoreticism:" the pursuit of theoretical purity at the expense of engagement with concrete politics. A text of continuing importance, his "Ideology and the Ideological State Apparatuses" stems from this period of self-criticism. In it he developed a distinctive and subsequently very influential "materialist" account of ideology as an "imaginary relation to real conditions of existence." On this account, embodied participation in the practices and rituals of the family, educational institutions, churches, voluntary associations of various kinds, and even trade unions (collectively termed "ideological state apparatuses"), formed individuals as "subjects," with a sense of self-identity appropriate to the position in society for which they were destined. This process was termed "interpellation." This was Althusser's main contribution towards a distinctively Marxist theory of the "superstructures," to complement Marx's economic theory, but it arguably erred too far in the structuralist direction, being unable to comprehend the "spontaneous" oppositional movements that were already exploding onto the streets and factories in France and elsewhere. Althusser was quick to acknowledge such failings, but it is arguable that the distinctiveness of Althusser's voice was less marked in his subsequent writings, which include autobiographical texts, as well as serious theoretical engagements with earlier philosophers and political theorists, notably Hegel, Machiavelli, and Spinoza. Althusser became increasingly estranged from the Communist Party, and came to recognize a growing crisis of Marxism itself. The inner distress which had been a permanent dimension of Althusser's life seems to have intensified until, in 1980, he confessed to killing his wife, and was committed to a psychiatric hospital. Since his death in 1990 there has been a resurgence of interest in his work, and there is a continuing stream of posthumous publications, some of which reveal previously unknown facets of his thought, and will require substantial efforts of revaluation of its significance.

Major Criticisms

The attempt to think the complexity of social formations, and to theorize with his concept of "conjunctures" the part played by contingency in historical change, are lasting achievements which still have much to offer for future social scientists. The account of ideology shares with Foucault's analysis of "power/knowledge" the common difficulty of adequately grasping the possibility and dynamics of resistance, and the conditions for autonomous agency. Within the Marxist tradition, Gramsci's parallel development of the concepts of civil society, hegemony and counter-hegemony are arguably more helpful in this respect. Despite his occasional insistence that he was not opposed to, and even endorsed, "moral humanism," Althusser never directly engaged in normative theorizing: historical materialism was to be developed as an explanatory theory, but adherence to a socialist politics was simply taken for granted. Arguably, again, the growing crisis of Marxism presaged a wider crisis of the whole socialist project which demanded direct engagement with the ethical critique of capitalism, most powerfully expressed in the rejected early works of Marx. Finally, the understandable priority accorded by Althusser to the overcoming of "economic determinist" versions of Marxism arguably led him away from Marx's own strong sense of the materiality of human existence. This latter has enabled some Marxists to advance distinctively Marxist approaches to our contemporary ecological predicament, and build bridges to the Green movement. The post-Althusserian emphasis on culture and discourse in abstraction from such material dimensions of social life has tended to obstruct such developments.

Bibliography

Althusser, L. (1969) [1965] *For Marx*. London: New Left Books.
Althusser, L. (1971) *Lenin and Philosophy and Other Essays*. London: New Left Books.
Althusser, L. (1976) *Essays in Self-Criticism*. London: New Left Books.
Althusser, L. (1990) *Philosophy and the Spontaneous Philosophy of the Scientists and Other Essays*. London: Verso.
Althusser, L. (1993) *The Future Lasts a Long Time*. London: Chatto and Windus.
Althusser, L. and Balibar, E. (1970) [1967] *Reading Capital*. London: New Left

Books.
Benton, T. (1984) *The Rise and Fall of Structural Marxism*. Basingstoke: Macmillan.
Elliott, G. (1987) *Althusser: The Detour of Theory*. London: Verso.
Elliott, G. (ed.) (1994) *Althusser: A Critical Reader*. Oxford: Blackwell.
Elliott, G. (1998) "Ghostlier Demarcations: On the Posthumous Edition of Althusser's Writings." *Radical Philosophy*, 90, July/August: 20–32.
Kaplan, A. E. and Sprinker, M. (eds.) (1993) *The Althusserian Legacy*. London: Verso.
Resch, R. P. (1992) *Althusser and the Renewal of Marxist Social Theory*. Berkeley: University of California Press.

4 | Hannah Arendt

Phillip Hansen

Ideas
Totalitarianism □ Public/private/social □ Thinking/judging/
willing □ Labour/work/action □ Banality of evil

Major books
The Origins of Totalitarianism (1973)
The Human Condition (1959)
The Life of the Mind (1978)
Between Past and Future (1977)
Eichmann in Jerusalem (1965)

Influences
Heidegger □ Jaspers □ Kant □ Marx □ Tocqueville

Biographical Details

Hannah Arendt (1906–75) is now recognized as one of the most important political theorists of the twentieth century. She is renowned for both
her work and her life – she was anything but a cloistered academic. Her
life history was entwined with the tumultuous events of the twentieth
century: Nazism and the Holocaust; war and Cold War; exile and the
refugee experience; imperialism, postcolonialism, and revolution; Vietnam, civil rights, and the international struggle for democracy (Young-
Bruehl 1982). A student of both Martin Heidegger and Karl Jaspers,
she is currently known as much, or more, for her relationships with them
as for the influence they exerted on her work. But it *is* her work which
will mark her legacy in the long run.

Normally, theorists who attain her stature are identified with a distinctive body of doctrine which can be transformed into a program of

political action, or at least an action-informing ideological perspective. But while there are specifically "Arendtian" themes, and a distinctive temper to her thinking, her position does not readily lend itself to such transformation. Nor would she have welcomed it. In *The Human Condition*, her best-known work of political theory, she claimed her purpose was "nothing more than to think what we are doing" (Arendt 1959: 5).

According to Arendt, such thinking had to be "thinking without a bannister" (Hill 1979: 336). The "bannister" was the Western tradition of political thought. This tradition provided the enduring context for political thinking. Yet Arendt believed it no longer either illuminated clearly our political experiences, or provided guides for political action. As a consequence of her complex relation to this tradition, Arendt has proven difficult to locate within the main currents of political thought. This has led to widely divergent interpretations of her work (Hill 1979; Hinchman and Hinchman 1994; Honig 1995; Calhoun and McGowan 1997). Even allowing that important political thinkers admit of different interpretations, the range of views is noteworthy. Perhaps, however, this is at it should be. Arendt's writings offer rich insights to theorists and scholars of diverse persuasions.

Key Theoretical Contributions

Two significant themes stand out both within the body of Arendt's work and against the backdrop of shifting contemporary theoretical concerns. These themes are *worldliness* and *plurality*. To grasp them requires an appreciation of the deeper structure and focus of Arendt's thinking.

Although her writings are generally accessible, Arendt is nonetheless a demanding thinker. Indeed, in a sense, she is not really a *political* thinker at all (see Arendt's (1965) use of a haunting citation from Sophocles's *Oedipus at Colonus* in *On Revolution*). She relies on the Western tradition of political thought, but, as noted earlier, she self-consciously distances herself from it at the same time. Drawn to the Greek *polis* for insights, she is at the same time neither a nostalgic classicist nor a "reluctant" modernist (cf. Benhabib 1996). But she is no unabashed admirer of post-Enlightenment modernity either. She once called herself a phenomenologist of sorts. This implies a quest for new clarity in confronting and assessing things. Such clarity requires a thinking space insulated from the pressures and claims of both ideology and conventional philosophy. Arendt's own metaphors of "thinking without a bannister" and of the "gap" between past and future where the thinking individual is situated (Arendt 1977) probably capture best what she is about.

Arendt confronts the traditional questions of political theory, but there is something fascinatingly elusive about this encounter. She offers a distinctive take on the ideas of "classical" (and not so classical) political thinkers, but she also encourages us to ask how we should understand political questions themselves. Her ideas "work" best when they recede in the face of our own rethinking about what it is important to know. That she is "right" or "wrong" about an issue is less significant than that we come away with a fresh sense of what the issues are.

The idea that Arendt helps us make sense anew about what we have thought we have always known or assumed is central to understanding worldliness and plurality. For Arendt, the "world" is the complex of institutions, practices, norms, and values which give human experience its identifiable character as both collectively organized and as unfolding in time and space. It is the objective domain within which we move and act, an order which lies between us and establishes, literally, our "interests:" the spaces between which unite while separating us at the same time. This world is a human artifice, a forum for the objectification of our capacities as *homo faber*, the creator of meaningful things. Without it, we would not be "at home" with ourselves or with others. As our habitation on earth, the world makes our lives as mortals bearable.

In bearing with others – "strangers forever" as Arendt puts it – we acknowledge and accept plurality: the reality that everyone is alike in that no one is exactly identical to anyone else, that individual human beings, and not an abstract, generic humanity, live on earth and inhabit the world. Respecting plurality means that we accept others in their "otherness." We are connected through our differences and not in spite of them. Plurality makes possible political ties among individuals that are more than instrumental, but less than intimate. It makes solidarity achievable.

Solidarity is central to a proper politics. Politics requires, and in turn makes possible, both worldliness and plurality. The core of a genuine politics is *action* – the capacity to take initiatives and insert ourselves through word and deed into events unfolding around us. Along with *labor*, which sustains life, and *work*, which builds the world, action constitutes "the human condition." All are needed and must be in a certain balance with each other if human capabilities are to be realized. Where this balance is maintained, another is also preserved. This is the balance between the *public* realm, the properly political space within which collective affairs are conducted, and the *private* realm, where the demands of both material and biological reproduction, and personal intimacy, are met.

In the modern world the boundaries demarcating these spheres have become blurred, with ominous consequences for modern politics. At the heart of this development is the triumph of the *social*. One of Arendt's most controversial and difficult ideas (cf. Pitkin 1998), "the social" refers to a fusion of public and private realms. This fusion is the result of the tendency for life-sustaining labor to increasingly define worthwhile human purposes at the expense of both world-constituting work and political action. A "laboring" society resembles a gigantic machine with humans as replaceable parts who are expected to "behave" by conforming to predictable rules. It is the kind of society within which someone like the Nazi functionary, Adolf Eichmann, could emerge and play a lethal role (Arendt 1965b).

Arendt's treatment of public, private, and social, as well as labor, work, and action, lays the groundwork for her consideration of plurality and worldliness. A common theme throughout her wide-ranging account of modern political life is the undermining of these qualities. Her magisterial and controversial treatment of totalitarianism (Arendt 1973) is the most extensive and haunting confrontation with the collapse of plurality and worldliness. But the fate of these also provides the backdrop to her discussions of a wide range of "everyday" phenomena in "normal" liberal democratic states, from problems with education to the role of lying in politics (Arendt 1972, 1977). Arendt suggests we have become victims of our own powers, with no appropriate political or social institutions within which they can be articulated or controlled.

It might seem that Arendt holds a tragic or pessimistic view of human experience, and some analysts have viewed her in this way. But such a view is misleading. Modern, and especially twentieth-century, politics may have undermined worldliness and plurality, but have not totally destroyed them. These capabilities have demonstrated surprising resiliency in unlikely places and settings. Revolution, the home of modernity's "lost treasure" of political action (Arendt 1965a), has provided evidence of them, even if actual revolutions have been largely unable to sustain them. The French Resistance in World War II generated among its members a solidarity which required and preserved them. And so, too, did certain elements of the international student movements of the 1960s. As well, the actions of "men" in "dark times" (Arendt 1968) cast light on human possibilities otherwise denied by prevailing political and social structures. For Arendt, nothing is inevitable – neither historical progress nor decline. Our tendency to think in terms of irresistible trends and historical necessity are central to the problems of the age.

What sort of political project comes out of this complex position? Because she defends free action as the core of a genuine politics, and the need for a public space of appearance within which the capacity for action can be displayed, Arendt may be considered a republican. But her's is a tough-minded republicanism. It owes more to Machiavelli than to Rousseau, to Tocqueville than to Marx. As suggested above, politics cannot involve relations between intimates – Arendt was always suspicious of fraternity as a political goal. On the other hand, it cannot be about instrumental ties among otherwise utterly self-absorbed individuals. Authentically political bonds bring together citizens who simultaneously acknowledge their connectedness and separateness, who know how to bear with each other. The truly political actor possesses judgment. This is the ability to put oneself in the place of another, to engage in representative thinking, to "go visiting" and see the common world from the multiplicity of perspectives which constitute it.

In the end, Arendt's republican politics is about a certain kind of solidarity. This is a solidarity of strangers who are neither *for* nor *against* but, rather, *with* each other as sharers in freedom of a common world. The dilemmas and horrors of the last two centuries reflect the all too evident absence of this solidarity. But, while under siege much of the time, the genuinely political qualities of freedom, action, and judging remain always as possibilities which can emerge unexpectedly, indeed, miraculously.

Major Criticisms

Given the demanding and often elusive nature of her categories, Arendt's work has been subjected to a wide range of criticisms. I want to mention briefly three sets of these.

One set contends that, as a defender of the *polis* as a political standard, Arendt holds an idealist, and as a consequence elitist and even anti-democratic, view of politics. She allegedly believed existing liberal democratic institutions were insufficiently political, and that we must recreate the *polis*, hierarchical structure and all, on modern soil. From this perspective, Arendt is seen as a conservative nostalgically hearkening back to a classical paradise lost. Much of the criticism of Arendt's earlier work took this form.

A second set of criticisms claims that Arendt defends a "decisionistic" and even potentially immoral conception of political action. The target here is the agonistic element in Arendt's understanding of action. This supposedly exempts it from those everyday moral and legal restraints which ensure that, in the pursuit of our goals, we respect the dignity of others by doing as little harm as possible to them. Arendt's close personal and intellectual ties to Martin Heidegger frequently provide the context for this assessment. In this light, she is viewed as a "political existentialist" whose ideas have unsavory antecedents (Kateb 1983; Jay 1985; Jay in Calhoun and McGowan 1997; Wolin 1995). (Postmodern analysts of Arendt of course assess these same influences more positively. Cf. Villa 1996).

A third set of criticisms argues that Arendt is insufficiently attuned to the realities of social and political power, and indifferent, if not actually hostile, to the complex array of political identities in modern societies, especially those shaped by race and gender. Her perceived hostility to the presence of economic or "social" motives in political life, coupled with a problematic interpretation of Marx, renders her unable to grasp the real forces at work shaping the modern state. And her ostensibly universalistic, Eurocentric conception of a genuine politics prevents her from appreciating the barriers to community, participation, democracy, and self-development which confront women and non-Europeans, as well as members of subordinate classes in modern industrial societies. Patriarchy and imperialism/colonialism elude her grasp; indeed in the eyes of some she is, wittingly or otherwise, a proponent of both. Such criticisms have been particularly well developed by contemporary femi-nist scholars and thinkers, and there is a burgeoning critical literature on Arendt from a feminist perspective (Honig 1995).

These criticisms raise worthwhile points. But many miss what I see as the core of her contribution: her capacity to stimulate the political imagi-nation by means of a distinctive appreciation of certain human qualities we are apt to forget or ignore, both in our theoretical reflections and in our political activities. Arendt illuminates for us what an activist politics, even a radical politics, demands by way of acknowledgment of, and respect for, those we struggle with – and against. At her best, she provides an antidote to the political posturing, the ideological blindness, the everyday delu-sions and hypocrisies about political life to which we are all prone. In my view, no other thinker engages us in quite this way.

Bibliography

Arendt, H. (1959) *The Human Condition.* Chicago: University of Chicago Press.
Arendt, H. (1965a) *On Revolution.* New York: Viking Press.
Arendt, H. (1965b) *Eichmann in Jerusalem,* revd. and enlarged edn. New York: Viking Press.
Arendt, H. (1968) *Men in Dark Times.* New York: Harcourt, Brace and World.
Arendt, H. (1972) *Crises of the Republic.* New York: Harcourt Brace Javanovich.
Arendt, H. (1973) *The Origins of Totalitarianism,* 3rd edn. New York: Meridian Books.
Arendt, H. (1977) *Between Past and Future.* New York: Penguin Books.
Arendt, H. (1978) *The Life of the Mind,* 2 vols. New York: Harcourt Brace Javanovich.
Arendt, H. (1982) *Lectures on Kant's Political Philosophy,* ed. R. Beiner. Chi-cago: University of Chicago Press.

Arendt, H. (1994) *Essays in Understanding*, ed. J. Kohn. New York: Harcourt, Brace.
Arendt, H. (1996) [1929] *Love and Saint Augustine*, ed. J. V. Scott and J. C. Stark. Chicago: University of Chicago Press.
Benhabib, S. (1996) *The Reluctant Modernism of Hannah Arendt*. Thousand Oaks, CA: Sage.
Calhoun, C. and McGowan, J. (eds.) (1997) *Hannah Arendt and the Meaning of Politics*. Minneapolis: University of Minnesota Press.
Canovan, M. (1992) *Hannah Arendt: A Reinterpretation of Her Political Thought*. Cambridge: Cambridge University Press.
Disch, L. J. (1994) *Hannah Arendt and the Limits of Philosophy*. Ithaca, NY: Cornell University Press.
Hansen, P. (1993) *Hannah Arendt: Politics, History and Citizenship*. Cambridge: Polity Press.
Hill, M. (ed.) (1979) *Hannah Arendt: The Recovery of the Public World*. New York: St. Martin's Press.
Hinchman, L. P. and Hinchman, S. K. (eds.) (1994) *Hannah Arendt: Critical Essays*. Albany: State University of New York Press.
Honig, B. (ed.) (1995) *Feminist Interpretations of Hannah Arendt*. University Park: Pennsylvania State University Press.
Jay, M. (1985) "The Political Existentialism of Hannah Arendt." In *Permanent Exiles: Essays on the Intellectual Migration from Germany to America*. New York: Columbia University Press.
Kateb, G. (1983) *Hannah Arendt: Politics, Conscience, Evil*. Totowa, NJ: Rowman and Allanheld.
May, L. and Kohn, J. (eds.) (1996) *Hannah Arendt: Twenty Years Later*. Cambridge, MA: MIT Press.
Pitkin, H. (1998) *The Attack of the Blob*. Chicago: University of Chicago Press.
Ring, J. (1998) *The Political Consequences of Thinking: Gender and Judaism in the Work of Hannah Arendt*. Albany: State University of New York Press.
Villa, D. (1996) *Arendt and Heidegger: The Fate of the Political*. Princeton, NJ: Princeton University Press.
Villa, D. (1999) *Politics, Philosophy, Terror: Essays on the Thought of Hannah Arendt*. Princeton, NJ: Princeton University Press.
Villa, D. (ed.) (2000) *The Cambridge Companion to Hannah Arendt*. Cambridge: Cambridge University Press.
Wolin, R. (1995) "Hannah and the Magician." *The New Republic*, October 9: 27–37.
Young-Bruehl, E. (1982) *Hannah Arendt: For Love of the World*. New Haven, CT: Yale University Press.

5 | Jean Baudrillard

Rex Butler

Ideas
Simulation □ Seduction □ Hyperreality □ Reversibility

Major books
The System of Objects (1968)
For a Critique of the Political Economy of the Sign (1972)
Symbolic Exchange and Death (1976)
In the Shadow of the Silent Majorities (1978)
Seduction (1979)
Simulacra and Simulation (1981)
The Perfect Crime (1995)

Influences
Bataille □ Lefebvre □ Marx □ Mauss □ Nietzsche □ Saussure

Biographical Details

How to write a biography of someone who can say in their most recent book: "The conventional universe of subject and object, of ends and means, of good and bad, does not correspond any more to the state of our world" (Baudrillard 1999: 28)? The career of French sociologist and theoretician Jean Baudrillard has been characterized at every stage by its unremitting radicality. From his early studies of the organization of domestic objects (*The System of Objects*, 1968), to his critiques of Foucault and Deleuze (*Forget Foucault*, 1987), to his later critiques of the very notion of critique (*The Perfect Crime*, 1995), little has escaped his eagle eye for the absurdities of modern life, his sharp, at times satirical, writing style, and his unsentimental yet bracing worldview.

Baudrillard began his academic career late, after working for a number of years as a secondary school German teacher. Employed at Nanterre University, he was already mixing in Situationist circles; and his department was certainly one of the focal points of the student and worker uprising that almost toppled the de Gaulle government in May 1968. Arguably the "failure" of this attempted revolution was to have a great impact on Baudrillard's work. Over the next few years he was to produce a series of ultra-leftist polemics, notably *The Mirror of Production* (1975) and *Symbolic Exchange and Death* (1976). These writings, however, already show Baudrillard moving beyond the conventional polarities of left and right, and a progressive disillusionment with the political process in whatever form. It is a tendency confirmed by the contemporaneous publications *Forget Foucault* and *In the Shadow of the Silent Majorities* (1978), which moreover mark a move away from any conventional sociology towards a more "transdisciplinary" set up. This corresponds also with Baudrillard establishing along with a number of others the journal *Traverses*, which comes out of Paris's Pompidou Center. This period of high productivity and inventiveness could be said to come to an end in 1987 with the publication of *Cool Memories*, whose opening passage reads: "It is just as probable that I have written the one – or two – best books I shall ever write. They are done with. That is how things go" (Baudrillard 1990a: 3). This final period coincides with Baudrillard leaving the French academic system at the first available opportunity. Thereafter he writes in a variety of forms: the travelogue of *America* (1988); the newspaper articles of *The Gulf War Will Not Take Place* (1991); and the fragments of *The Transparency of Evil* (1990) and *The Illusion of the End* (1992). We might see this as a moment of increasing disillusionment and melancholy in Baudrillard's life and work, but this would be to give it a subjective, biographical meaning that he would reject. Rather it might correspond to something objective in the world itself, a certain running down or loss of vitality.

Key Theoretical Contributions

As implied by the above, it is possible to divide Baudrillard's career into three distinct stages. The first, which encompasses the work from *The System of Objects* to *Symbolic Exchange and Death*, lies within the orbit of conventional sociology. The former attempts to provide a structuralist analysis of domestic objects, inspired equally by Lefebvre and Barthes; the latter wants to speak against the exclusion of death in contemporary Western societies as opposed to "primitive" ones, inspired to various extents by Freud, Mauss, and (though he is rarely mentioned) Ariès. In between these, there are two other important books: *The Society of*

Consumption (1970), which analyzes how need and consumption are precisely *produced* within advanced capitalism; and *For a Critique of the Political Economy of the Sign* (1972), a collection of essays treating such diverse topics as fetishism, the mass media, and the art auction.

In each of these early studies there is a prescient – and, we would say, undervalued – attempt to translate the discoveries of Saussure, Lévi-Strauss, and Lacan into the domain of everyday life. Baudrillard's fundamental insight is that it is the object's *sign value* that precedes both its use- and exchange-values. Thus in *The System of Objects* he can argue that it is the differential logic of the series that makes possible the uniqueness of the model. In *The Society of Consumption* he is able to show how even the apparently biological fact of need is the creation of a rivalrous symbolic order involving prestige and competition. In *For a Critique of the Political Economy of the Sign*, in demonstrating that use- and exchange-values operate as ideological alibis allowing the further extension of sign value, he can state in abstract form: "$\dfrac{EcEV}{UV} = \dfrac{Sr}{Sd}$ or: exchange-value is to use-value what the signifier is to the signified" (Baudrillard 1981: 127).

In *The Mirror of Production* and *Symbolic Exchange and Death* Baudrillard will want to think what is excluded from this fraction. In *The Mirror of Production* it is called the "radical presentness, the denegation of finality, of poetic speech" (Baudrillard 1975: 165); and in *Symbolic Exchange and Death* it is called death, the gift, or symbolic exchange. In the first it is characterized positively and in the second negatively; but what is crucial is that in both it is a form of reciprocality or reversibility, which for all its Maussean/Bataillean associations is not something material but a kind of analytic remainder or leftover. (And one of the most intriguing theoretical tasks would be to think through the similarities between Baudrillard's critique of Marx in *The Mirror of Production* and Derrida's "deconstruction" of him in *Specters of Marx,* employing a similar notion of the "spectral" as that which always returns.)

We might date a second period in Baudrillard's work from *Forget Foucault* to *Fatal Strategies* (1983). This is a period of great theoretical fecundity for Baudrillard, in which he publishes no fewer than seven books and develops the terms with which he is principally to be associated: simulation, seduction, the masses, the fatal. It is also a period when he first becomes widely known in the English-speaking world, where he is to have his major impact. It is also the period, finally, when he moves beyond the widest definition of sociology and towards what we might call "theory." It is the thinking through of the consequences of this that is perhaps Baudrillard's most important contribution and that will provide the greatest difficulties for his interpreters.

We might summarize the chief concern of this period in the words of "The Precession of Simulacra" from *Simulacra and Simulation* (1981): "A hyperreal sheltered from the imaginary, and from any distinction between the real and imaginary" (Baudrillard 1983b: 4). It is this generalized condition – which he had begun to work out from his first publications – that Baudrillard was to analyze in detail during this time. It is no longer seen as the specific outcome of industrial production, but as a phenomenon covering all aspects of contemporary life: sociology, anthropology, sexuality, architecture. And although it can take a variety of forms – the over-production of goods, the desire for "authenticity," terrorism (whether by terrorists themselves or the state combating terrorism) – these are merely the symptoms of a single underlying cause: the coming too close of models to reality. What simulation is is a crisis of representation. It is the literally catastrophic effect of the loss of that distance proper to representation.

What happens when systems reach this state of over-perfection or over-saturation? They no longer resemble reality but only themselves. Beyond a certain point, they are mysteriously afflicted by glitches, breakdowns, short-circuits. (The signs of this are many in Baudrillard: the phenomenon of the masses in sociology; power failures in New York; the erotics of sexual intrigue. As are the names Baudrillard gives it throughout his work: not only waste, symbolic exchange, and reversibility, but seduction, the feminine, objective irony, and theory.) Crucially however – and this complex point escapes even Baudrillard himself at times – the relationship of these two phenomena, let us call them simulation and seduction, is not strictly oppositional. Seduction arises not only at the end of systems when they are too perfect, but is also what allows them to become like this. Seduction is not simply the end or collapse of a system of simulation but its *limit* – a limit that occurs at every point during it.

In this sense, Baudrillard's critique is properly "transcendental." It attempts to think the conditions of possibility of a system of rationality (which also turn out to be the conditions of its impossibility). We might in this regard compare Baudrillard to a number of other theorists of "difference:" Derrida, most obviously, but also – surprisingly – Lyotard, Deleuze, and even Foucault. In each of their *oeuvres* we find a thinking of that difference required for resemblance; a difference that will allow them to prise apart the usual terms of identity. In Baudrillard's work, that is, we have the conceptualization of an impossible, unrepresentable "seduction" that makes the seeming "reality" of the world possible. As he writes in *The Perfect Crime*: "For the world betrays itself by appearances, which are the clues to its non-existence, the traces of the continuity of the nothing" (Baudrillard 1996: 1).

Perhaps if Baudrillard can be understood to be adding anything to the general field of French poststructuralism, it is in raising the question of how this kind of thinking proceeds, what effects it has in the world, what its status or reality might be. For it seems to us that, if in one way his work is less original or at least eccentric than is usually thought, in another he goes further than many in developing a truly Nietzschean "critique of critique." It is in the publications of this third and last period such as *The Perfect Crime* and *The Impossible Exchange* (1999) that Baudrillard asks: is critique guided by the values of truth, progress, and objectivity? Is it a response to the real or does it bring reality about? Does it offer another point of view onto the world or is it the extrapolation of tendencies already implicit in this world?

Major Criticisms

Virtually from the start of his career Baudrillard has been the subject of virulent criticism. In part this can be explained by the stridency of his pronouncements and the strength of his rhetoric. At first this takes the form of a utopian, perhaps even poetic, ultra-leftism, but later it derives from a conception of the outbidding of theory having to match the hyperbole of the world ("Better to die from extremes than from the extremities" states the epigraph to *The Transparency of Evil*). This, of course, is not to the taste of those who desire moderation or at least an empirical grounding in their theory. Thus the common objections that Baudrillard does not define his terms (Poster in Kellner 1994); that he does not argue using evidence or that he is factually incorrect (Norris 1992; Rojek and Turner 1993; Levin 1996); or that things are not as bad as he makes out, that we do not need such extreme measures as he advocates (Kellner 1989).

Undoubtedly, all this is true. However, it is also to beg the question, not to grasp Baudrillard's argument in its own terms. Thus to seek to discredit Baudrillard's argument by appeal to Marxism, as Douglas Kellner (1989) does, is to miss the logical point that it is premised upon a *rejection* of Marxism and its rhetoric of productivity, dialectical resolution, and the liberation of humankind. Likewise, to criticize Baudrillard for getting the facts wrong – or, inversely, to praise him for getting them right – is not to understand that his work contests the very notion of referentiality, whether in the systems he analyzes or in his own work. Rather the more telling criticism of Baudrillard – one that would require patient analysis and not simple condemnation or support – is that he often does not develop consistently his own best insights, that his work lacks a kind of methodological rigor that would make it even stronger. Certainly, after a period of great popularity, Baudrillard's influence appears to be waning. However, we would suggest that it is actually by emphasizing the affinities of his work to that of his fellow *soixante-huitards* that the most compelling readings of it will emerge, in a sense according it the academic respectability it has done so much to avoid.

Bibliography

Baudrillard, J. (1970) *La Société de consommation* [The Society of Consumption]. Paris: Denoël.

Baudrillard, J. (1975) *The Mirror of Production*. St. Louis: Telos.

Baudrillard, J. (1981) [1972] *For a Critique of the Political Economy of the Sign*. St. Louis: Telos.

Baudrillard, J. (1983a) [1978] *In the Shadow of the Silent Majorities*. New York: Semiotext(e).

Baudrillard, J. (1983b) *Simulations*. New York: Semiotext(e).

Baudrillard, J. (1987) *Forget Foucault*. New York: Semiotext(e).

Baudrillard, J. (1988) *America*. London: Verso.

Baudrillard. J. (1990a) *Cool Memories*. London: Verso.

Baudrillard, J. (1990b) [1983] *Fatal Strategies*. New York: Semiotext(e).

Baudrillard, J. (1990c) [1979] *Seduction*. New York: St. Martin's Press.

Baudrillard, J. (1993a) [1976] *Symbolic Exchange and Death*. London: Sage.

Baudrillard. J. (1993b) [1990] *The Transparency of Evil*. London: Verso.

Baudrillard, J. (1994) [1992] *The Illusion of the End*. Cambridge: Polity Press.

Baudrillard, J. (1995) *The Gulf War Did Not Take Place*. Sydney: Power Publications.

Baudrillard J. (1996a) [1995] *The Perfect Crime*. London: Verso.

Baudrillard, J. (1996b) [1968] *The System of Objects*. London: Verso.

Baudrillard, J. (1999) *L'Échange impossible* [The Impossible Exchange]. Paris: Galilée.

Gane, M. (1991) *Baudrillard: Critical and Fatal Theory*. London: Routledge.

Gane, M. (ed.) (1993) *Baudrillard Live: Selected Interviews*. London: Routledge.

Genosko, G. (1994) *Baudrillard and Signs: Signification Ablaze*. London: Routledge.

Grace, V. (2000) *Baudrillard's Challenge: A Feminist Reading*. London: Routledge.

Kellner, D. (1989) *Jean Baudrillard: From Marxism to Postmodernism and Beyond*. Stanford, CA: Stanford University Press.

Kellner, D. (ed.) (1994) *Baudrillard: A Critical Reader*. Oxford: Blackwell.

Levin, C. (1996) *Jean Baudrillard: A Study in Cultural Metaphysics*. New York: Prentice-Hall.

Norris, C. (1992) *Uncritical Theory: Postmodernism, Intellectuals and the Gulf War*. London: Lawrence and Wishart.

Rojek, C. and Turner, B. (eds.) (1993) *Forget Baudrillard?* London: Routledge.

6 | Zygmunt Bauman

Ian Varcoe

Ideas
Modernity/postmodernity □ Culture □ Socialism □
Hermeneutics □ Ambivalence □ Legislator □ Interpreter □ Seduction/
repression □ Consumer society

Major books
Culture as Praxis (1973)
Memories of Class (1982)
Legislators and Interpreters (1987)
Modernity and the Holocaust (1989)
Modernity and Ambivalence (1991)
Intimations of Postmodernity (1992)
Postmodern Ethics (1993)
Work, Consumerism and the New Poor (1998)
Globalization (1998)
Liquid Modernity (2000)

Influences
Adorno □ Baudrillard □ Douglas (Mary) □ Foucault □ Gramsci
□ Horkheimer □ Lévi-Strauss □ Lévinas □ Marx □ Simmel

Biographical Details

Zygmunt Bauman (b. 1925) has always been interested in culture; culture is for this eminent Polish–British sociologist fundamental. "Postmodernity" is opened up through a consideration of art movements (Bauman 1992b). Bauman has had a major impact on cultural studies.

He has always been opposed to the Durkheim–Parsons tradition in which the social system or society is pre-set. Social relations are already hardened into an established social reality, to which the actor must adapt or adjust. (This also puts him in opposition to similar forms of Marxism that stress structure over and above the creative side of humans in their collective life.) Bauman starts from the active side. However, he does not do this using the actor, the active individual (as this would lead into liberalism). Rather, for him, humans are, together, structuring, order-needing, order-creating creatures. Their struggles and strivings are carried on in the field of culture, of which "social structure" is only the sedimented result at any given time, i.e., what appears to be solid (in Antonio Gramsci's sense of common sense). What Bauman constantly reminds us is this: it could be otherwise, and his (generic) concept of culture encapsulates this.

If postmodernity is characterized by plurality of life forms or "language games," modernity was marked by the disciplinary power of the pastoral state. Modernity is a regime intolerant of ambiguity, i.e., those things that sit astride the barricades, the slimy (Sartre, *le visqueux*), that are neither one thing nor the other and therefore threaten the order which is a culture-driven pursuit of a utopia.

Key Theoretical Contributions

So, rather than culture being secondary, something "added on," a sort of superstructure (or system additional to the social system: Parsons) to the hard reality of already set social relations, something that merely makes meaning possible, that allows for the possibility of there being norms (in the Durkheim manner, *représentations collectives*), Bauman reverses the "Durksonian" formula, structure first, culture second (culture serving structure); he sees structure as a temporary phase, a provisional moment in the cultural process, which is human life as a basically meaning-generating, structuring-attempt, conducted always and willy-nilly by all humans, *qua* human beings, living in the world.

Bauman mapped this out from almost the earliest point in his development, and the conception has stayed with him through the treatment of both modernity and postmodernity. The crucial insight is from anthropology, namely that "weeds" are plants that look wrong in the garden, that "dirt" is matter out of place. There are no essential weeds, no inherently dirty things. Rather, these things are produced by the drive to create order out of chaos itself. Order-creating "crusades" generate ambivalence or "waste." And they will continue to do so. They cannot therefore succeed; this is Bauman's underlying (cultural) metaphysic – and it is characteristic, indeed constitutive, of modernity, which is nothing more than a drive to create order. It is doomed. We can see this now. Our awareness of this is the postmodern sensibility. Postmodernity is modernity conscious of itself, aware of its own limits, namely that in the drive to fulfill its vocation it cannot but generate ambivalence – in greater and greater amounts.

Modernity and postmodernity are conceived as opposites, and in essentially cultural terms, the first as an ordering drive by states and intellectuals, the second as the relaxation of this drive, and the development of a (cultural) awareness of this. The source of these ideas is the "early Marx" of the theory of praxis, but stripped of its focus on labor in the narrow sense. Human beings shape the world and are shaped by it, and in the process they develop and extend a cultural heritage which is what makes them human.

Bauman's thought is that of one imbued with the idea that social reality is cultural. Thus "memories" of class, where a way of seeing the world becomes increasingly out of touch with a changing reality (Bauman 1982); postmodernity as modernity aware of itself (Bauman 1992b); and sociology as an attitude or set of questions, a way of trying to order experience, rather than a substantive slice of the "real world" (Bauman 1990a). With culture Bauman not only dissolves the opposition between structure and action or agency as a "problem," but also that between stasis and change: structuring is always ongoing in the perpetual dialectic interplay between freedom and dependence, power and the attempt to escape it. Drawn forward by hopes of the future (of which socialism is one form, modernity another), pervaded by the Enlightenment ideals that retain their validity through thick and thin, praxis as culture, or culture as praxis, involves humans structuring their world and simultaneously attempting to escape the consequences of that ever-temporary crystallization, temporary that is because always a threat to freedom and creativity. The human condition is thus Janus-faced, both seeking order and trying always to escape from the constraints of an alien order. Bauman clearly favors personally the active side of this single equation both as a socialist and as a sociologist. The task of the sociologist is to understand and latterly to foster ambivalence by questioning features of the lifeworld that seem from a commonsense viewpoint fixed and unquestionable. Socialism was curiously a *design* for freedom, inherently paradoxical. Now, the intellectual can hope to foster freedom as an interpreter between and within lifeworlds. If culture is the primary reality, the medium and outcome, to use Giddens's terminology, of human life, culture specialists, intellectuals, have a prime role – as either legislators *or* interpreters. At the same time, if freedom is part of culture, culture is the source of human emancipation. Culture liberates, or can do so. It is to it that socialism belongs and appeals, as a utopia, a horizon of hope, a conception of an alternative, a counter-culture to capitalism, and it is intellectuals who are charged with a unique vocation through their involvement in cultural creation. Bauman conceives culture as having a partly critical and therefore emancipatory edge.

Bauman incorporates into culture as one side of the concept what Anglo-American anthropological theory led Western sociology to leave out, as being too close to the commonsense, culturally loaded, elitist notion of culture, namely the idea of creativity. Restoring this to the concept as one side of a two-sided enterprise was an extremely fruitful early conceptual move from which much else in Bauman's extended *oeuvre* follows. It allows culture to re-enter *social* theory – in a fuller sense than heretofore permitted – and to serve as the main figure in it, rather than being peripheral. Why? Because Durksonian sociology makes culture peripheral; and those who simply want to supplement this tradition end by *substituting* culture as freedom; but they fail to see that culture is *both*, i.e., it is both what has crystallized and what is ongoing against that crystallization – so far. Culture is both behavior trimmed, cut to shape, limited, *and* it is behavior before it has been so trimmed. Durksonian sociology sees only the trimmed behavior and structuralizes it – obscuring the fact that it is *only* culture. Normal behavior is always socialized behavior. This completely obscures the fact that behavior is inherently (i.e., before everything) neither for nor against any status quo. It is just free activity. Freedom comes first. This is parallel to the later argument of *Postmodern Ethics* (Bauman 1993).

In *Postmodern Ethics* Bauman proposed *a priori* that the moral impulse was innate, that is *pre-social*, rather than the product of society. Bauman holds generally that the civilizing mission of modern cultural crusades is a power-driven phenomenon. It operates from the "top down" so to speak. The comfortable illusion that "we are more civilized than they" must be challenged by a critical theory that exposes the "will to power" involved in modernity, *sans* ethics.

In addition to civilization theory, Bauman is opposed to communitarians. Modern society destroyed forever the proximity of neighbors who were both physically and morally "face to face." It created a world of strangers who are physically close but morally distant (Simmel). A postmodern strategy should accept this. And it should be genuinely tolerant (rather than as so easily is the case, indifferent to others). Artificial communities, beloved of some intellectuals today, are not the solution. Down this road lies ethnic exclusiveness and nationalism, things that the world, the postmodern world, if its opportunities are grasped, can and should, learn to do without.

It is crucial to Bauman's view that structuring is ongoing, all the time; we never start from a clean slate, we are both free (structuring) and unfree (structured). And by this token some are freer than others, some in being free in effect structure the world *for* others.

Inequality is a crucial part of this conception of the human condition. So, in a sense, "conflict theorists" are met: conflict is not an alternative to order, but endemic to the human condition, and therefore not something to be championed separately against order, another equally one-sided option if elevated to a norm, such as the "equilibrium tendency" of Talcott Parsons. This is something Bauman holds against the models of the early Anthony Giddens – who centers the knowledgeable actor, free of preexisting dependency, no appreciation being therefore later possible of the "hard" fact of inequality, because of this starting point foregrounding knowledgeability – and the ideal speech situation of Jürgen Habermas. The Habermasian ideal state would be a static one, whereas we always encounter ambivalence, so that the future is always open in a way that sociological models must reflect if they are to be realistic ones. Bauman's watchword would be: "Keep open the alternative."

Bauman suggests that Habermas's ideal speech situation, were it ever to be realized, would be a state of static unfreedom. It is not helpful if social reality is seen, as correctly it must be, as a constant flux between ordering and a critique of that attemptedly imposed structure that is another form of ordering.

Major Criticisms

Bauman's concept of culture is a highly flexible notion. It has enabled him to stay out of some arguably rather fruitless debates between "false oppositions" such as structure–agency, change–stability, etc. We may designate as potential critics of Bauman those traditions of which, and theorists of whom, he is himself critical; and to this roster add some specific areas crucial for Bauman's analyses where empirical research might well cause one to differ from him.

Bauman's picture of modernity may well be decidedly too restrictive. Research on consumers and consumption is beginning to present a more differentiated picture than the one he paints. His attribution of the Nazi genocide to a generic modernity flies in the face of the body of scholarship – historical and sociological – indicating a *Sonderweg* (special way or path of modernization) in the case of Germany (Varcoe 1998). Lévinasian, Habermasian, Durkheimian, and Eliasian scholars would no doubt question his somewhat summary depiction of these figures. Of course one could easily extend this list. And the whole issue of the timing and dynamics of the transitions Bauman depicts in very broad-brush terms will provoke other scholars.

His, however, is a remarkable achievement. In the 1990s Bauman drew back somewhat from "postmodernity." He returned to critical commentary focusing upon inequality. He repudiated postmodern theory at one point (Bauman 2000). Central concerns for him were politics and the virtual disappearance of a sphere in which there might be some meeting between public issues and private troubles.

Bibliography

A complete bibliography of Bauman's writings to 1995 can be found in Kilminster and Varcoe (1996).

Bauman, Z. (1972a) *Between Class and Elite: The Evolution of the British Labour Movement: A Sociological Study*, trans. Sheila Patterson. Manchester: Manchester University Press.

Bauman, Z. (1972b) "Praxis: The Controversial Culture–Society Paradigm." In *Rules of the Game: Cross-Disciplinary Essays in Scholarly Thought*, ed. Theodor Shanin. London: Tavistock.

Bauman, Z. (1972c) "Culture, Values and Science of Society." *The University of Leeds Review*, 15, 2: 185–203.

Bauman, Z. (1976a) *Socialism: The Active Utopia*. London: George Allen and Unwin.

Bauman, Z. (1976b) *Towards a Critical Sociology: An Essay on Common-sense and Emancipation*. London: Routledge and Kegan Paul.

Bauman, Z. (1978) *Hermeneutics and Social Science: Approaches to Understanding*. London: Hutchinson.

Bauman, Z. (1982) *Memories of Class: The Pre-History and After-Life of Class*. London: Routledge and Kegan Paul.

Bauman, Z. (1987) *Legislators and Interpreters: On Modernity, Post-Modernity and Intellectuals*. Cambridge: Polity Press.

Bauman, Z. (1988) *Freedom*. Milton Keynes: Open University Press.

Bauman, Z. (1989a) *Modernity and the Holocaust*. Cambridge: Polity Press.

Bauman, Z. (1989b) "Hermeneutics and Modern Social Theory." In *Social Theory of Modern Societies: Giddens and his Critics*, ed. David Held and John B. Thompson. Cambridge: Cambridge University Press.

Bauman, Z. (1989c) "Strangers: The Social Construction of Universality and Particularity." *Telos*, winter, 78: 7–42.

Bauman, Z. (1990a) *Thinking Sociologically*. Oxford: Blackwell.

Bauman, Z. (1990b) "Effacing the Face: On the Social Management of Moral Proximity." *Theory, Culture and Society*, 7, 1: 5–38.

Bauman, Z. (1991a) *Modernity and Ambivalence*. Cambridge: Polity Press.

Bauman, Z. (1991b) "Social Manipulation of Morality – Moralizing Actors, Adiaphorizing Action." *Theory, Culture and Society*, 8, 1: 139–53.

Bauman, Z. (1992a) *Mortality, Immortality, and Other Life Strategies*. Cambridge: Polity Press.

Bauman, Z. (1992b) *Intimations of Postmodernity*. London: Routledge.
Bauman, Z. (1992c) "Soil, Blood and Identity." *The Sociological Review*, 40, 4: 675–701.
Bauman, Z. (1993) *Postmodern Ethics*. Cambridge: Polity Press.
Bauman, Z. (1994) *Alone Again: Ethics after Certainty*. London: Demos.
Bauman, Z. (1995) *Life in Fragments: Essays in Postmodern Morality*. Oxford: Blackwell.
Bauman, Z. (1996) "On Communitarians and Human Freedom: or, How to Square the Circle." *Theory, Culture and Society*, 13, 2: 79–90.
Bauman, Z. (1997) *Postmodernity and its Discontents*. Cambridge: Polity Press.
Bauman, Z. (1998a) *Globalization: The Human Consequences*. Cambridge: Polity Press.
Bauman, Z. (1998b) *Work, Consumerism and the New Poor*. Buckingham: Open University Press.
Bauman, Z. (1999a) *In Search of Politics*. Cambridge: Polity Press.
Bauman, Z. (1999b) [1973] *Culture as Praxis*, 2nd edn. London: Sage.
Bauman, Z. (2000) *Liquid Modernity*. Cambridge: Polity Press.
Beilharz, P. (2000a) *Zygmunt Bauman: Dialectic of Modernity*. London: Sage.
Beilharz, P. (ed.) (2000b) *The Bauman Reader*. Oxford: Blackwell.
Kilminster, R. and Varcoe, I. (1992) "Appendix: An Interview with Zygmunt Bauman." In *Intimations of Postmodernity*, Zygmunt Bauman. London: Routledge.
Kilminster, R. and Varcoe, I. (1996) "Introduction: Intellectual Migration and Sociological Thought." In *Culture, Modernity and Revolution: Essays in Honour of Zygmunt Bauman*, ed. Richard Kilminster and Ian Varcoe. London: Routledge.
Morawski, S. (1998) "Bauman's Ways of Seeing the World." *Theory, Culture and Society*, 15, 1: 29–38.
Nijhoff, P. (1998) "The Right to Inconsistency." *Theory, Culture and Society*, 15, 1: 87–112.
Smith, D. (2000) *Zygmunt Bauman: Prophet of Postmodernity*. Cambridge: Polity Press.
Varcoe, I. (1998) "Identity and the Limits of Comparison: Bauman's Reception in Germany." *Theory, Culture and Society*, 15, 1: 57–72.
Varcoe, I. and Kilminster, R. (1996) "Addendum: Culture and Power in the Writings of Zygmunt Bauman." In *Culture, Modernity and Revolution: Essays in Honour of Zygmunt Bauman*, ed. Richard Kilminster and Ian Varcoe. London: Routledge.

7 | Ulrich Beck

Joost van Loon

Ideas
Risk society □ Subpolitics □ Reflexivity □ Modernization □
Individualization

Major books
The Risk Society: Towards a New Modernity (1992)
Ecological Politics in an Age of Risk (1995)
The Reinvention of Politics (1997)
The World Risk Society (1999)

Influences
Habermas □ Luhmann □ Marx □ Weber

Biographical Details

Despite a growing erosion of disciplinary boundaries, Ulrich Beck (b. 1944) is one of today's best-known sociologists to have kept a recogniz-able disciplinary rigor in his approach to social theory. Alongside Jürgen Habermas, Axel Honneth, and the late Niklas Luhmann, he stands out as one of the major contemporary German theorists. His best-known work, *The Risk Society* (1992), has been a bestseller not only in sociol-ogy but across a wide range of academic and para-academic publication lists. It contains a most illuminating reflection on the transformative impact that "risk-perception" has had on the organization of modern Western society, and the challenges it creates for developing a politics and ethics of "sustainable development," not exclusively in ecological terms, but in the widest possible sense of social, political, cultural, and moral concerns. In his more recent works on cosmopolitan democracy Beck attempts to trace several logical conclusions from his previous assertions in terms of dealing with changing institutional and political landscapes not only of modern Western society but the entire global social order. Here he elaborates on the concepts of reflexive modernization and subpolitics that have emerged out of his writings on the risk society. A most remarkable feature of those reflections is his willingness to embrace ambivalence, not as part of a secret Hegelian plot to overthrow it for a new synthesizing historicism, but to skillfully trace a possible path between utopianism and nihilism, that may lead us to reconcile ourselves with a human-being that is not destined for either heaven or hell.

The attraction of Beck's work for students of contemporary sociology may be found in the combination of highly original theoretical insights and thorough reflections on key insights from classical sociology, most notably the works of Marx and Weber. A clear feature of his writing is his refusal to be reduced to a commentator on either of them, or any other theorists for that matter. Beck is an original scholar in that he brings together insights from a range of sources and perspectives, but always maintains his own line of argument as the primary guide for engaging with other works.

Key Theoretical Contributions

Whenever the term "risk" is uttered in the context of a sociological inquiry, the name of Beck will inevitably crop up. His name is widely associated with the concept of "risk society," the title of his most famous book translated in English in 1992. As far as book titles go, this is probably one of the most effective and oft-cited examples of how to label the type of society we live in. The concept of risk society stands alongside other characterizations such as "postmodern society," "information society," "network society," and "postindustrial society." However, after a quick glance at his publication list, it will become apparent that Beck's contributions to contemporary social and cultural theory are not confined to issues of risk alone.

In *Risk Society* Beck puts forward the argument that the developments of science and technology have generated major problems for industrial society, which he treats as a type of "modernity." He understands industrial society through a combined reading of Marx and Weber as capitalist and rationalist. It is primarily based on the production and distribution of *goods*, for which scarcity functions as the main regulatory principle. The problem with this is that the institutions of industrial society have not been designed to handle and process the production and distribution of "bads," which he predominantly conceptualizes as the risks and hazards that emerge with industrial production. The main argument he puts forward is that whereas these risks and hazards have been the undesirable latent side-effects of industrialization from the beginning, it is only with their manifestation – which could be traced back to the early 1970s "Limits to Growth" debates – that they start to undermine the institutions of industrial modernity. That is to say, somewhere in our relatively recent past, a qualitative change occurred in the perception of social order as based on flows of goods and "bads" rather than goods alone. This change in perception has led to a crisis in the way in which modern Western society organizes and manages its institutions and functions. This crisis, it could be argued, is the transition period between industrial modernity and something else. The interregnum is referred to as the (world) risk society.

In other words, and in contrast to what has been claimed by some of his critics (Alexander 1996; Levitas 2000; Scott 2000), Beck is neither arguing that industrial society was less risky, nor that the risk society has simply replaced the industrial society. Scarcity still matters and social class is still relevant, especially when considering exposure to a wide variety of (often industrial) risks. However, what is different is the relative relevance of scarcity in comparison to risk, and class relations in comparison to risk relations. Risk places a whole new reflection on class politics, one that provides a rather different arrangement of "alienations." This is not simply a matter of addition (i.e., both scarcity and risk), but one of transcoding: risks turn scarcity into something else, a distorted mirror-image of itself. The language of risk is infectious and contagious. It induces everything into its own properties. As a result, it makes a mockery of the positions held in the traditional class struggle which would turn every risk into a health-and-safety issue. In the face of the catastrophic potential of a nuclear or genetic disaster, class struggle indeed ceases to be all-embracing.

Central to understanding the complexity of the risk society thesis is a sense of the cultural dynamics that Beck stresses as being central to the "phenomenon" of risk. These cultural dynamics involve not only the pivotal role of sense-making and perception in the actualization of risk, but also what could be called the communicative logic that underscores the very possibility of "action," of social movements, political parties, institutions, including science and mass media, and corporations. Understanding the full extent of the central role of communication in the risk society thesis requires a more detailed appreciation of the wide-ranging influences of, among others, the works of Luhmann and Habermas on the development of Beck's thought.

With both Luhmann and Habermas, Beck shares an analysis of modernization as increased complexity and ambivalence. The silent presence of Durkheim can also be felt here, as this complexity is produced by ever increasing differentiation. Similar to Luhmann and unlike Durkheim, however, Beck does not project "integration" accompanying the inevitable "differentiation" engendered by modernization. In other words, his conception of the social is derived from an idea of complexity and instability – social organization is an accomplishment, not a matter of fact. Luhmann's insistence on the improbability of communication, however, receives less attention in Beck's work. Beck is more concerned with the way in which different systems affect each other, which may mean breakdown as well as synthesis. He shares with Luhmann a fascination for the complexity of open systems, although unlike Luhmann, Beck does not take autopoiesis as the sole model of systemic development. That is to say, whereas for Luhmann systems would ultimately resort to self-enclosure in order to cope with and reduce the complexity and enable the continuation of communications, Beck acknowledges self-enclosures (for example, individualization as disembedding) as one strategy among others (for example, individualization as reembedding). Moreover, he does not share Luhmann's political quietism.

Beck's own political ideals are much closer to those of Habermas. Like Habermas, Beck has a maintained commitment to a sense of modernity as emancipation, and more specifically, a faith in reasoned deliberation (communicative action) as the main political means by which this emancipation is to be realized. Although Beck's politics are more eclectic and pragmatic than the philosophically based ideas of Habermas, the latter's thought has clearly influenced that of Beck. His emphasis on "another modernity," which in close association with Anthony Giddens and Scott Lash he consistently termed "reflexive modernity" (Beck, Giddens, and Lash 1994), must be seen in this light. What is at stake here is to repoliticize social theory in terms of enabling a critical self-confrontation that is already offered to us in terms of risk, and extending these to reflect on the way in which the institutions of modern society have failed to address risk-related issues properly, because they are still captivated by categories and concepts from a previous era.

Reflexivity, then, is for Beck the central concept in understanding the communicative logic of the risk society, or better, it is that which will enable us to engage the risk society more positively in pursuit of an alternative modernity. Reflexivity is an effective concept in a critique of instrumental rationality, which – because simply motivated by a desire to maximize effectivity and efficiency – does not engender affect and cannot develop a concern for being, which is necessarily a priority in the risk society. Reflexivity is essentially connected to skepticism and doubt, which are advocated by Beck not in an ethos of despondency but as disclosures of other possible futures. Indeed, there are traces of an accomplished nihilism in Beck's later works. In this sense, it is false to describe the risk society either in terms of utopianism or nihilism. The right word to use here is ambivalence.

What makes the production and distribution of "bads" so potent in the contemporary world is the impossibility of evading their implications. Systemic closures such as those generally offered by science in the form of "expertise," governments in the form of "legislation," and media in the form of "moral panic," are no longer an option, as we are all implicated in this worldwide web of risk technologies. That is to say, reflexivity disassembles autopoiesis and reassembles communication flows into hybrid systems (Van Loon 1999). Closures offered by expertise, legislation, and moral panics are not met with trust in the systems that produced them. The technical fix can no longer be performed.

Science and its technologies of visualization have fundamentally transformed the "see-no-evil, hear-no-evil" principle that accompanied the focus of the visible and quantifiable aspects of risks and dangers commonly associated with industrial production. "Leave it to the experts" is no longer an acceptable slogan, in the same way as "trust me, I'm a doctor" is no longer convincing. They have become standard jokes in Hollywood films. As invisibility is no longer an excuse for non-decision and non-action, the full implications of the catastrophic potential of industrial production are increasingly becoming part of everyone's being-in-the-world. This catastrophic potential is engendered by the indeterminable character of risks and hazards, which has subsequently eroded the politics of security of the capital-finance and insurance complex upon which so much of contemporary capitalism depends.

Major Criticisms

Whereas it would be unfair to read the risk society thesis as a venture in either social or technological determinism, giving an account of how human perceptions or technology have changed the world, there is a danger of either over-inflating the role of a collective consciousness, here primarily defined as "risk-awareness," or – inversely – over-inflating the political–economic infrastructure of social changes. Beck has been accused by some of his critics as either being too pessimistic (Levitas 2000), or too optimistic (Rose 2000), for either ignoring agency or overstating its potential. Beck already anticipated such criticism in the turn to a critique of subpolitics in *The Reinvention of Politics* (1997). This, however, may not provide enough of an antidote to the suggestion that perceptions and cognitions could change the world on their own. That is, there resides an inherent bias towards reason, consciousness at the expense of, for example, unconscious desires and drives which are often not at all reasonable (see Lash 2000). This problem is generally found in Habermasian political philosophy. The main weakness here is not its inherent "idealism," but the lack of understanding of the origins of reason itself. By treating it as primarily human, the collective consciousness is reduced to a cacophony of individual insights, all competing for attention in the public sphere. This competition is further complicated by the involvement of a wide range of interests, which will not be purified through reasoned deliberation but merely take on more deceptive appearances. It is no wonder that governments are more inclined to give primacy to the voice of a kind of scientific expertise that does not tolerate dissent. Scientists are at a clear advantage here, since their truths are alleged to have come directly from "reality" (via "measurements" and "instruments of perception").

What Beck perhaps has failed to acknowledge explicitly thus far is what motivates "faith in reason." Whereas deliberative practices undoubtedly enhance the degree and intensity of participative democracy in the public sphere, there remains an unexplored metaphysical dimension to reason, highlighted by the term "faith," which neither Beck, nor for that matter Habermas or Luhmann, have addressed. Having said that, his obvious appreciation of ambivalence and his boundless creativity in dealing with complex issues may actually enable Beck to address these issues more sensibly and innovatively than many of his contemporaries, who remain trapped by the aporia of modern social thought. His reflections on skepticism and doubt towards the end of *The Reinvention of Politics* already signal the beginnings of a more philosophical turning to address issues of reflexivity in terms of ambivalence.

Bibliography

Alexander, J. (1996) "Critical Reflections on Reflexive Modernization." *Theory, Culture and Society*, 13, 4: 133–8.

Beck, U. (1992) *The Risk Society: Towards a New Modernity*. London: Sage.

Beck, U. (1995) *Ecological Politics in an Age of Risk*. Cambridge: Polity Press.

Beck, U. (1997) *The Reinvention of Politics: Rethinking Modernity in the Global Social Order*. Cambridge: Polity Press.

Beck, U. (1999) *The World Risk Society*. Cambridge: Polity Press.

Beck, U., Giddens, A., and Lash, S. (1994) *Reflexive Modernization: Politics, Tradition and Aesthetics in the Modern Social Order*. Cambridge: Polity Press.

Lash, S. (2000) "Risk Culture." In *The Risk Society and Beyond: Critical Issues for Social Theory*, ed. B. Adam, U. Beck, and J. Van Loon. London: Sage.

Levitas, R. (2000) "Discourses of Risk and Utopia." In *The Risk Society and Beyond: Critical Issues for Social Theory,* ed. B. Adam, U. Beck, and J. Van Loon. London: Sage.

Rose, H. (2000) "Risk, Trust and Scepticism in the Age of the New Genetics." In *The Risk Society and Beyond: Critical Issues for Social Theory,* ed. B. Adam, U. Beck, and J. Van Loon. London: Sage.

Scott,. A. (2000) "Risk Society or Angst Society." In *The Risk Society and Beyond: Critical Issues for Social Theory,* ed. B. Adam, U. Beck, and J. Van Loon. London: Sage.

Van Loon, J. (1999) "Mediating the Risks of Virtual Environments." In *Environmental Risks and the Media,* ed. S. Allan, B. Adam, and C. Carter. London: Routledge.

8 | Daniel Bell

Malcolm Waters

Ideas
End of ideology □ Postindustrial society □ Cultural contradiction

Major books
The End of Ideology (1960)
The Coming of Postindustrial Society (1973)
The Cultural Contradictions of Capitalism (1976)

Influences
Aron □ Rousseau □ Schumpeter □ Weber

Biographical Details

Daniel Bell was born in 1919 in the Lower East Side of New York City, his family having migrated from Eastern Poland. He was originally named Bolotsky, but this was changed to Bell when he was placed in the legal care of an upwardly mobile paternal uncle. Not withstanding this development, Bell experienced the full gamut of poor, immigrant Jewish experience: Yiddish as the first language; Hebrew school; ethnic street gangs; petty crime; racketeering; and the public poverty of waterfront shacks. By his own supposition, these experiences of poverty predisposed him to join the Young People's Socialist League

Bell entered the City College of New York as an undergraduate in 1935, majoring in classics. After graduating in 1938 he spent a year in graduate school at Columbia University, but without any apparent result. He left, for reasons unexplained, and spent most of the next twenty years working as a journalist mainly at the *New Leader* and then as Labor Editor at *Fortune*. He became an academic at Columbia in 1958, receiving a Ph.D. in 1960 for a compilation of his published work. He moved to Harvard in 1969 and became Henry Ford II Professor of Social Sciences in that university in 1980.

The key features of Bell's biography are that in the 1940s he experienced a Damascene turn away from the Marxism of his youth; that he operated at the center of an influential group of mainly Jewish intellectuals known as the New York Circle; that as a consequence, and against his own claims to the contrary, he is widely regarded as a neoconservative; that he was probably the most famous sociologist of his generation; that this fame came from his role as a public intellectual and adviser to government rather than from a direct influence on social theory.

Key Theoretical Contributions

Daniel Bell's theory is historical and substantive rather than formal and analytic. It proposes that society is organized in three realms: the techno-economic structure (sometimes the "social structure"), the polity, and culture.

The techno-economic structure (TES) is the realm of economic life, the arena of social arrangements for the production and distribution of goods and services. Such activities imply applications of technology to instrumental ends and result in a stratified occupational system. The axial principle of the modern TES is functional rationality. The lifeworlds of the TES are "reified" worlds in which the individual is subordinated to roles specified in organizational charts.

The polity is a system of societal authority involving the distribution of power, legitimated in modern society by reference to the consent of the governed. The axial structure is a system of representation that allows general consent to be expressed through organized arrangements – that is, political parties, lobby groups, and social movements – that can funnel claims to the center.

Bell's version of culture is much narrower than the conventional sociological or anthropological definitions that specify it as the overall pattern or shape of life in a society. He restricts his interest in culture to the arena of expressive symbolizations that always address the universal and irreducible fundamentals of human existence, the nature and meaning of death, tragedy, heroism, loyalty, redemption, love, sacrifice, and spirituality. The axial principle of modern culture is self-expression and self-realization.

The direction and the pattern of change in each of the realms are fundamentally different. In the TES change is linear or progressive, involving an upward curve in production and efficiency. In the polity the pattern of change consists in alternation between opposing configurations, e.g., between oligarchy and democracy. By contrast, cultural change is recursive, cyclically revisiting fundamental issues. Because the rhythm of change is different in each realm the realms will often be disjunctive; that is, normatively contradictory. Disjunction is the fulcrum of change and a central feature of modern society.

Bell explores this disjunctiveness of modern society through three more specific theoretical constructs. Perhaps the best known is the "postindustrial society." It argues that contemporary societies are or will be going through a shift from industrial society, "a game against fabricated nature" centering on the manufacturing and processing of tangible goods by semi-skilled factory workers and engineers, to postindustrial society, "a 'game between persons' in which an 'intellectual technology,' based on information, rises alongside of machine technology." The main features are that "the majority of the labor force is no longer engaged in agriculture or manufacturing but in services, which are defined, residually, as trade, finance, transport, health, recreation, research, education, and government"; the core will be scientists and engineers and together they will become a knowledge class that displaces the propertied bourgeoisie; and theoretical knowledge, as opposed to practical or traditional knowledge, is the "axial principle."

Bell takes his central and most controversial idea about the polity, "the end of ideology," from Camus via Aron (see Waxman 1968: 27–48). Ideology, for Bell, emerges to fill the psychic gap left by secularization and is therefore a nineteenth-century development. "Today [i.e., the 1960s]," Bell asserts, "these ideologies are exhausted" due to violent oppression by communist regimes, the welfare state, and the emergence of such new philosophies as existentialism and humanism. Bell is not, it must be stressed, entirely triumphalist about this development, mourning the spent passions of intellectualized politics and pleading for the retention of utopias as focuses for human aspiration.

Doubtless the most sociologically influential of Bell's contributions is his analysis of the contradictions of modern culture: "Modernity is individualism, the effort of individuals to remake themselves, and, where necessary, to remake society in order to allow design and choice." It implies the rejection of any "naturally" ascribed or divinely ordained order, external authority, and collective authority, in favor of the self as the sole point of reference for action.

The question is, how the self is to be fulfilled – by hedonism, by acquisitiveness, by faith, by the privatization of morality, or by sensationalism?

The initial pattern of "bourgeois society" was one of unification between entrepreneurship and personal economic responsibility in the TES, liberal resistance to state constraints in the polity, and an emphasis on expressing the self, as against tradition, in culture. The shift to a more hedonistic response, Bell argues, could only be confirmed once modernizing changes had also taken place in the realm of social (techno-economic) structure which could multiply possibilities for consumption. The primary contradiction of modern culture lies between norms of hedonism and norms of work discipline, that is between culture and social structure. But there is also an enormous contradiction within the social structure itself: a good worker delays gratification but a good consumer looks for immediate gratification.

Modern artistic culture has three important characteristics: an emphasis on medium, rage against order, and "the eclipse of distance"; that is, it denies content, opposes bourgeois morality, and seeks to represent the inner emotions rather than the external world. The largest contradiction of modern culture is that it persists in the face of this attack upon itself.

Major Criticisms

Analytic imprecision is the key weakness of the theoretical account of the postindustrial society. First, as Nichols indicates, Bell denies any claim that he is theorizing an end to capitalism and class. However, throughout the book, and particularly in the sections on stratification, it is clear that in Bell's view neither society as a whole nor the TES alone will be structured by capital accumulation in the future. This formulation surely must be designed to deny the reality of business power in a claim that is perhaps a little too anti-Marxist. Second, Bell forecasts the development of an enlarged communal state as if it can only happen in some future society. In fact, liberal corporatist states have long existed elsewhere than in the USA and have frequently successfully managed to balance claims within a reasoned political philosophy.

Bell's analysis of culture is both theoretically and normatively problematic. Everywhere Bell identifies radical contradictions between developments that do not really contradict each other at all. The biggest disjunction apparently lies between a culture that celebrates the self and a TES that requires the subordination of the self to discipline. However, an alternative interpretation of these processes is possible. In such an interpretation, the TES requires not self-discipline but merely a non-internalized compliance with rules in return for compensation. The primary source of commitment in the TES is therefore a radicalized individualism that links firmly to the gratification of the untrammeled self. On this alternative view, the fit between the instrumental worker, the yuppie entrepreneur, the rapacious consumer, and a spectacular, dehierarchized artistic arena is indissoluble.

Bell's explanation for the rise of modernism is that technology released the demonic self from its religious jail. Several full-blown alternative arguments suggest that the "self," demonic or otherwise, is a modern construction rather than a foundational reality. Foucault, for example, argues that sexuality was not constrained under premodern conditions but was embedded within kinship. For him, bourgeois society "discovered" sexuality and defined its perversities so that it could control it, precisely by means of discipline. For Foucault, as for Giddens, society is replete with authoritarian practices, elitist imposts, and bureaucratic controls. If the self strains to express itself against such constraints it is surely a little dismissive to treat that effort as inauthentic or as mere opinionism. Bell's value-stance on culture is not merely conservative but elitist. His derogations of popular culture and of postmodernism must be read as a claim for not merely authoritative but authoritarian cultural standards.

Perhaps even more than the great sociological theorists of the nineteenth century, Daniel Bell has been the prisoner of his time, his circumstances, and his value-commitments. He appears unable sufficiently to step out of specifically American sociohistorical developments to see his theory generalized and adopted widely. Moreover, this incapacity leads him into fundamental errors about power and class and about the relationship between general cultural standards and individual expression.

Bibliography

Bell, D. (1947) "Adjusting Men to Machines." *Commentary*, 79–88.
Bell D. (ed.) (1955) *The New American Right*. New York: Doubleday.
Bell, D. (1964) "Twelve Modes of Prediction." *Daedalus*, 93: 845–80.
Bell, D. (1965) [1960] *The End of Ideology*. Glencoe, IL: Free Press.
Bell, D. (1966) *The Reforming of General Education*. New York: Columbia University Press.
Bell, D. (1967) *Marxian Socialism in the United States*. Princeton, NJ: Princeton University Press.
Bell, D. (1968) *Towards the Year 2000*. Boston: Beacon Press.
Bell D. (1970) *Work and Its Discontents*. New York: League for Industrial Democracy.
Bell, D. (1973) *The Coming of Postindustrial Society*. New York: Basic Books.
Bell, D. (1976) *The Cultural Contradictions of Capitalism*. New York: Basic Books.
Bell, D. (1980) *The Winding Passage*. Cambridge: Abt.

Bell, D. (1982) *The Social Sciences since the Second World War*. New Brunswick, NJ: Transaction Press.

Bell, D. (1987) "The World and the United States in 2013." *Daedalus*, 116: 1–31.

Bell, D. (1990) "The Misreading of Ideology." *Berkeley Journal of Sociology*, 35: 1–54.

Bell, D. and Kristol, I. (eds.) (1969) *Confrontation*. New York: Basic Books.

Bell, D. and Kristol, I. (eds.) (1970) *Capitalism Today*. New York: New American Library.

Bell, D. and Kristol, I. (eds.) (1981) *The Crisis in Economic Theory*. New York: Basic Books.

Bloom, A. (1986) *Prodigal Sons*. New York: Oxford University Press.

Brick, H. (1986) *Daniel Bell and the Decline of Intellectual Radicalism*. Madison: University of Wisconsin Press.

Jumonville, N. (1991) *Critical Crossings*. Berkeley: University of California Press.

Kumar, K. (1978) *Prophecy and Progress*. Harmondsworth: Penguin Books.

Kumar, K. (1995) *From Postindustrial to Postmodern Society*. Oxford: Blackwell.

Leibowitz, N. (1985) *Daniel Bell and the Agony of Modern Liberalism*. Westport, CT: Greenwood Press.

O'Neill, J. (1988) "Religion and Postmodernism." *Theory, Culture and Society*, 5: 493–508.

Rose, M. (1991) *The Postmodern and the Postindustrial*. Cambridge: Cambridge University Press.

Steinfels, P. (1979) *The Neoconservatives*. New York: Simon and Schuster.

Wald, A. (1987) *The New York Intellectuals*. Chapel Hill: University of North Carolina Press.

Waters, M. (1996) *Daniel Bell*. London: Routledge.

Waxman, C. (ed.) (1968) *The End of Ideology Debate*. New York: Simon and Schuster.

9 | Jessica Benjamin

Kay Torney Souter

Ideas
Intersubjectivity □ Gender □ Recognition □ Inclusion □
Identification

Major books
The Bonds of Love (1986)
Like Subjects, Love Objects (1995)
Shadow of the Other (1998)

Influences
Freud □ Mahler □ Marcuse □ Stern □ Winnicott

Biographical Details

Jessica Benjamin (b. 1946) is perhaps the first practicing psychoanalyst to attempt to bring object relations theory and interpersonal psychoanalysis into serious dialogue with the central questions of poststructuralist feminist thought. Identifying a "cultural lag" in the response of psychoanalysis to questions of gender and sexuality, Benjamin's work brings the insights of feminist questions about identity to bear on misogynist and normalizing, and sometimes homophobic, tendencies within the mainstream tradition of clinical and theoretical psychoanalysis.

Benjamin's family background in left-wing politics was a formative influence on her intellectual life. Her father was a communist in the 1920s, but left the party in the 1940s in protest at its authoritarian aspects. Benjamin thus grew up in an atmosphere of somewhat baffled progressivism, surrounded by people who had been associated with left-wing politics, but for whom the forces of anti-communism had limited what could be achieved. The rise of the New Left (civil rights, the antiwar movement, and later feminism) in the late 1960s provided her with a new forum in which to explore political life and possibility. She studied in Frankfurt in the late 1960s – at the height of the student movement there – where she was able to study the connections between critical social theory and psychoanalysis, an interest from her first reading of Marcuse in 1966. She returned to the US in 1973 to work on the connections between psychoanalysis and social theory under Richard Sennett at New York University. Her doctoral work in the mid-1970s concerned the opposition between internalization of the object and recognition by the other, a focus which has continued to dominate much of her subsequent work.

In 1980 she entered the NYU postdoctoral program in Psychoanalysis and Psychotherapy, one of the relatively few American training programs which then accepted applicants who were not medically qualified. It was an important moment in the rise of relational psychoanalysis in the United States, and many who became important in that field trained with her. In 1988 she joined with Stephen Mitchell, Emannuel Ghent, and others to start a new relational wing of the training program, a wing which founded the journal *Psychoanalytic Dialogues*. Benjamin was simultaneously training and working with a group of feminist analysts, including Muriel Dimen, Virginia Goldner, and Adrienne Harris, with whom she ran a seminar on psychoanalysis and feminist issues during the mid-1980s to 1990s. This group later began the journal *Studies in Gender and Sexuality*. This range of clinical, political, and intellectual experiences meant that she was unusually placed for a practicing psychoanalyst, and in a position to bring philosophical and political insight to bear on current debates about the construction of gender.

Benjamin's theoretical model of psychoanalysis draws on a number of approaches which construct themselves as mutually exclusive, "the only thing worth knowing," in order to understand the problem of maternal subjectivity and its effect on the developing child. Her own practice maintains the intrapsychic emphasis of British Object Relations and combines it with the intersubjective emphasis of New York Relational Psychoanalysis, itself something of a blend of Habermasian philosophy, the work of Harry Stack Sullivan on the interpersonal, Kohutian self-psychology, and British object relations. Finally, she is influenced by the developmental models of childhood proposed by the empirical studies of childhood conducted by psychoanalysts Margaret Mahler and Daniel Stern. She uses British Object Relations (a combination of Kleinian and Middle School approaches), which proposes that subjectivity comes into being by its interaction with a primary carer, to critique the Lacanian orientation of academic feminism, in an attempt to bring the two traditions into "fruitful dispute" (Benjamin 1995: 15), rather than allowing them to stand constructed as mutually exclusive. Her argument is that where the Object Relations tradition has understood much more about the nature of identification, feminism, including Lacanian feminism, has much more to say about difference.

Benjamin rarely uses the conventional structure of the psychoanalytic theorist, where a theory is closely tied to a series of lengthy "clinical illustrations," but structures her work more like a social theorist: referring to other research and theory, with brief (often one-line) clinical examples. Her work sets out to resist the splitting tendency which is close to universal in both psychoanalysis and feminism, insisting on the importance of the "non-exclusivity" of different psychoanalytic models, and the value of maintaining a dialectical tension in theory. On the one hand, she uses the insights of clinical experience to question some of the conventions of the feminist philosophy of the 1990s, in particular those which suggest that "identity" is little more than an epistemological or formal construct. On the other, she uses her background in feminism and critical social theory to require the psychoanalytic institution to reconsider some of its more antiquated approaches to sexuality and gender.

Key Theoretical Contributions

Jessica Benjamin works and writes as a relational psychoanalyst, one who assumes the centrality of intersubjective phenomena, the two-person as opposed to the one-person psychic domain. Her academic training in critical social theory and feminism unites with her clinical experience to allow her to bring into dialogue several fields which have been represented as antithetical to each other: various (and sometimes warring) psychoanalytic traditions, and the insights of the feminist theory of the 1980s and 1990s. She combines these theoretical perspectives to reconfigure the psychoanalytic idea of what interpersonal relations and the development of a gendered self might involve. It is crucial to her argument that an intersubjective perspective be interwoven with other psychoanalytic approaches, rather than being put forward as a "more correct" school of psychoanalytic thinking which should supersede earlier models – an antagonistic approach to controversy which is endemic in the psychoanalytic tradition. For Benjamin, it is important politically as well as theoretically to develop a model of selfhood which is built on an interpersonal *as well as* an intrapsychic approach.

Her work addresses several areas which have been comparatively neglected by the various schools of psychoanalytic thought. These center on the tendency of psychoanalysis "to collapse other subjects into the rubric *objects*" (ibid: 29), especially where the first "object," the mother, is concerned; its institutionalization of rigid heterosexual Oedipal triangulation as the goal of maturity; and its often naturalizing or normative response to the structure of gendered identity. She approaches these areas of neglect by working across different theoretical positions: prying open a "space between" them (analogous to D. W. Winnicott's "potential space," where creative work can happen). Her goal is to avoid the binary mode, where one approach is ideologically sound and its opposite is heretical. Consequently, she insists that the intersubjective model, where minds always exist in exchange and dialogue with other minds, can coexist with the intrapsychic model in all its messy irrationality. Likewise (though with reservations about the binary inherent in Lacanian theory), she argues that Lacanian constitutive Lack can coexist with the object relations position that subjectivity comes into being by attention from the Other. In challenging the hermetic separation of different schools of psychoanalytic thought, and bringing different areas into dialogue, she works to decenter and "refigure" the psychoanalytic theory of development: "This ...would be analogous to Freud's idea of deferred action, *Nachtraeglichkeit* (see Laplanche and Pontalis, 1973). According to this approach, later integrations would retain and refine earlier positions, changing their appearance, yet not obliterating them, enabling a flexible oscillation between levels of experience" (ibid: 71).

From this championing of an "over-inclusive" psychoanalytic viewpoint, Benjamin approaches the development of gendered subjectivity and the representation of the maternal. Feminism has long been suspicious of psychoanalysis's attitude to women in general and the maternal in particular. Rather than ignoring or attacking this suspiciousness, Benjamin uses it in her first book, *The Bonds of Love* (1986), to analyze the relationship between the mother and the developing infant/child with the tools of intersubjective psychoanalysis and clinical–empirical studies of infant development. *The Bonds of Love* describes and analyzes the psychological processes leading to erotic domination. Benjamin argues the traditional feminist case that women's subordination to men is a "paradigmatic expression of splitting" (Benjamin 1995: 18), in which male denial of maternal subjectivity and repudiation of identification with the mother leads to denigration of the female. This position involves a critique of traditionally understood Oedipal structuring of the psyche with its consequent splitting of capacities into Subject and Other. Benjamin builds on the work of Margaret Mahler in the 1970s and Daniel Stern in the 1980s, whose theories of infant development were based on psychoanalytic observations of the actual interactions of mothers and infants in a relatively controlled setting. Mahler framed her observations of, for example, the storminess of the 2-year-old's "rapprochement crisis," in classic Freudian terms, as a matter of the infant's imperious need to separate from the mother, and Stern discussed similar material in more intersubjective terms, as a matter of discovering the existence of other minds. Arguing that previous accounts had been relatively father- or infant-centered, Benjamin insists that a developing sense of the mother as a subject in her own right is a normal part of psychic development, and that the idea of a presocial maternal symbiosis involves wishful reconstruction, "reading backwards through the lens of loss." She brings the work of D. W. Winnicott to bear on separation issues, suggesting that it is the reality that the object "survives destruction" (Winnicott 1991) which allows the developing child to "recognize" the mother's subjectivity and autonomy.

In fact, Benjamin argues that the "intersubjective space," an interpersonal counterpart of Winnicott's "potential space," which is created by the child achieving intersubjective recognition of the Other, and understanding that its "object" is in fact a subject in her own right, is what can provide the impetus to break up the pre- and antisocial dyad of mother and infant. Traditionally, Freudians and Lacanian theorists have argued that a "third term," some external force, typically the father, is needed to rescue the dyad from what is variously represented as primitive symbiosis or psychotic bliss. Benjamin's case is that this solution to undifferentiation simply preserves maternal idealization, as issues pertaining to anger are simply displaced onto the rival "third term," rather than worked through in the relationship with the mother. If the intersubjective space is preserved as an area where the fantasy of unity and omnipotence can be mourned and worked through, Benjamin argues that the need for the splitting defenses of the Oedipal, where object love and identification are polarized, can be avoided.

In short, Benjamin takes issue with the idea that identification and object-love are the simple inverses that the Oedipal triangle suggests. Rather, she suggests this belief is a problem of Oedipal "stuckness," and that identificatory love may well be the basis of healthy object-love. This is especially important in understanding of the development of boys. Full gender capacity, she argues, includes the capacity to "play" with multiple identifications, and the child becoming able to think of the mother as a subject in her own right, someone who can be subject as well as object. Importantly, intersubjective reality and fantasy always coexist.

In her later work Benjamin addresses the concerns of feminist theorists: in particular, epistemological issues to do with the construction of knowledge; philosophical ones to do with the avoidance of polarities in discourse; and questions in poststructuralist discourse. She insists that a developmental view need not lead to "normative goals" of sexuality, but (in what is close to the Kleinian idea of psychic shuttle) that developmental levels can be revisited throughout life, whether in play or in distress.

Major Criticisms

Clinical psychoanalysis has some objections to Benjamin's methods and ideas. She provides a less clinical–empirical framework for her argument than is usual in the Anglophone psychoanalytic establishments, and has been criticized for a tendency to illustrate her assertions with such brief clinical illustrations that they offer little in the way of evidence. It is also sometimes argued that her concentration on the intersubjective leads her to devalue the intrapsychic, thus substituting social psychology for psychoanalysis.

The main criticisms of Benjamin's work, however, result from her concentration on the role of the mother, and her attempts to bring conflicting psychoanalytic paradigms into dialogue. Her earlier work, too, was thought to pay insufficient attention to the possibility of homosexuality as a healthy choice. Her continual attempt to work across and between theoretical models, and particularly between the "philosophical and psychoanalytic register[s]" (Benjamin 1995: 20), sometimes leads to irritation as proponents of individual models object to her diverging from the usual approaches. Thus, clinical psychoanalysis occasionally objects to the amount of postmodern theory packed into her writing. Postmodern feminism sometimes objects to her work on intersubjectivity as normative and essentializing, and her treatment of the maternal as romanticizing. Critical theory is wary of her treatment of rationality.

Much of this criticism can be summarized as objecting that "recognition" risks the sacrifice of "difference." Benjamin herself argues strenuously that, on the contrary, she wants to establish a tension between difference and identification as paradox rather than to sacrifice one or the other.

Bibliography

Alford, C. F. (1989) *Melanie Klein and Critical Social Theory: An Account of Politics, Art and Reason Based on her Psychoanalytic Theory*. New Haven,

CT: Yale University Press.

Benjamin, J. (1986) *The Bonds of Love: Psychoanalysis, Feminism and the Problem of Domination*. London: Virago.

Benjamin, J. (1995) *Like Subjects, Love Objects: Essays on Recognition and Sexual Difference*. New Haven, CT: Yale University Press.

Benjamin, J. (1998) *Shadow of the Other: Intersubjectivity and Gender in Psychoanalysis*. New York: Routledge.

Mahler, M., Pine, F., and Bergmann, A. (1975) *The Psychological Birth of the Human Infant*. New York: Basic Books.

Meehan, J. (1994) "Autonomy, Recognition and Respect: Habermas, Benjamin, Honneth." *Constellations*, 1, 2: 270 –85.

Stern, D. (1985) *The Interpersonal World of the Infant*. New York: Basic Books.

Winnicott, D. W. (1991) [1969] "The Use of an Object and Relating through Identifications." In *Playing and Reality*. London: Routledge.

10 | **Walter Benjamin**

Howard Caygill

> ***Ideas***
> Aesthetics □ Modernity □ Experience □ Aestheticization of
> Politics □ Technology
>
> ***Major books***
> *The Origin of the German Mourning Play* (1928)
> *One Way Street* (1928)
> *The Arcades Project* (1999)
>
> ***Influences***
> Adorno □ Horkheimer □ Critical theory □ Arendt □ Scholem

Biographical Details

Walter Benjamin was born into a prosperous Jewish family in Berlin in 1892. His childhood in the rapidly expanding metropolis was recorded in his autobiographical memoirs from 1932, *A Berlin Chronicle* and *A Berlin Childhood around 1900*. In these texts Benjamin recalls the city as an enigma, full of strange objects and inexplicable actions, a perspective on the world that he sustained in his later work. His early education was marked by a mute resistance to the authoritarian culture of the Prussian school and an enthusiasm for the educational reforms proposed by Gustav Wyneken and the prewar youth movement in Germany. From 1912 Benjamin studied at the University of Freiburg with the neo-Kantian philosopher Heinrich Rickert, at the University of Berlin with Georg Simmel, and at the University of Munich with the art historian and philosopher of art Heinrich Wölfflin. He gained his Ph.D. at the University of Bern in 1919, where he had been in exile from conscription in

Germany, with a dissertation on *The Concept of Criticism in German Romanticism*.

During the difficult early years of the Weimar Republic Benjamin unsuccessfully pursued the possibility of an academic career in the German University. In the mid-1920s he abandoned this ambition and pursued a successful career as a public intellectual active in publishing for the booming newspaper industry and broadcasting on the new radio networks. Forced to leave Germany after the Nazi "seizure of power" in 1933 both as a Jew and a radical leftist, Benjamin lived largely in exile in Paris, where he worked on a large-scale project on the Paris Arcades. In 1940, during an attempt to escape the German occupation of France, Benjamin committed suicide in the Spanish border town of Port Bou. His writings were preserved by Theodor Adorno, Hannah Arendt, and the Gestapo archive in East Germany and were fitfully published in the 1950s and 1960s. Since their publication and translation they have become increasingly important as an influence on the New Left and later on the formulation of the field of cultural studies.

Key Theoretical Contributions

From his very earliest writings connected with the prewar youth movement, such as *The Metaphysics of Youth* (1913–14) and *Two Poems by Friedrich Hölderlin* (1914–15), Benjamin sought to combine philosophy and criticism. His critique of philosophy developed in *On Language as Such and on the Language of Man* (1916), and *On the Programme of the Coming Philosophy* (1918) sought to extend the range of the concept of experience that informed contemporary neo-Kantian philosophy to include language and the experience of everyday life. Benjamin fused the linguistic metacritique of philosophy with literarature to produce a new form of philosophizing and criticism in which the experience of the work of literature is corrected by philosophical reflection at the same time as that reflection is enriched by the work of literature. The medium for this encounter of philosophy and criticism was the long critical essay, a genre Benjamin perfected in the study *Goethe's Elective Affinities*, published in 1924, and which he continued to practice throughout the 1920s and 1930s in his essays on nineteenth-century writers such as Gottfried Keller and Charles Baudelaire and contemporaries such as the Surrealists, Brecht, Doblin, Kafka, and Kraus. Viewed as a whole, the essays add up to a startling reading of the emergence of literary and philosophical modernism and its relationship with the broader processes characteristic of the development of social and political modernity.

The essayistic confrontation of philosophy and criticism was extended to the dimensions of a treatise in Benjamin's *The Origins of the German Mourning Play* published in 1928. The work combines a philosophical analysis of the relationship between language and the experience of melancholy and mourning, an aesthetic justification of the concept of allegory recovered by the contemporary German expressionist movement, and an erudite reading of the largely forgotten genre of German baroque drama. These divergent lines of inquiry are contained by the broader ambition to reconstruct the origins of modernity in the Reformation. The 1921 fragment *Capitalism as Religion* allows *The Origins of the German Mourning Play* to be read as a contribution to the debate around the Protestant ethic inaugurated by Max Weber at the beginning of the century. Benjamin not only examines the melancholy ethic attendant upon the Protestant concept of sin, but also what might be called the "Protestant Aesthetic" of allegory characterized by an intense distrust of meaning and appearances. The text announces the growing significance of social theory for Benjamin's work, not only that of Weber, but also of George Sorel (*Critique of Violence*) , Georg Lukács (*History and Class Consciousness*), and Carl Schmitt (*The Concept of the Political*).

The project of the comprehensive recovery of the origins of modernity and modernism informing *The Origin of the German Mourning Play* was to be repeated with different materials – the cultural history of nineteenth-century Paris – in the incomplete *Arcades Project*. An important preliminary to the turn from literary criticism to cultural history was the text *One Way Street* published alongside *The Origin of the German Mourning Play* in 1928. With its aphoristic style and typographical experimentation *One Way Street* would seem to represent the modernist antithesis to the antiquarian erudition of its companion text, but the relationship between the two books is rather closer and more complex. *One Way Street* marks the development of Benjamin's extension of the prevailing concept of experience to include not only the experience of language but also that of everyday life. The book combines evocations of the destruction of the certainties of everyday life during the German inflation with fragmentary reflections on the urban experience of contemporary Berlin and Paris. In addition, *One Way Street* offers a preliminary sketch of the social theory of technology that Benjamin had been developing during the 1920s and which would play an important role in the *Arcades Project* .

Most of Benjamin's work in the 1930s was in some way connected with the work on the *Arcades Project*. This had begun life in 1927 as a projected joint article with Franz Hessel prompted by the destruction of the nineteenth-century arcades of central Paris. The project soon exceeded these modest bounds to become a vast, never to be completed cultural history of nineteenth-century Paris. The surviving alphabetically organized archive along with the outline *Paris, the Capital of the Nineteenth Century* (1935) show that the ambition of the project was to combine and exceed the achievements of the *The Origin of the German Mourning Play* and *One Way Street*. As in the former, Benjamin attempts a reconstruction of the origins of modernity, but with the focus falling this time not on the fate of the Reformation but on that of the French Revolution as revealed in the revolutions of the nineteenth century staged in Paris. And while the earlier focus on language and literary modernism is not abandoned, maintained in the studies of Baudelaire and Hugo that Benjamin considered publishing separately from the rest of the project, it is now extended to include a vast range of cultural historical materials drawn from the everyday life of nineteenth-century Paris.

The use of a broad range of archive material was intended to illustrate the tension between political and technological radicalism that Benjamin considered central to nineteenth-century Parisian culture. The guiding motif of the arcade exemplifies this tension, being at once the direct outcome of technological developments in iron and glass architecture and the utopian revolutionary impulse towards a democratic and transparent metropolitan community. The positive image of modernity that for Benjamin emerged from this coincidence of technological development and political imagination was subsequently lost, and much of the *Arcades Project* traces this loss in the fate of the arcade – its transformation from innovative public space into the department store. The account of Haussmann's urban reforms presents a similar picture, with the technological possibilities for a redrawing of the map of Paris being directed toward the goal of "strategic beautification" in the interests of the existing order. It is within this account of the fate of the French and industrial revolutions that Benjamin situates the modernism of Baudelaire and Hugo, contrasting their literary techniques and their melancholic and ecstatic responses to the tension between the forces of the political and technological modernization of Paris.

Benjamin consistently claimed during the 1930s that the *Arcades Project* was intended to form a constellation between the nineteenth century and the present – the 1930s. His other well-known writings of the period, such as *The Author as Producer, Franz Kafka*, the Brecht commentaries, and the *The Work of Art in the Age of Mechanical Reproduction*, draw on the results of the *Arcades Project* to imagine a new relationship between art, revolution, and technology. Perhaps the most significant historical constellation is that between "strategic beautification" of nineteenth-century Paris and the contemporary fascist "aestheticization of politics." By tracing the origins of the reactionary uses of technology and aesthetics Benjamin sought better to understand what seemed to him the fascist fate of modernity and the potential for resistance in what he described at the close of the *Work of Art* essay as the "politicization of art" intimated by cinema and other new mass media. His last work, the *Theses on the Philosophy of History* (1940), sustains the case for establishing a critical constellation of the present with its forgotten past, but conspicuously without the positive prognosis of the politicization of art.

Major Criticisms

Since his death and the posthumous publication and republication of his writings, the significance of Benjamin's contribution has undergone a number of changes. The early phases of his reception tried to ally his work with the neo-Marxism of the Frankfurt School of Adorno and Horkheimer, separating it from the "crude" Marxism of Brecht and in the face of objections to any Marxist claim on his work from Hannah Arendt, who situated Benjamin within a German tradition of romantic criticism, and of Benjamin's friend Gershom Scholem who insisted upon his debts to the Jewish mystical tradition. The focus of the early phase of debate – the extent and nature of Benjamin's Marxism – has since shifted to one between his contribution as a philosopher and as a cultural historian. However, even this opposition is increasingly being questioned, especially in the light of the comprehensive translation project undertaken by Harvard University Press, which has made available in English the complete range of Benjamin's texts.

Bibliography

Adorno, T. W. (1995) [1967] *Prisms*, trans. Samuel and Shierry Weber. Cambridge, MA: MIT Press.
Arendt, H. (1968) "Walter Benjamin 1892–1940." In *Men in Dark Times* San Diego: Harcourt Brace Jovanovich.
Benjamin, A. and Osborne, P. (2000) *Walter Benjamin's Philosophy: The Destruction of Experience*. Manchester: Clinamen Books.
Benjamin, W. (1970) *Illuminations,* trans. H. Zohn. London: Jonathan Cape.
Benjamin, W. (1973) *Understanding Brecht*, trans. A. Bostock. London: Verso.
Benjamin, W. (1977) *The Origin of German Tragic Drama*, trans. J. Osborne. London: Verso.
Benjamin, W. (1979) *One Way Street and Other Writings*, trans. E. Jephcott and K. Shorter. London: Verso.

Benjamin, W. (1983) *Charles Baudelaire: A Lyric Poet in the Era of High Capitalism*, trans. H. Zohn and Q. Hoare. London: Verso.

Benjamin, W. (1994) *The Correspondence of Walter Benjamin, 1910–1940*, trans. M. R. Jacobsen and E. M. Jacobsen. Chicago: University of Chicago Press.

Benjamin, W. (1996) *Selected Writings: Volume 1 1913–1926*, ed. M. Bullock and M. W. Jennings. Cambridge, MA: Harvard University Press.

Benjamin, W. (1999a) *The Arcades Project*, trans. H. Eiland and K. McLaughlin. Cambridge, MA: Harvard University Press.

Benjamin, W. (1999b) *Selected Writings: Volume 2 1927–1934*, ed. M. W. Jennings, H. Eiland and G. Smith. Cambridge, MA: Harvard University Press.

Brodersen, M. (1996) *Walter Benjamin: A Biography*. London: Verso.

Buck-Morss, S. (1989) *The Dialectics of Seeing: Walter Benjamin and the Arcades Project*. Cambridge, MA: MIT Press.

Caygill, H. *Walter Benjamin: The Colour of Experience*. London: Routledge.

Caygill, H. and Coles, A. (1998) *Walter Benjamin for Beginners*. Cambridge: Icon Books.

Eagleton, T. (1981) *Walter Benjamin, or Towards a Revolutionary Criticism*. London: New Left Books.

Handelman, S. A.(1991) *Fragments of Redemption: Jewish Thought and Literary Theory in Benjamin, Scholem and Levinas*. Bloomington: Indiana University Press.

Jennings, M. (1987) *Dialectical Images: Walter Benjamin's Theory of Literary Criticism*. Ithaca, NY: Cornell University Press.

McCole, J. (1993) *Walter Benjamin and the Antinomies of Tradition*. Ithaca, NY: Cornell University Press.

Mehlmann, J. (1993) *Walter Benjamin for Children: An Essay on his Radio Years*. Chicago: University of Chicago Press.

Nagele, R. (ed.) (1988) *Benjamin's Ground: New Readings of Walter Benjamin*. Detroit, MI: Wayne State University Press.

Scholem, G. (1981) *Walter Benjamin: The Story of a Friendship*, trans. H. Zohn. Philadelphia, PA: Jewish Publication Society of America.

Smith, G. (ed.) (1989) *Benjamin: Philosophy, History, Aesthetics*. Chicago: University of Chicago Press.

Witte, B. (1991) *Walter Benjamin: An Intellectual Biography*, trans. J. Rolleston. Detroit, MI: Wayne State University Press.

Wolin, R. (1994) *Walter Benjamin: An Aesthetic of Redemption*. Berkeley: University of California Press.

11 | Homi Bhabha

Bart Moore-Gilbert

Ideas
Ambivalence □ Hybridity □ Mimicry □ Third space

Major books
Nation and Narration (1990)
The Location of Culture (1994)

Influences
Bakhtin □ Benjamin □ Derrida □ Fanon □ Foucault □ Kristeva □
Lacan

Biographical Details

Along with Edward Said and Gayatri Spivak, Homi Bhabha (b. 1949) is
a member of what Robert Young's *Colonial Desire* (1995) calls "the Holy
Trinity" of postcolonial theorists. The trio has been instrumental in the
rapid expansion of contemporary postcolonial studies, the founding text
of which is Said's *Orientalism* (1978). Bhabha's influence has been out
of all proportion to the volume of his published work. His only single-
authored book is *The Location of Culture* (1994), a collection of (sometimes heavily rewritten) essays published previously. In revising and
extending both Fanon's and Said's accounts of colonial relations, it has
made him one of the most influential theoreticians of diasporic culture
(he himself was born in India, was university-educated in Britain, and
now works in the United States) and of contemporary
"multiculturalisms" in the West.

Key Theoretical Contributions

The first phase of Bhabha's career (approximately 1980 to 1988) is distinctive for its questioning of the system of binaries which underwrites the account of colonial relations in both Said's *Orientalism* and the better-known work of Fanon, such as *The Wretched of the Earth* (1961). Bhabha suggests that such tensions, contradictions, and polarities as *Orientalism* does note in colonial relations are illegitimately resolved and unified by Said's conviction of the unidirectionality and intentionality of colonial knowledge as will to power. Meanwhile he suggests that Fanon's later work relies too much on psychically and phenomenologically fixed models of colonial identity. For Bhabha, such ideas ironically reinforce the very divisions between colonizer and colonized on which colonial discourse itself relies.

For Bhabha, the relationship between colonizer and colonized is more complex and politically ambiguous than the previous figures suggest, primarily because of the contradictory play of psychic affect and identification in colonial relations (desire for as well as fear of the Other, for example). In this respect, Bhabha's main methodological debts are to Lacan, whose radical revisions of Freudian models of identity-formation underlie Bhabha's foundational premise that "identity is only ever possible in the *negation* of any sense of originality or plenitude, through the principle of displacement and differentiation ... that always renders it a liminal reality." The adaptation of Lacanian theory to analysis of colonial relations was in fact anticipated in Fanon's *Black Skin, White Masks* (1952), which for Bhabha offers a much more enabling path than *The Wretched of the Earth*. Fanon's text is valued for its focus on intersubjective negotiations (rather than the "public sphere" of law, economic relations, and the army, for instance) and for conceiving of such engagements in terms of dynamic and shifting, rather than binary and static, modes of operation.

Indeed, Bhabha's early essays reconfigure the very category of "the political" as it is understood by early Said and late Fanon. Bhabha sites it in this shifting and often unconscious affective area "in-between" the dominant and subordinate cultures, across which an unstable traffic of continuously (re)negotiated psychic identifications and (re)positionings is in evidence. Bhabha concludes that while psychic "ambivalence" on the part of both "partners" in the colonial relationship points to a certain complicity between them, it also opens up unexpected and hitherto unrecognized ways in which the operations of colonial power were circumvented by the native subject, through a process which might be described as psychological guerrilla warfare.

This involves a radical reconceptualization of anti-colonial politics. On the one hand, Bhabha posits an "intransitive" model of resistance, which recuperates the resistance which is written out in *Orientalism*, without reinscribing the sovereign subject of Fanon's later work. For Bhabha, colonial power is immanently liable to destabilization, or what might be termed "resistance from within," for three principal reasons. First, following Foucault's *The History of Sexuality* (1976), Bhabha suggests that, like all forms of power, colonial authority "unintentionally" incites "refusal, blockage, and invalidation" in its attempts at surveillance. Secondly, following Lacan's *Four Fundamental Concepts of Psychoanalysis* (1973), Bhabha argues that the gaze of colonial authority is always troubled by the fact that colonial identity is partly dependent for its constitution on a colonized Other and can never, therefore, be foundational. Both these kinds of resistance are illustrated in Bhabha's discussion of "mimicry" and "hybridization," colonial strategies which work to consolidate power by inducing colonized subjects to imitate the forms and values of the dominant culture. For Bhabha, such strategies can never fully succeed because they also always require the subordinate to remain at least partially different from the dominant in order to preserve the structures of discrimination on which the latter's power is based. Thirdly, following the Derrida of *Writing and Difference* (1967), Bhabha suggests that "intransitive" resistance derives at least in part from the vicissitudes to which all language, including the language of power, is intrinsically liable, especially through the play of "repetition" and the structure of *différance*. Thus "Englishness" itself, once "translated" into the alien context of the Indian colonial arena, becomes only "a partial presence, a (strategic) device in a specific colonial engagement, an appurtenance of authority."

In contrast to such kinds of "intransitive" resistance, however, Bhabha's early work also explores resistance in more (ostensibly) conventional terms as "transitive" and active, which nonetheless also diverges from standard accounts of anti-colonial resistance. First, the colonized subject can return, and consequently directly challenge, the colonizer's gaze. Secondly, the mimic subject can also refuse to return the colonizer's gaze which, Bhabha suggests, also destabilizes colonial authority. A refusal to satisfy the colonizer's "narrative demand" for recognition is, for Bhabha, an equally effective act of political as well as psychic resistance.

Since the late 1980s Bhabha has devoted himself primarily to analysis of the legacies of colonial history, and traditional discourses of race, nation, and ethnicity, in contemporary cultural relations in the post- (or neo-)colonial era. Bhabha is especially preoccupied by questions of cultural exchange and identification which are not overdetermined by problems of geographical distance and overt forms of political inequality, as in colonialism, but by the contiguity of cultures sharing the same (metropolitan) space and relations of ostensible, if often illusory, equality. Such issues involve Bhabha in a complex set of negotiations between postcolonialism and postmodernism. On the one hand, he seems to suggest that insofar as colonial repression and genocide represent events as catastrophic as the Holocaust or Hiroshima, the disillusionment with modernity's ideologies of reason, progress, and humanism which underwrites the "closure" of modernity in one strand of postmodernism is justified. However, Bhabha also suggests that modernity cannot be considered complete because in certain crucial respects the putatively postmodern world replicates and perpetuates certain negative aspects of modernity. This is nowhere so apparent as in the contemporary West's rearticulation of the social, political, and economic structures (and ideological forms of Othering) which characterized the colonial history accompanying the Enlightenment and its legacies. Consequently, Bhabha proposes what he calls a "postcolonial contramodernity" which, by reinscribing the repressed histories and social experiences of the formerly colonized, generates the same destabilizing relationship to postmodernity as colonial history represented for the West's earlier claim to modernity and Enlightenment.

While stressing this alternative conception of modernity as open (or "unfinished"), as a means through which new sites, times, and kinds of enunciation are made possible for the formerly colonized, however, Bhabha scrupulously avoids a reinscription of modernity as constituted by progress towards a synthesis or resolution of historical and cultural differences and tensions. Bhabha's recent writing is strongly anti-teleological and anti-dialectical insofar as such efforts at synthesis will tend to efface the cultural particularity and specificity of the formerly colonized within a "higher" term. Bhabha proposes instead a conception of "cultural difference" which does not simply aspire to equivalence or equality with the dominant, and resists any process of sublation which may preserve the former authority of the dominant. Instead his model of cultural "difference" respects and preserves the peculiar and multiple histories and identities of the historically marginalized.

Cultural difference in Bhabha's sense, however, is not to be understood simply as that which remains beyond the attempt of one culture to "integrate" or "translate" another. While Bhabha is at pains to deny the liberal, cultural relativist concept of "the family of man," together with what he sees as postmodernism's "celebration of fragmentation, *bricolage*, pastiche, or 'simulacrum,'" he stresses that the relationship of postcolonial or migrant experience to the dominant culture is not simply antagonistic. For this reason he opposes what he calls the doctrine of "cultural diversity" which, like the regime of apartheid, seeks to inscribe absolute and ontological relations of difference between cultures. Equally, Bhabha seeks to "revise those nationalist or 'nativist' pedagogies that set up the relation of Third World and First World in a binary structure of opposition." Instead, such binaries are to be displaced by means of concepts like the hybrid "third space."

Major Criticisms

Productive though Bhabha's intervention in the postcolonial field has undoubtedly been, both phases of his career have excited a considerable amount of criticism. In his work on colonial discourse, Bhabha has been accused of minimizing more material forms of resistance to colonial rule, and privileging instead discursive modes of resistance, with the implication that the critic who unpicks the symbolic and narrative ordering of the hegemonic order becomes the prime locus of opposition to the dominant. This raises the question of how effective the kinds of resistance which Bhabha identifies actually were in colonial history, or could be if adapted to the present moment. Bhabha's recourse to psychoanalytic theory raises other difficult questions. First, he does not really consider whether psychoanalysis may be a specifically "First World" form of knowledge which, as such, may not be unproblematically translatable to analysis of (post)colonial problematics. Secondly, Bhabha has been accused of illegitimately conflating the psychic identities of the colonizer and colonized to produce a unitary model of the colonial subject which discounts the crucial material differences in their situations. Another important line of criticism is that Bhabha overlooks the problems posed to his analytic models by class and gender differentials on both sides of the colonial equation. Finally, one could argue that Bhabha fudges the question of the degree to which some of the kinds of "active" resistance he outlines are in fact conscious or not and can therefore legitimately be understood to constitute the grounds of political action.

In terms of Bhabha's more recent work, a number of criticisms suggest themselves. While he claims to be attempting to "provide a form of the writing of cultural difference in the midst of modernity that is inimical to binary boundaries," his concepts often rely on the very structures he is trying to undermine for their effectivity. "Hybridity," perhaps the key concept throughout his career in this respect, obviously depends upon a presumption of the existence of its opposite for its force. This leads to the danger that the "hybrid" may itself become essentialized or fixed. Kristeva (an important point of reference throughout Bhabha's second phase) warns in *Women's Time* (1979) that the insistence that sexual difference is constructed in irreducibly biological terms may lead eventually to the practice of an inverted sexism. This is the same order of problem which Bhabha faces insofar as, more often than not, he presents the "non-hybrid" alternatives to the postcolonial, notably Western neocolonialism and Third World nationalism, in unitary terms which do not do justice to their manifest internal contradictions and differentiated histories. Thus, in tracking the ways that (post)modernity constitutes itself as such in relation to a non-Western Other, for instance, Bhabha makes only the most token reference to the parallel processes of the Othering of women and subordinate classes within the discourses of the (post)Enlightenment – as well as to (post)modernity's initial impetus, its engagement with its own (pre)modern history.

Bibliography

Ahmad, A. (1992) *In Theory: Classes, Nations, Literatures*. London: Verso.
Bhabha, H. (ed.) (1990) *Nation and Narration*. London: Routledge.
Bhabha, H. (1994) *The Location of Culture*. London: Routledge.
Byrne, E. (forthcoming) *Homi Bhabha*. London: Macmillan.
McClintock, A. (1993) "The Return of Female Fetishism and the Fiction of the Phallus." *New Formations*, 19, spring.
Moore-Gilbert, B. (1997) "The Babelian Performance." In *Postcolonial Theory: Contexts, Practices, Politics*. London: Verso.
Parry, B. (1994) "'Signs of Our Times': A Discussion of Homi Bhabha's *Location of Culture*." *Third Text*, 28–8.
Young, R. (1990) "The Ambivalence of Bhabha." In *White Mythologies: Reading History and the West*. London: Routledge.

12 | Maurice Blanchot

Kevin Hart

Ideas
Community □ Contestation □ The Outside □ Friendship □
Experience

Major books
The Unavowable Community (1988)
The Blanchot Reader (1995)
Friendship (1997)
The Infinite Conversation (1997)
The Station Hill Blanchot Reader (1998)

Influences
Bataille □ Hegel □ Heidegger □ Lévinas □ Mallarmé

Biographical Details

The author's note to *L'Espace littéraire* (1995) reads: "Maurice Blanchot, novelist and critic, was born in 1907. His life is entirely devoted to literature and to the silence appropriate to it." These sentences are clearly intended to deflect any biographical interest in Blanchot, and until quite recently they worked very well indeed. His acquaintances perhaps knew that he was born in Quain in Saône-et-Loire, that he attended university at Strasbourg where he met his lifelong friend Emmanuel Lévinas, that he met his other great friend, Georges Bataille, in 1940, and that he participated joyfully and lucidly in the events of May 1968. His more distant readers have had to content themselves with his enigmatic novels, *récits*, and a body of literary criticism that is almost as haunting and perplexing as the fiction. Blanchot, so the story goes, is unlike any other French intellectual: he has effaced himself from the public world. Until

Lire published an unauthorized photograph of him in 1985, no one knew what he looked like.

In May 1968 only those with long memories would have recalled that Blanchot the left-wing revolutionary was the same man who wrote for the far right-wing press in the 1930s. When his political columns in *Le Rempart, L'Insurgé*, and especially *Combat* were rediscovered in the 1970s and 1980s the Blanchot who came into focus was not the "novelist and critic" committed to silence but an articulate and fiery monarchist. Like Charles Maurras, the young Blanchot affirmed the values of pre-revolutionary France; unlike Maurras, Blanchot had no link with Action Française, and unlike some of Maurras's disciples at *Je Suis Partout* he did not collaborate with the Nazis. What Blanchot wanted, above all, was a national revolution that would revive a weak France. Instead, in 1940 France was occupied by Germany.

It would be a mistake to picture a disappointed Blanchot of the early 1940s simply retreating from politics to the comfort of literature. He had been reviewing fiction and poetry while also commenting on politics. Literature for him hardly brought serenity, as *Thomas l'obscur* (1941) and *Aminadab* (1942) show. Besides, his attraction to the "space of literature" did not distract him from his moral responsibilities. During the war he resisted the occupying forces and, in particular, hid Lévinas's wife and daughter from the Nazis. From 1949 to 1957 he lived in the south of France, in Eze, far from the center of French culture; and in these years he produced several of his finest works: the new version of *Thomas l'obscur* (1950), *Au Moment voulu* (1951), *Celui qui ne m'accompagnait pas* (1953), *L'Espace littéraire* (1955), and *Le Dernier homme* (1957). Returning to Paris he identified himself with the leftist opposition to de Gaulle, contributing to the revolutionary *Le 14 Juillet* and helping to draft the "Manifesto of the 121" (1958) which supported French soldiers who refused to fight against the Algerians. In 1968 he wrote a good deal of *Comité*, yet when students and workers opposed Israel he distanced himself from them. Even the absence of antisemitism, he realized, was insufficient to prevent antisemitic acts.

In 1998 there appeared Christophe Bident's biography of Blanchot. Bident debunks the myth of Blanchot as an absent presence, a ghostly figure, and presents him instead as an "invisible partner" in the world of French intellectual life. So intently, though, does Bident present the life in terms of the work that the author's note in *L'Espace littéraire* comes close to being confirmed. Yet over the years Blanchot had changed in some respects: "writing" had come to replace "literature," and he talked less of "silence" and more of the endless "murmur" of language.

Key Theoretical Contributions

One index of Blanchot's standing among French writers is the admiration for his writing expressed by Georges Bataille, Gilles Deleuze, Jacques Derrida, Michel Foucault, Edmond Jabès, and Emmanuel Lévinas. Testimony to the originality and power of his fiction, especially *Thomas the Obscure*, *The Madness of the Day*, and *Death Sentence*, is common. Most of his work has now been translated into English, and one could find no better resource than *The Station Hill Blanchot Reader* (Quasha 1998). In Blanchot the border between fiction and criticism has never been smooth and continuous, and with *Awaiting Oblivion, The Infinite Conversation, The Step Not Beyond*, and *The Writing of the Disaster* it is interrupted as a matter of principle. That said, I will focus on his critical and theoretical writings, paying particular attention to what is valuable for social theory in his work.

Of primary importance for understanding the contemporary transformation of the human sciences, Foucault thinks, is Blanchot's notion of the Outside; and Foucault's personal commitment to it is confirmed by Deleuze, who points out that his friend wished to position himself here. For anyone familiar with *The Space of Literature* this will seem odd, since the Outside is evoked there as something only novelists and poets brush against when writing, and it is described as menacing, sordid, and suffocating. Blanchot has in mind the moment when the writer loses contact with everyday life and is exposed to language working without an organizing intelligence: a great murmur of what has been said, could have been said, and perhaps will be said. Fascinated, the writer must nonetheless break free from this vision of the Outside in order to begin the work. Blanchot calls this glimpse of the Outside the "original experience," and he values those works that posit themselves by way of this experience. It is felt keenly in the writings of Mallarmé and Kafka.

The original experience is existential rather than aesthetic, Blanchot thinks. Death has two aspects. The first is a relationship of possibility: my death appears to me as the possibility of my impossibility. This is the language of Heidegger's *Being and Time* (1927), although Blanchot stresses that Hegel also construes death in terms of possibility, as the labor of the negative: the movement of the dialectic that constitutes history. Death can also approach me as the impossibility of all possibility, however. Here I am opened to the endlessness of dying, a task that can never be completed because in dying there is no negativity. We can say that I am confronted by death while, in dying, I have already become an anonymous and neutral "one." It is Blanchot's central contention that in giving oneself over to writing one passes from the first to the third person, from "I" to "one," and is consequently exposed to the infinite movement of dying. Of course, an author may ignore the original experience and simply produce a bestseller or even a masterpiece, but the work that matters – prose by Beckett, poetry by Celan – will involve the original experience. In reading it one follows the inexorable movement of writing, its demural to become a fixed work. Regardless of its length, this kind of writing is a fragment. It does not answer to a unity.

For this reason Blanchot distances himself from Jean-Paul Sartre's insistence that literature should be socially engaged. To be sure, any piece of writing has a dialectic; it is meaningful because language is thoroughly social. Yet literature is not only a work but also out of work: a portion of an endless movement of writing that cannot be properly assigned a cultural or social value. Indeed, Blanchot conceives writing as endless contestation; all power, even its own, is called into question. This does not lead to anarchy, Blanchot thinks. As late as the early 1960s, when he was involved in the project of a *Revue internationale*, he insisted that infinite contestation led to the recognition of literature as a "power without power." Without denying this, Blanchot started to change his way of phrasing matters. Partly due to the influence of Derrida's early essays, Blanchot began to prefer the word "writing" over "literature." By 1969 he could give pride of place in one of his most significant books to the judgment that writing is "an anonymous, distracted, deferred and dispersed way of being in relation" (Blanchot 1997 [1969]: xii).

The Outside, as figured here, answers to writing rather than to literature; and it is this adjusted version of the notion which Deleuze and Foucault prize. In *The Space of Literature* the writer brushes against the Outside when leaving the security of the journal, which merely records daily events, for the dangerous experience of literature. With *The Infinite Conversation* the situation has changed. Now the Outside is construed in terms of the everyday as well as art. One thing that remains constant in both accounts is Blanchot's insistence that, strictly speaking, one cannot experience the Outside. Since the Outside is neutral and does not participate in any dialectic, there is nothing that can offer itself to consciousness. In passing from the first to the third person, from "I" to "one," we encounter the Outside as a limit, and in describing this we are constrained to speak of the "experience of non-experience."

Blanchot grounds his reflections on the everyday in Henri Lefebvre's critique of everyday life. More rigorously than Lefebvre, though, he makes the everyday itself into a perpetual critique of philosophy and religion. Everyday life excludes God because it allows no beginning or end; it frightens heroes because there is nothing for them to do; it refuses distinctions between true and false, subject and object; and opens a space of radical nihilism. Blanchot asks us to understand this view of things in the strongest possible sense: not as a fall from an ideal but as an affirmation of human community. A community is not formed by reference to a dialectic (as in Hegel) or in a moment of fusion (as in the fascist state), but in the dispersed and mobile way of being in relation, the model for which is writing.

Community, here, is not a contract of reciprocal rights and obligations between distinct selves who retain the power to say "I." Rather, it interrupts such models, opening up the vista of an anonymous relation of double dissymmetry between people who live in the third person, as "one" rather than "I." Blanchot glimpsed this neutral way of being, this relation without relation, in May 1968, and associates it with a communism that is forever to come. The smallest and most tender of communities is that between two friends. Yet friendship is not to be confused with camaraderie; it prizes discretion, is characterized by fidelity, and maintains itself in a relation of mutual openness to the other person. Friendship does not unify two individuals; it fractures totality and exposes friends to the strangeness of the Outside.

Major Criticisms

Blanchot is less than plain in specifying the scope and strength of his claims about literature. His reflections on the "original experience" are based on a narrow range of modern European writers. Although he admits that his privileged texts speak in a dialectical as well as a neutral language, it is unclear why, since the neutral contests cultural and social values, those fragmentary texts which affirm the original experience should be accorded a special place in his reflections. Also, although Blanchot's most persistent target is unity, he takes very little interest in describing it or telling us exactly what is wrong with it. Whether he objects to a unity of parts or of stages, for instance, is not specified. One consequence of this is that, to a theologian, his dismissal of God as the ground of all unity seems uninformed. God is one, yet unity is not one of his primary attributes. And to a philosopher, his critique of the subject is at best impressionistic: perhaps the subject is dispersed, but we still need to know what constitutes personal identity over time.

Blanchot has been sharply criticized, especially by Jeffrey Mehlman, for his contributions to the right-wing press in the 1930s (Mehlman 1983; Gill 1996). The dossier on Blanchot's wartime activities had in fact been opened by Michael Holland and Patrick Rousseau some years before in *Gramma* (1976), and Holland has since insisted that "no suspicion hangs over Maurice Blanchot's life, as there are those well placed to attest" (Holland 1995: 13). In self-condemnation, however, Blanchot has said that merely to refer to Maurras in March 1942, as he did in a review, was "detestable and inexcusable" (Gill 1996: 210). Tzvetan Todorov claims that "before the war Blanchot became the spokesman for a certain antisemitism" (Todorov 1987: 61), although it is not clear exactly what the "certain" refers to here and what evidence there is to support the claim. More generally, Todorov takes Blanchot to task for rejecting values and embracing a post-Nietzschean nihilism. Knowing what we know about the Gulag and the Nazis, he says, should make us think twice before we deride universal values. Besides, Blanchot the severe critic of totality has been "singularly tolerant with respect to Soviet totalitarianism" (ibid). All in all, perhaps Blanchot's criticisms of unity are of more interest in practice, in his criticism and fiction, that in his theoretical pronouncements.

Bibliography

Bident, C. (1998) *Maurice Blanchot, partenaire invisible: essai biographique* [Maurice Blanchot, Invisible Partner: Biographical Essay]. Seyssel: Éditions Champ Vallon.

Blanchot, M. (1943) *Faux pas* [False Step]. Paris: Gallimard.

Blanchot, M. (1948a) *La Part du feu*. Paris: Gallimard. Trans. C. Mandell, *The Work of Fire*. Stanford, CA: Stanford University Press, 1995.

Blanchot, M. (1948b) *Le Très-haut*. Paris: Gallimard, 1948. Trans. A. Stoekl, *The Most High*. Lincoln: University of Nebraska Press, 1996.

Blanchot, M. (1949) *Lautréamont et Sade*. Paris: Éditions de Minuit. Partially trans. B. Wall, "Marquis de Sage." *Horizon*, 20 (Dec. 1949–Jan. 1950): 423–52.

Blanchot, M. (1955) *L'Espace littéraire*. Paris: Gallimard. Trans. A. Smock, *The Space of Literature*. Lincoln: University of Nebraska Press, 1982.

Blanchot, M. (1959) *Le Livre à venir* [The Book to Come]. Paris: Gallimard.

Blanchot, M. (1962) *L'Attente l'oubli*. Paris: Gallimard. Trans. J. Gregg, *Awaiting Oblivion*. Lincoln: University of Nebraska Press, 1997.

Blanchot, M. (1969) *L'Entretien infini*. Paris: Gallimard. Trans. S. Hanson, *The Infinite Conversation*. Lincoln: University of Nebraska Press, 1997.

Blanchot, M. (1971) *L'Amitié*. Paris: Gallimard. Trans. E. Rottenberg, *Friendship*. Stanford, CA: Stanford University Press, 1997.

Blanchot, M. (1973) *Le Pas au-delà*. Paris: Gallimard. Trans. L. Nelson, *The Step Not Beyond*. Albany: State University of New York Press, 1992.

Blanchot, M. (1977) *Le Dernier homme,* new edn. Paris: Gallimard. Trans. L. Davis, *The Last Man*. New York: Columbia University Press, 1987.

Blanchot, M. (1980) *L'Écriture du désastre*. Paris: Gallimard. Trans. A. Smock, *The Writing of the Disaster*. Lincoln: University of Nebraska Press, 1986.

Blanchot, M. (1981) *The Gaze of Orpheus and Other Literary Essays,* trans. L.

Davis, ed. P. A. Sitney. Barrytown, NY: Station Hill Press.

Blanchot, M. (1983a) *Après coup précédé par Le Ressassement éternel*. Paris: Éditions de Minuit. Trans. P. Auster, *Vicious Circles: Two Fictions and "After the Fact."* Barrytown, NY: Station Hill Press, 1985.

Blanchot, M. (1983b) *La Communauté inavouable*. Paris: Éditions de Minuit. Trans. P. Joris, *The Unavowable Community*. Barrytown, NY: Station Hill Press, 1988.

Blanchot, M. (1986) *Michel Foucault tel que je l'imagine*. Montpellier: Éditions Fata Morgana. Trans. J. Mehlman, "Michel Foucault as I Imagine Him," in *Foucault/Blanchot* by M. Foucault and M. Blanchot. New York: Zone Books, 1990.

Blanchot, M. (1994) *L'Instant de ma mort*. Montpellier: Éditions Fata Morgana. Trans. E. Rottenberg, *The Instant of My Death/Demeure*. Stanford, CA: Stanford University Press, 2000.

Blanchot, M. (1996a) *Les Intellectuels en question: ébauche d'une réfelxion*. Paris: Fourbis. Trans. M. Holland, "Intellectuals Under Scrutiny" in *The Blanchot Reader*. Oxford: Blackwell, 1995.

Blanchot, M. (1996b) *Pour l'amitié* [For Friendship]. Paris: Fourbis.

Bruns, G. L. (1997) *Maurice Blanchot: The Refusal of Philosophy*. Baltimore, MD: Johns Hopkins University Press.

Char, R. et al. (1997) "Dossier Maurice Blanchot." *Ralentir Travaux*, 7.

Clark, T. (ed.) (2000) *Oxford Literary Review*, special issue on Blanchot, 22 .

Collin, F. (1986) *Maurice Blanchot et la question de l'écriture* [Maurice Blanchot and the Question of Writing], revd. edn. Paris: Gallimard.

Derrida, J. (1986) *Parages* [Locality]. Paris: Galilée.

Derrida, J. (1998) *Demeure: Maurice Blanchot*. Paris: Galilée. Trans. E. Rottenberg, *The Instant of My Death/Demeure*, ed. M. Blanchot and J. Derrida. Stanford, CA: Stanford University Press, 2000.

Gill, C. B. (ed.) (1996) *Maurice Blanchot: The Demand of Writing*. London: Routledge.

Gregg, J. (1994) *Maurice Blanchot and the Literature of Transgression*. Princeton, NJ: Princeton University Press.

Hess, D. M. (1999) *Politics and Literature: The Case of Maurice Blanchot*. New York: Peter Lang.

Hill, L. (1997) *Blanchot: Extreme Contemporary*. London: Routledge.

Holland, M. (ed.) (1995) *The Blanchot Reader*. Oxford: Blackwell.

Holland, M. and Rousseau, P. (1976) "Topographie-parcours d'une (contre) revolution." *Gramma*, 5: 8–43.

Josipovici, G. (ed.) (1982) *The Siren's Song: Selected Essays by Maurice Blanchot*, trans. S. Rabinovitch. Brighton: Harvester Press.

Laporte, R. (ed.) (1999) *Maurice Blanchot*, special issue of *Revue des sciences humaines*, 253.

Lefebvre, H. (1947) *Critique de la view quotidienne*. Paris: Grasset. Trans. J. Moore: London: Verso, 1991.

Lévinas, E. (1975) *Sur Maurice Blanchot*. Montpellier: Éditions Fata Morgana. Trans. M. B. Smith, "On Maurice Blanchot." In *Proper Names* by E. Lévinas. Stanford, CA: Stanford University Press, 1996.

Mehlman, J. (1983) *Legacies of Anti-Semitism in France*. Minneapolis: University of Minnesota Press.

Mesnard, P. (1996) *Maurice Blanchot: le sujet de l'engagement* [Maurice Blanchot: The Subject of Engagement]. Paris: L'Harmattan.

Pepper, T. (ed.) (1998) "The Place of Maurice Blanchot." Special issue of *Yale French Studies*, 93.

Quasha, G. (ed.) (1998) *The Station Hill Blanchot Reader: Fiction and Literary Essays*. Barrytown, NY: Station Hill Press.

Schulte Nordholt, A.-L. (1995) *Maurice Blanchot: l'écriture comme expérience du dehors* [Maurice Blanchot: Writing as Experience of the Outside]. Geneva: Librairie Droz.

Sinety, P. de. (ed.) (1998) "Maurice Blanchot." Special issue of *L'Oeil de boeuf*, 14/15.

Surya, M. (ed.) (1990) *Lignes*, special issue on Blanchot, 11, September.

Todorov, T. (1984) *Critique de la critique*. Paris: Éditions du Seuil. Trans. C. Porter, *Literature and its Theorists*. Ithaca, NY: Cornell University Press, 1987.

Ungar, S. (1995) *Scandal and After-effect: Blanchot and France Since 1930*. Minneapolis: University of Minnesota Press.

13 | Pierre Bourdieu

Don Miller

Ideas
Theory of practice □ Reflexive sociology □ Agency □ Habitus □
Field □ Symbolic capital □ Cultural capital □ Symbolic violence

Major books
The Algerians (1962)
Outline of a Theory of Practice (1977)
Reproduction in Education, Society and Culture (with J. C. Passeron) (1977)
Algeria 1960 (1979)
The Inheritors (with J. C. Passeron) (1979)
Distinction (1984)
Homo Academicus (1988)
The Logic of Practice (1989)
In Other Words (1990)
The Political Ontology of Martin Heidegger (1991)
Language and Symbolic Power (1991)
Practical Reason (1998)
Acts of Resistance (1998)
The Weight of the World (1999)
Pascalian Meditations (2000)

Influences
Aron □ Canguilhem □ Durkheim □ Heidegger □ Husserl □ Lévi-Strauss □ Pascal

Biographical Details

Pierre Bourdieu (1930–2002), Professor of Sociology at the Collège de France and Director of Studies at the École des Hautes Études en Sciences Sociales, was the son of a postman, in the province of Bearn in the south of France. He was educated with the elite, while not identifying himself as one of them, at the École Normale Supérieure. He carried out ethnographic research in war-torn Algeria between 1958 and 1961, in particular among the acephalous Kabyle, the site for the development of many of the concepts central to his theory of practice as he struggled to understand the reproduction of sociocultural cohesion and of law and order in the face of an absence of overt rules and authority. Between 1959 and 1960 he also carried out ethnographic research in the region of his birth. From 1962, Bourdieu's research focused on French society, researching and theorizing the processes by which the formation and transformation of structured cultural differences in French society are central to the reproduction of structured social inequalities, of class divisions. Initially, Bourdieu (with Jean Claude Passeron) focused on the French education system, secondary and tertiary, as an ideological practice, which serves to reproduce what it claims to destroy:

> Indeed, among all the solutions put forward throughout history to the problem of the transmission of power and privileges, there surely does not exist one that is better concealed, and therefore better adapted to societies which tend to refuse the most patent forms of the transmission of power and privileges, than that solution which the educational system provides. (Bourdieu 1977b: 488)
>
> By doing away with giving explicitly to everyone what it implicitly demands of everyone, the educational system demands of everyone alike that they have what it does not give. This consists mainly of linguistic and cultural competence and that relationship of familiarity with culture which can only be produced by family upbringing when it transmits the dominant culture. (Ibid: 494)

The language confronts us and makes us work at the reading process and through the clever juxtaposition of concepts reveals the contradictions inherent in everyday social life. As he struggles to reveal and explain what ideologies deny; as he reflexively demands as much of himself as of others, a critical search for the unintended consequences of academic concepts, theories and practices, Bourdieu presses "the discursive limits of sociology," attempting to convey "more information than print can possibly support," demanding "a competence, at least, in poetry, in a field more accustomed to literal prose" (Lemert 2000: 104–5).

As we turn to review Bourdieu's approach to social and cultural practice it is important to note that he is, like Foucault, a self-declared disciple of the historian of science Georges Canguilhem, who became the focus in the 1950s and 1960s for opposition to the existentialism and personalism of Sartre. It is Canguilhem's descendants who have provided us with the most enlightening theories of social and cultural practice: Lévi-Strauss, Dumont, Foucault, Bourdieu. It is the Canguilhem heritage that lies behind Bourdieu's concentration on agency rather than the individual in his theory of practice. It is our agency, not "us," that is the focus of his sociological attention.

Key Theoretical Contributions

Through all of his studies Bourdieu has remained the ethnographer. In maintaining a position of constant reflexivity he cultivates a perspective based in his own anthropological experience in Algeria, that of the marginalized observer for whom even the most familiar and commonsensical becomes exotic and strange, in need of explanation (Bourdieu 1988: xi).

Bourdieu's theory of practice is the linchpin of all his work; his *Outline of a Theory of Practice* (1977a) the work that must be read if his studies of education, taste, art, language, and the state are to be understood, as they must, as part of a larger coherent sociological enterprise. It is here that he develops the concepts that have remained central to his work. It is here too that the vital links between, on the one hand, his ethnographic work among the Kabyle, and on the other, his copious writings on French society, philosophy, social theory, and the academy are explained.

Bourdieu's theory of practice focuses on agency, on the processes through which individuals creatively contribute to the formation and transformation, the "reproduction," of the social structures which channel and limit their life chances. This agency is affected as people strategically orient themselves to the socially and culturally defined and structured environments of which they are part and through which they strategically seek to satisfy their needs and aspirations. Their strategic practice is structured by their sociocultural environment, by their "habitus," a concept central to Bourdieu's theory of practice, consisting of structured dispositions which are the basis for ongoing structuration. Society's strategic agents are thus disposed to compete for honor, for symbolic capital, on myriad but related fields of thought and action. Their cultural competence and effectiveness on any particular field of action is dependent on the accumulation of the relevant cultural capital, the cultural resources that they can strategically expend on the interweaving fields of their practice. Those with privileged access to restricted cultural capital exercise symbolic violence upon those who cannot access the cultural capital required to succeed in those fields of practice, such as education, which yield potent symbolic capital.

Agents are also represented as the producers and reproducers of "objective meaning" whose "actions and works are the product of a *modus operandi* of which he or she is not the producer and has no conscious mastery" (Bourdieu 1977a: 79). "It is because subjects do not, strictly speaking, know what they are doing that what they do has more meaning than they know" (ibid). To transcend the false consciousness that blinds us to the "objective realities," the sociologist must engage in a *methodological objectivism* (ibid: 21). But Bourdieu warns of the tendency "to slip from the model of reality to the reality of the model" (ibid: 29): "Methodological objectivism ... demands its own supersession" (ibid: 72). We must escape "the realism of the structure" by passing "from the *opus operatum* to the *modus operandi*, from statistical regularity or algebraic structure to the principle of the production of this observed order" (ibid). So the people we study regain their individuality, their creativity, and we the sociologists, via a methodological objectivism, expose the meaning that they do not know but which they unknowingly create.

Through the study of education, of language, of taste, of the relationship between the state and education, and through his recent, politically more active and polemical engagement with the inhumanity of neoliberalism as it generates insecurity and despair in the workplace, Bourdieu consistently demonstrates that class structures, and those based on gender, race, or ethnicity, are not imposed from above or created by the ethnographer but subtly reproduced through the containment of cultural dispositions within class groups.

Major Criticisms

Bourdieu has stimulated a vast amount of discussion within and beyond the academy and has been the object of wide-ranging and often vehement criticism. Bisseret (1979) long ago accused Bourdieu of essentialism. More recently, Alexander (1995) has accused him of determinism, materialism, and reductionism among other damnations, despite viewing Bourdieu as "the most impressive living embodiment of [the] neo-Marxist tradition" (ibid: 128). Bourdieu has constantly denied any primary or important link to Marx or Marxism. And this is where the most substantive criticism lies in relation to Bourdieu's theory of practice: his focus is on symbolic capital rather than real capital and until very recently on symbolic violence rather than overt physical oppression and suffering. The most cogent critique of Bourdieu in these terms is provided by Callinicos, who sees Bourdieu's own rejection of Marxism as allowing him "to affect a position of radical theoretical and political novelty" (Callinicos 1999: 95), but at a price. Callinicos continues: "But whatever fruits this stance may have borne in his sociological writings, its effect now is to deprive him, in the struggle on which he has now embarked, of precious – one is inclined to say essential – intellectual capital" (ibid). The crux of the matter is that in all of Bourdieu's writings "the economy itself tends simply to be taken for granted and left unanalyzed" (ibid: 90).

The publication by Bourdieu and Wacquant (1999) of a provocative polemic against the hidden, unrecognized imperialism of concepts central to much apparently radical current debate, "multiculturalism" and "globalization" in particular, prompted a string of critical responses not only to the article but to Bourdieu's sociology in general. For some (French 2000; Werbner 2000), Bourdieu too readily extrapolated from the French situation to America and on to the rest of the world, and in a tirade of criticism, Wieviorka (2000) revealed many of the conflicts inherent in the field of French sociology, accusing Bourdieu above all of sociological terrorism.

Much of Bourdieu's work is insular and fails to engage with others in the field, and the tendency to take the economy for granted is an enduring problem with his theorizing. But these shortcomings pale into insignificance when considered alongside what he has brought to sociology, anthropology, philosophy, and cultural studies. As one of the most important sociologists of our time (indeed of all time) Bourdieu not only presents us with a theory of social and cultural practice which, in its constant reflexivity, steers a delicate course through those "isms" that attract loyalty rather than critical reevaluation – functionalism, structuralism, voluntarism, existentialism, poststructuralism, postcolonialism – but his theorizing is constantly grounded in the praxis of research into specific social and cultural processes and representations. He retains a central focus on the traditional subject matter of sociology, what Dahrendorf called "the vexatious fact of society," through his commitment to revealing and understanding the structures that contain but at the same time are formed and transformed by the practices of the strategic agents that are our multiple and shared social selves.

Bibliography

Alexander, J. (1995) *Fin de Siècle Social Theory*. London: Verso.
Bisseret, N. (1979) *Education, Class Language and Ideology*. London: Routledge and Kegan Paul.

Bourdieu, P. (1962) *The Algerians*. Boston: Beacon Press.
Bourdieu, P. (1977a) *Outline of a Theory of Practice*. Cambridge: Cambridge University Press.
Bourdieu, P. (1977b) (with J. C. Passeron) *Reproduction in Education, Society and Culture*. London: Sage.
Bourdieu, P (1979a) *Algeria 1960*. New York: Cambridge University Press.
Bourdieu, P. (1979b) (with J. C. Passeron) *The Inheritors*. Chicago: University of Chicago Press.
Bourdieu, P. (1980) *Le Sens pratique*. Paris: Editions de Minuit.
Bourdieu, P. (1982) *Ce que parler veut dire*. Paris: Fayard.
Bourdieu, P. (1984) *Distinction*. London: Routledge and Kegan Paul.
Bourdieu, P. (1988) *Homo Academicus*. Cambridge: Polity Press.
Bourdieu, P. (1989) *The Logic of Practice*. Cambridge: Polity Press.
Bourdieu, P. (1990) *In Other Words*. Cambridge: Polity Press.
Bourdieu, P. (1991a) *Language and Symbolic Power*. Cambridge: Polity Press.
Bourdieu, P. (1991b) *The Political Ontology of Martin Heidegger*. Cambridge: Polity Press.
Bourdieu, P. (1996) *The State Nobility*. Cambridge: Polity Press.
Bourdieu, P. (1998a) *On Television*. New York: New Press.
Bourdieu, P. (1998b) *Practical Reason*. Cambridge: Polity Press.
Bourdieu, P. (1999) *Male Domination*. Cambridge: Polity Press.
Bourdieu, P. (2000) *Pascalian Meditations*. Cambridge: Polity Press.
Bourdieu, P. and Wacquant, L. J. D. (1992) *An Invitation to Reflexive Sociology*. Chicago: University of Chicago Press.
Bourdieu, P. and Wacquant, L. J. D. (1999) "On the Cunning of Imperialist Reason." *Theory, Culture and Society*, 16, 1, February.
Bourdieu, P. et al. (1999) *The Weight of the World*. Cambridge: Polity Press.
Callinicos, A. (1999) "Social Theory Put to the Test of Politics: Pierre Bourdieu and Anthony Giddens." *New Left Review*, 236, July/August.
Callinicos, A. (2000) "Impossible Anti-Capitalism?" *New Left Review*, New Series, 2, March/April.
French, J. D. (2000) "The Missteps of Anti-Imperialist Reason: Bourdieu, Wacquant and Hanchard's *Orpheus and Power*." *Theory, Culture and Society*, 17, 1, February.
Friedman, J. (2000) "American Again, or the New Age of Imperial Reason? Global Elite Formation, its Identity and Ideological Discourses." *Theory, Culture and Society*, 17, 1, February.
Lemert, C. (2000) "The Clothes Have No Emperor: Bourdieu and American Imperialism." *Theory, Culture and Society*, 17, 1, February.
Ven, C. (2000) "Intellectuals, Power and Multiculturalism." *Theory, Culture and Society*, 17, 1, February.
Werbner, P. (2000) "Who Sets the Terms of the Debate? Heterotopic Intellectuals and the Clash of Discourses." *Theory, Culture and Society*, 17, 1, February.
Wieviorka, M. (2000) "Contextualizing French Multiculturalism and Racism." *Theory, Culture and Society*, 17, 1, February.

14 | Manuel Castells

Nick Stevenson

Ideas
Information society □ Networks □ Social movements □
Globalization □ Identity

Major books
The Urban Question: A Marxist Approach (1972)
The Information City (1989)
The Information Age, 3 vols (1996–8)
Technopoles of the World (with P. Hall) (1994)

Influences
Althusser □ Baudrillard □ Foucault □ Giddens □
Gramsci □ Habermas

Biographical Details

For many, Manuel Castells (b. 1942) is among the most important social thinkers of his generation. He has been described as the author of the postindustrial age and the most important sociologist since Max Weber. Castells is a genuinely global academic, having held posts in Paris, Madrid, Montreal, Barcelona, Tokyo, and California among others. During his early career he was heavily influenced by the Marxist structuralist thought of Louis Althusser. His first major work, *The Urban Question* (1972), was subtitled *A Marxist Approach*. However, by the time he came to write *The Informational City* (1989) Castells had become more closely associated with the attempt to rethink a rapidly changing world while distancing himself from Marxist scholasticism (Webster 1995).

Politically, however, Castells remains passionately concerned with questions of exclusion and social justice in the context of what he calls the "network society." These issues have been forcibly pursued in his three-volume study of the informational age, which will probably embody Castells's most enduring contribution to the social sciences (Castells 1996, 1997, 1998).

Key Theoretical Contributions

Castells argues that the emergent "information society" is primarily born out of the changing relationship between global capitalism, the state, and new social movements. However, it is the development of the "informational economy" that is central to his attempt to rethink the dynamics of postindustrial society. In this new economy it is the application of knowledge and technology in customized production that best ensures economic success. The technological level of the enterprise is a much better guide to its competitiveness than older indices like labor costs. The rapid development of informational technology in the 1970s in Silicon Valley, USA enabled capital to restructure itself after the impacts of a worldwide recession. "Informationalism" has allowed organizations to achieve increasing flexibility in terms of more knowledge-dependent and less hierarchical structures. New technology has enabled large structures to coordinate their activities worldwide, while building in reflexive inputs to both quickly respond to the current state of the market and benefit from economies of scale (Castells and Hall 1994). Hence, whereas industrialism was oriented towards economic growth, informationalism is more concerned with the development of knowledge and the creation of networks. The digitalization of knowledge bases allows information to be processed and stored across huge distances. Thus capitalism is becoming less dependent upon the state and more upon the ability of a common informational system to transmit knowledge across distanciated networks (Castells 1996).

The dominance of the flows of capital as opposed to the locality of labor has heightened processes of social exclusion. The new informational economy is characterized by simultaneous processes of economic development and underdevelopment. The "black holes" of the informational economy include people who are culturally out of communication with mainstream society. That is, while informationalism has led to the growth of employment within the higher tiers of management, there has also been a substantial reduction in low-skilled employment and heightened exclusion of the earth's poorer regions from the flows of global capital. These excluded zones (that cannot be mapped onto any simple

North–South divide) have responded to such processes by operating "perverse" forms of inclusion. This has fostered the expansion of illegal and criminal economies within inner-city ghettos and the planet's most marginalized economies.

The dominance of the informational economy also has definite cultural effects. Television in particular and the media in general have become central and defining institutions in modern society. Castells illustrates this by pointing to the fact that television currently frames the language and types of symbolic exchange that help define society. Unless a social movement, set of ideas, or commercial product appears on television it may as well not exist. The media then do not so much determine political agendas, as provide the background and context to political and social struggles. The centrality of modern communications in contemporary culture therefore does not deliver a mass culture, but what Castells calls a culture of "real virtuality." The idea of a mass culture has now been surpassed by a media environment where messages are explicitly customized to the symbolic languages of the intended audience. The future will not so much be governed by a homogeneous mass-produced culture repressing human diversity, as by a diversified popular culture where competitive advantage comes through product differentiation and audience segmentation. For Castells (1996), "we are not living in a global village, but in customized cottages globally produced and locally distributed."

"Scandal politics" develops within the general context of an increasingly televisual society that has come to the fore against a backdrop where political concerns are frequently played out and reported as a cynical and strategic game. This privileges the presentation of political issues in a fast-paced and punchy style, which in turn prioritizes the culture of the soundbite. Further, the visualization and corresponding trivialization of political issues through television gives an added emphasis to the "personalities" rather than the substantive issues at stake in political debate. Television then produces a binary politics where complex positions are boiled down into digestible categories. The personalization of politics and the decline of ideological contrasts between the major political parties produces the grounds for the central forms of struggle in the age of informational politics.

Castells (1997) characterizes a variety of social movements as developing highly skillful media techniques in largely reactive and defensive responses to economic globalization. By this he means that the movements under review do not so much articulate a vision of a future emancipated society; rather they are a more conservative attempt to preserve current social identities. For Castells (ibid: 69), "people all over the world resent loss of control over their lives, over their environment, over their jobs, over their economies, over their governments, over their countries, and, ultimately, over the fate of the Earth." The task then of any oppositional movement must be to connect local experiences to a more global agenda. Defensive reactions to globalization can be seen in a range of fundamentalist and communalist political movements and cultural struggles the world over. As the democratic state becomes increasingly reduced to an empty shell, the new sites of power lie in images and information codes. As Castells (ibid: 359) puts it, the "sites of this power are people's minds." However, given the new vitality of information and culture in the network society, the mobilization of peoples through information flows and networks is likely to be short lived.

These considerations point towards not only a new politics but also a new society in the making. For example, Castells (1997) argues that the patriarchal family, the focal point of patriarchalism, is being progressively challenged. The combined forces of the increased visibility of diverse sexual practices, the massive incorporation of women into paid work, growing control over biological reproduction, and new self-definitions offered by new social movements are the social forces that are redefining gendered relations. The shaking of heterosexual norms and the disruption of the patriarchal family (primarily through the emergence of singles lifestyles and households, divorce, the practice of "living together," and greater autonomy in reproduction) have meant that there is an increasing diversity of family types on offer. Castells perceives that, despite the fact that men continue to be more socially privileged, a reactive politics is unlikely to serve their long-term interests. Hence, to begin the process of rebuilding society the emergence of more egalitarian families is crucial to the remaking of civil society in the face of exclusion and fundamentalism. It will then be our capacity to escape the traps of communalism and the free market, coupled with a renewed respect for nature, social justice, and human rights, that is most likely to point to a generative politics. However, whatever new forms our societies take in the future we are at this point caught in the social and cultural morphology of the network (McGuigan 1999; Urry 2000).

Major Criticisms

By viewing Castells in terms of the tradition of critical theory we might argue that he takes a less "pessimistic turn" than is evident in Habermas and the early Frankfurt School. What Castells most clearly provides is a social and historical understanding of the emergence of the "information society." Like Adorno's and Horkheimer's account of the culture industry and Habermas's notion of the public sphere, the "informational society" opens out a new critical paradigm. Yet if one of the main agendas of critical theory is present, others are absent. Missing from Castells's account is a more normative analysis that would provide us with a critical standpoint from which to evaluate social change. In answer to this charge I think Castells would make two responses. The first is that implicit in much of what he says there is an agenda that seeks to map out the possibilities for democracy and social justice. Secondly, that it is not for "experts" like him to hand down blueprints for social change; the history of socialism has surely put paid to the desirability (or even feasibility) of getting social reality to conform to the wishes of the intellectual vanguard. While these are important considerations (especially in the context of Castells's Althusserianism) such reasons should not be allowed to detach critical theory from moral and ethical agendas. To put the point bluntly: if it is worth arguing that the public sphere is becoming increasingly infected by a form of cynical reason and "show" politics, it is also worth making some broad suggestions on how we might begin to construct an alternative. Further, if the media are becoming increasingly central to the self-definition of democratic societies then radical change will only come through citizens increasing their involvement and participation within wider media and political cultures. The question as to how democratic societies help foster public involvement as opposed to private withdrawal, communicative concerns as opposed to instrumental strategies, and publicly engaged pluralistic identities as opposed to passively construed cultures, is central to the concerns of Castells's work. In doing this we should indeed avoid adopting the legislative ambitions of the expert, while also side-stepping thinking that fails to open new critical possibilities. It is not that Castells believes that the world could not be otherwise, but that he misses the implications a moral and ethical agenda could have for our common futures (Stevenson 1999).

Castells, as we have seen, poses some difficult questions for those seeking to promote a cosmopolitan agenda. How do we ensure that cosmopolitan orientations are spread more widely within society? Is it the case that those of a cosmopolitan orientation are most likely to be found among elites, within global cities, and in fields such as education? How might more cosmopolitan dispositions become an ordinary part of everyday life? These questions are particularly pressing given the emphasis Castells places on social movements as "reactions" to globalization. Yet in connection to these agendas we might criticize Castells for not being concerned enough to connect global dimensions to a cosmopolitan defense of human rights and cultural difference (Beck 1998). These criticisms are, however, minor when juxtaposed to the massive contribution Castells has made in helping us understand our runaway world.

Bibliography

Beck, U. (1998) *Democracy Without Enemies*. Cambridge: Polity Press.

Castells, M. (1972) *The Urban Question: A Marxist Approach*. Oxford: Blackwell.

Castells, M. (1989) *The Informational City: Information Technology, Economic Restructuring and Urban–Regional Process*. Oxford: Blackwell.

Castells, M. (1996) *The Information Age: Economy, Society and Culture, Vol. 1: The Rise of the Network Society*. Oxford: Blackwell.

Castells, M. (1997) *The Information Age: Economy, Society and Culture, Vol. 2: The Power of Identity*. Oxford: Blackwell.

Castells, M. (1998) *The Information Age: Economy, Society and Culture, Vol. 3: End of Millennium*. Oxford: Blackwell.

Castells, M. and Hall, P. (1994) *Technopoles of the World: The Making of Twenty-First Century Industrial Complexes*. London: Routledge.

McGuigan, J. (1999) *Modernity and Postmodern Culture*. Buckingham: Open University Press.

Stevenson, N. (1999) *The Transformation of the Media: Globalization, Morality and Ethics*. Harlow: Longman.

Urry, J. (2000) *Sociology Beyond Societies: Mobilities for the Twenty-First Century*.

Webster, F. (1995) *Theories of the Information Society*. London: Routledge.

15 | Nancy J. Chodorow

Diana Tietjens Meyers

Ideas
Relational self □ Revalued femininity □ Co-parenting □ Personal
meaning □ Identity

Major books
The Reproduction of Mothering (1978)
Feminism and Psychoanalytic Theory (1989)
The Power of Feelings (1999)

Influences
Freud □ Loewald □ Winnicott

Biographical Details

Nancy Chodorow is among today's most influential psychoanalytic feminists. A Professor of Sociology and a practicing psychoanalyst, Chodorow brings interdisciplinary erudition and extensive clinical experience to bear on key theoretical issues. Chodorow and her cohort of psychoanalytic feminists have rescued psychoanalytic theory and method from the critiques 1960s feminists rightly leveled at Freud's account of gender and restored feminist appropriations of psychoanalysis to intellectual respectability and political relevance. *The Reproduction of Mothering* (1978) gives an account of how women's exclusive responsibility for childcare in the nuclear family perpetuates the sexual division of labor between female nurturers and male earners. *Feminism and Psychoanalytic Theory* (1989) reprints a number of her essays. One group of essays revisits the construction of gendered identities; another focuses on central psychoanalytic concepts, e.g., the nature of the self and intersubjectivity; a third defends psychoanalysis's contribution to feminist theory. Her book *The Power of Feelings* (1999) engages with psychoanalysts, postmodern feminists, and anthropologists. Highlighting the creativity of individual intrapsychic processes, Chodorow presents a non-deterministic conception of the role of culture in the constitution of individual identity.

Key Theoretical Contributions

Chodorow's groundbreaking book *The Reproduction of Mothering* asks not only why gender is so satisfying to women but also why it is so harmful to them. Isolating what she takes to be a universal feature of childcare – women's exclusive responsibility for nurturing children – Chodorow explains how that allocation of responsibility perpetuates women's primary parenting.

The starting point for infants of both sexes is a state of primary narcissism in which they cathect being fused with their primary caregiver and their dependence upon this person. Since infants love their relationship to their mother, their earliest emotional orientation is not individualistic, but social. Thus, the need for human connection provides the emotional framework in which the self emerges, and the self gains its distinctive identity through interaction with others. The self, regardless of the individual's sex, is relational. Yet women want to become primary parents, and men do not. Why?

For Chodorow, this asymmetrical commitment to parenting stems from childrearing practices that develop girls' capacities to empathize with and respond sensitively to others and that concomitantly suppress boys' relational capacities. Against Freud, Chodorow argues that the Oedipus complex is not the watershed moment in the development of gender, but rather that gender is consolidated in the pre-Oedipal period. That primary parenting is invariably women's responsibility results in differences in the length and quality of the pre-Oedipal attachment to the primary parent that in turn bring about this gender bifurcation.

Mothers identify strongly with their daughters and delay separating from them. Girls respond in a complementary way. They identify with their mothers in a context of ongoing and intense love. Thus, their acquisition of feminine traits and goals is continuous with their earliest attachment to their mother and, for that reason, virtually unshakeable. Moreover, because of this continuity, women's ego boundaries are permeable, and they do not experience emotional ties as threatening to their identity. In other words, women are inclined to follow in their mothers' footsteps by having children, and they are emotionally equipped to give children the warmly solicitous care they need. All that remains for the girl to accomplish in the Oedipal period is to add her father to her emotional constellation, thus enriching her inner life, further strengthening her relational capacities, and acquiring heterosexual desires.

In contrast, mothers act to distinguish their sons from themselves. They underscore boys' masculinity, and they may insinuate an amorous element into their behavior towards their sons. This sexualization of the pre-Oedipal period pressures boys into an early Oedipal stance. But a masculine identity is hard to come by. Since fathers almost never function as primary parents and are seldom present as role models, boys must gain their gender identity by learning abstract rules and observing remote exemplars. Moreover, achieving a masculine identity requires that men take the draconian and emotionally wrenching step of disavowing their attachment to their mothers. Repudiating their mothers and repressing whatever residue of femininity they may find in themselves, they supplement their masculine code by defining masculinity negatively as the not-feminine, i.e., as emotional detachment. Founded more on contempt for their mothers than on love for their fathers, men's gender identity is rigid yet precarious. Heavily invested in defending sharply demarcated ego boundaries and in maintaining control, men are neither disposed to assume nor prepared to assume the demands of childcare.

Still, it remains puzzling why mothering should be women's destiny. After all, women's relational capacities could find outlets in adult relationships with other women or with men. Several factors militate against these outcomes. First, although most women take men as their primary erotic objects, men remain emotionally secondary for them, for girls do not break off their primary emotional attachment to their mothers. Second, masculine socialization discourages men from entering into the kind of intimate, affectionate relationships women seek. Third, in a society organized around monogamous heterosexuality and nuclear families, lesbian relations as well as close friendships with other women are difficult to sustain. Bereft of other interpersonal possibilities, women turn to children. With their children they can recreate the mother–child fusion that, according to psychoanalytic theory, all adults yearn to regain, and their relational capacities are put to constructive, socially condoned use.

Now, it might seem that societies that organize childcare in this way have chanced upon a happy allocation of responsibilities, but this is hardly Chodorow's assessment. She diagnoses a number of serious personal and social problems that are traceable to women's exclusive responsibility for childcare. This system distorts both women's and men's personalities: women lack independent control over their lives, and men lack emotional connection to other people. Moreover, people who grow up under this regime have trouble, even as adults, respecting their mothers' individuality – they tend to oscillate between recognizing these women's distinct needs and treating them as all-purpose nursemaids who should always be on call. In contrast, fathers are accepted throughout life as people who have their own interests and who are entitled to assert them. Thus, women's primary parenting reinforces dichotomous gender expectations and roles.

To avoid instilling gendered defects in children, Chodorow claims, primary parents must be individuals who can give care freely. Women whose unresolved conflicts and lack of options compel them to become primary parents overinvest in their children and project inappropriate demands on them. Moreover, these women unwittingly help to perpetuate male dominance, for they raise boys who stake their masculinity on devaluing women as a group while they raise girls who stake their femininity on a life of subordinate domesticity.

In Chodorow's view, it is only by replacing women's exclusive mothering with a practice of co-parenting that these problems can be overcome. If fathers are emotionally available to their sons, boys will not grow up dismissing emotional warmth as feminine, and masculine identity will be formed in the context of a close, ongoing relationship. More secure in their own identity, less troubled by intimacy, men will be equally capable of good parenting. Likewise, if fathers share the work of caring for their daughters and mothers go to work outside the home, girls will cease to worship men as symbols of freedom and independence and stop equating femininity with unflagging devotion to others. Women, then, will not experience self-development as conflicting with feminine identity and will be emotionally free to pursue careers. Caregiving will be a genuine choice for both women and men, and the traditionally feminine work of caregiving will be accorded its true value.

In the interim between *The Reproduction of Mothering* and *The Power of Feelings* Chodorow reorients her thinking in several major respects. Eschewing the universalism and essentialism for which her earlier work on gender identity was criticized, she focuses on individuated identities, the intrapsychic processes that shape them, and the impact of culture on the evolution of individuated identities. Her undiminished commitment to the relational self is the principal point of contact between the two phases of her scholarship.

In *The Power of Feelings* Chodorow addresses three key controversies: (1) the relation between culture and the constitution of individual identity, (2) the role of unconscious fantasy in conferring meaning on experience, and (3) the epistemology of the interpersonal sciences. The title Chodorow gives her book tips off readers to where she thinks the main resistance to her views lies. She is engaged in reclaiming the "power of feelings," i.e., the capacity of unconscious fantasy to process cultural and interpersonal experience in individually distinctive ways, to endow the people one interacts with and one's physical environment with per-sonal meaning, and to spur intrapsychic and behavioral change. Her project, then, is to explicate individual depth and creativity. But it is also to develop a dual-pronged critique: on the one hand, a critique of psychoanalytic theories that see the present as determined by the past or that see gendered people as products of biological programming or uni-versal fantasies; on the other hand, a critique of anthropological theories that see people as constructed by cultural discourses or social structures. Her account of personal meaning undergirds these critiques.

The concept of personal meaning knits together two of Chodorow's most important themes: individuality and creativity. According to Chodorow, we "need to cross what might be called the horizontal view of cultural mean-ing – thick description, multiplicity, polysemy, webs of meaning, forests of symbols – with a vertical view, in which each individual's internal history is its own emotionally polysemic web of continually created unconscious and conscious personal meaning, animated by fantasies, projections, and introjections." For Chodorow, the capacities for unconscious fantasizing, projecting, and introjecting are innate, and individuals start using these ca-pacities before they acquire a language. From the beginning, infants are developing a distinctive subjective perspective. After they are initiated into language and culture, their innate, non-conscious experience-processing capacities continue to individualize their subjectivity and to impart emo-tional meaning to their encounters and their relationships. In the lifelong process of becoming unique individuals, people "avail themselves" of, but also customize inputs from, their respective cultural and interpersonal con-texts to create personally meaningful lives. Thus, gender identity is not a culturally mandated set of internalized attributes. Rather, each individual creates their own "personal–cultural gender."

Chodorow's epistemology is anchored in the processes of transfer-ence – projection, introjection, and the defenses. These are the same relational processes through which gendered selves emerge. Since trans-ference and countertransference are integral to subjectivity, the key to objectivity is to be reflective about one's transferences, and reality is an interpersonal construction through which personal meanings are shared. Like the self, reality is relational.

Major Criticisms

Some of the problems in *The Reproduction of Mothering* are (regrettably) typical of 1970s feminist theory. The book's universalistic rhetoric denies women's difference. Its univocal account of femininity and masculinity overlooks the ways in which race, class, and ethnicity inflect gender

(Spelman 1988). Assuming a heterosexual couple and a nuclear family marginalizes the lives of single mothers and lesbian couples. Chodorow acknowledges these failings but maintains that psychoanalytic theory can accommodate diverse social positions and family structures.

Other objections cannot be met so easily. *The Reproduction of Mothering* implicitly blames mothers, i.e., members of a subordinated group, for reproducing male dominance. It downplays the role of political and economic structures in perpetuating women's subordination (Lorber et al. 1981; Young 1983). In advocating that mothers and fathers co-parent their children, it deplores opting for single motherhood, female childrearing collectives, or parenting with a lesbian partner. The polarized conception of gender that frames Chodorow's argument compromises her vision of emancipation (Meyers 1992).

In my view, the principle difficulty with Chodorow's current account of gender and subjectivity is that it has gone to the opposite extreme. Whereas *The Reproduction of Mothering* construes gender as the engine of male dominance, *The Power of Feelings* represents gender as innocuous. Gender poses no serious threat to women's interests, for individuals possess prodigious transformational powers. To discuss the relations between culture and individuality without discussing power and social hierarchy is to minimize culture's role in enforcing domination and subordination. My concern, then, is that Chodorow underestimates the damage that patriarchal cultures inflict on individuals and consequently ignores the need for a political response to culturally transmitted norms and stereotypes.

Bibliography

Chodorow, N. J. (1978) *The Reproduction of Mothering*. Berkeley: University of California Press.

Chodorow, N. J. (1989) *Feminism and Psychoanalytic Theory*. New Haven, CT: Yale University Press.

Chodorow, N. J. (1999) *The Power of Feelings*. New Haven, CT: Yale University Press.

Lorber, J., et al. (1981) "On *The Reproduction of Mothering*: A Methodological Debate." *Signs*, 6: 500–14.

Meyers, D. T. (1992) "The Subversion of Women's Agency in Psychoanalytic Feminism: Chodorow, Flax, Kristeva." In *Revaluing French Feminism*, ed. N. Fraser and S. Bartky. Bloomington: Indiana University Press.

Spelman, E. V. (1988) *Inessential Woman*. Boston: Beacon Press.

Young, I. M.. (1983) "Is Male Gender Identity the Cause of Male Domination?" In *Mothering*, ed. J. Trebilcot. Totowa, NJ: Rowman and Allanheld.

16 | Gilles Deleuze

Claire Colebrook

Ideas
Transcendental empiricism □ Immanence □ Schizoanalysis

Major books
Difference and Repetition (1994)
Anti-Oedipus (with Félix Guattari 1977)

Influences
Bergson □ Nietzsche □ Spinoza

Biographical Details

Gilles Deleuze (1925–95) was a French philosopher who spent the early part of his career writing studies of those philosophers who he felt challenged the dominant ideas of the present. Like most French thinkers of his day, Deleuze was influenced by Marxism, psychoanalysis, phenomenology, and existentialism, but he radically challenged all these modes of thought with his own canon of philosophers, including Bergson, Spinoza, Leibniz, Hume, and Nietzsche. The second part of Deleuze's career was less conventional and interpretive, and more explicitly creative. Deleuze always considered himself to be a philosopher and maintained the specificity of philosophy in contrast to science and art. But he also felt that philosophy was continually recreated by encounters with other modes of thought. He wrote books on cinema – a new mode of presentation that he believed opened new styles of thinking – books on literature and fine art, and he also co-authored a number of highly interdisciplinary works with the French psychoanalyst Félix Guattari.

Key Theoretical Contributions

Deleuze described his own philosophical position as "transcendental empiricism." A *transcendental* approach does not begin from any presupposed starting point, but asks how any starting point is possible. *Transcendence* or the "transcendent" is what lies outside or beyond experience. So, in many ways, a theory that is *transcendental* is critical of *transcendence*, critical of any assumed outside to experience. Deleuze was critical of philosophies that explained the world or life from some ground or foundation, such as consciousness, culture, the subject, language, or history. A truly transcendental theory, he argued, needed to begin, not from some being, but from a "genetic element" (the becoming or process from which any being emerges). "Genesis" is that from which any thing or being is given or becomes; it is not another *thing*, and so it is not actual but virtual. The task of philosophy, Deleuze argued, is to think this "plane" of virtual becoming or genesis from which actual beings are perceived. Philosophy is therefore empiricism: the commitment to remaining within experience, and *not* assuming some being or foundation that lies outside the becoming of experience. Philosophy is the attempt to think the virtual whole of life and becoming, freed from its restrictions to the actual viewpoint of human perception. We don't assume or begin from a foundation or being; philosophy is not limited by what is actual or already exists. Philosophy is open to the future, to the possibilities and virtual openings that are *real* if not actual. Empiricism is a commitment to the given or experience, but a *transcendental* empiricism insists that experience cannot be enclosed within any actual limit.

We have to think experience *immanently*: not as the experience *of* some subject or being, but as a pre-human plane of life or becoming. We begin from a single "plane" of experience, and *then* we explain how certain beings (such as the human, the subject, or consciousness) emerge or have their genesis. One of the words Deleuze uses to describe this "genetic element" or immanent becoming of life is "desire." There are not beings – such as men, animals, or organisms – who *then* have desires for other beings or things which they lack. Desire is not based on lack, or one thing needing another. Rather, there is a flow of desire prior to all needs or distinct things – pure life as an *intense* continuum. It is from the force or affirmation of flows of desire, which "cut" into each other and "code" themselves onto each other, that extended and actual objects are formed. (Think of the flow of light cutting into the pre-human biotic soup.) This cutting or coding, or the "synthesis" of the flow of intense life into extended beings is, Deleuze argues, pre-human, collective, and historical.

There is a passive and pre-human synthesis of singularities before there are active and extended human subjects. All of Deleuze's philosophy was aimed at thinking the "becoming" of life without assuming that this becoming was the becoming *of* some being.

One of the most important consequences of Deleuze's insistence on becoming was his rejection of the once dominant idea of the "social construction of reality." Deleuze was a contemporary of both phenomenology and structuralism. In different ways both these movements argued that any reference we make to the world or reality is meaningful. We always experience the world *as* this or that thing, either through the structures of language (structuralism) or through the meanings of human life (phenomenology). This means that experience is conditioned or structured by concepts or language. The problem with such theories that focus on the conditions of experience, Deleuze argues, is that they fall into the illusion of "transcendence." They assume some condition for experience outside experience; they assume some starting point or being as the beginning of explanation (even if this starting point is as general as "culture," "language," or "society"). The illusion comes about because we are asking the wrong type of question: we try to explain how subjects come to know the world, and so we have to invent some means – such as language or culture – which provides a mediating term. But how did we divide the subject from the world in the first place? The question already assumes a distinction between two types of being: subjects and the reality that that they know or construct. An immanent philosophy or empiricism, Deleuze argues, is more radical than this. We need to begin by asking how, from a single flow of life, we came to think of subjects as distinct from the world. What is the genesis of the subject; how did we form the image of "man"? Deleuze gives two broad answers. The first is philosophical; the second is political.

We think of experience as the experience *of* a subject because of the very nature of life, for life bears the possibility of its own "internal illusions." Deleuze refers to a number of philosophers to make this claim, but the most important is probably Bergson. Life is an infinitely complex flow of difference. In order to act and live we organize intense qualities into extended objects. We don't just live the pure chaos of an ever-changing experience. It's because we need to live and act that we don't perceive the full complexity of life, but only those sections that interest us. I think of myself as a subject set over against a world that I perceive; and I think of the world as *matter*. The main point of all this, for Deleuze, is not just that the flow of life is synthesized into objects but that this synthesis is pre-human and passive. "We" don't construct reality; and it is not language or culture that produces the experienced world. The genetic element is life in general in all its different modes of becoming, including all manner of syntheses. In addition to the structures and syntheses of language and culture, there are genetic, animal, chemical, geological, and imperceptible "becomings."

Deleuze's second critique of transcendence is more explicitly political. The notion of "man" as the origin of synthesis or becoming has a political history. This history is recounted in *Anti-Oedipus*, the first volume that Deleuze co-authored with Félix Guattari. This history begins from the "primitive" flow of life: tribal relations organized or "assembled" around collective body parts. In the next stage of "despotism" or barbarism these assemblages are "overcoded" by the imposition of an external terrorizing body (of the king or despot): the tribal territories are organized by some higher body of law. No longer defined immanently – by their own assembling – these groups are limited by some outside point or figure (the body of the despot). At this stage the external body is literal or actual. In the third – capitalist or civilized – stage, it is not the despot's body that terrorizes the territories, it is the virtual image of man. We imagine that we are all unified because we are all "human" and that the essence of human life was there all along, waiting to be liberated by modernity. This is the illusion of subjectivism.

Deleuze and Guattari also tie capitalism to a specific mode of desire, desire as lack. Capitalism and modernity have the Oedipal fantasy at their heart. We tend to begin the explanation of desire from the notion of the person, the person who constantly desires reunification with his first maternal object of desire but then sublimates this demand by identifying with his father and social recognition. Desire is explained from an original loss, and from a relation between three socially defined roles of father, mother, and child. The Oedipal family, Deleuze and Guattari argue, takes the modern political formation of the family and uses it to explain desire in general. But the image of the private family is the outcome of a collective political history, where the first objects of investment are not persons (such as the mother and father), but body parts (the totem phallus or anus) and intensities (experiences of pain in scarring, tattooing, and incising). It is the barbaric despot and then the king who are the original figures of law and prohibition. In modernity the figure of masculine law is, however, internalized, so we come to recognize the father, fascist, or authority "in" us all. We subject ourselves to law, not because we are governed from without, but because we obey the human nature that is in all of us. Deleuze and Guattari referred to their own radical politics as a form of schizoanalysis: here we don't begin with the psyche or man, but with the parts and micro-investments from which the image of man is formed. We need to trace the image of the private person or ego back to its collective investments. This can be done historically: from investment in body-parts, to the body of the despot and king as founder of law, and finally to the bourgeois subject as the agent of capitalism which "we" all are. Philosophy is the ethical counterpart of the enterprise, for philosophy aims to think the virtual becoming or whole of life prior to any of its constituted, human, or synthesized forms.

Major Criticisms

Possibly the most significant criticism that can be leveled against Deleuze concerns the very aim of transcendental empiricism. If we want to think "life" freed from any specific point of view or actual being, then we will have to reform the very criteria of what it is to think, and possibly have to recreate the very grammar of our languages. This is why Deleuze so often appealed to literature and cinema as the sites for a philosophy or thinking to come. Deleuze's insistent anti-humanism and his commitment to thinking the radical immanence of life led him to forge highly idiosyncratic styles and vocabularies, which are highly resistant to translation and may indicate the limits of his project. This is why there are also very few explicit criticisms of Deleuze to date. Making one's way through his vocabulary and corpus tends to be a task for devotees alone. To put one obvious problem most crudely, there may be something overly optimistic about Deleuze's philosophy. *Can* we free ourselves from the "illusion" of a transcendent law to which we are all subjected, and would such joyful freedom and innocence necessarily be a good thing? It may well be, as Deleuze insisted, that the idea of an original lack or loss at the heart of experience is an illusion. But there are two ways we can respond to this illusion. The first way is to abandon all sense of loss and origins and affirm the immanence of life; this is Deleuze's project. The second is to accept that human life is constituted by an *illusion* of loss and lack, and while there may be no lost origin, we nevertheless need to recognize its fantasmatic effects in psychic life.

Bibliography

Deleuze, G. (1972) *Proust and Signs*, trans. R. Howard. London: Allen Lane/ Penguin Books.
Deleuze, G. (1983) *Nietzsche and Philosophy*, trans. H. Tomlinson. London: Athlone Press.
Deleuze, G. (1984) *Kant's Critical Philosophy: The Doctrine of the Faculties*, trans. H. Tomlinson and B. Habberjam. London, Athlone Press.

Deleuze, G. (1986) *Cinema 1: The Movement-Image,* trans. H. Tomlinson and B. Habberjam. Minneapolis: University of Minnesota Press.

Deleuze, G. (1988a) *Foucault,* trans. S. Hand. London: Athlone Press.

Deleuze, G. (1988b) *Spinoza: Practical Philosophy,* trans. R. Hurley. San Francisco: City Lights.

Deleuze, G. (1989) *Cinema 2: The Time-Image,* trans. H. Tomlinson and R. Galeta. Minneapolis: University of Minnesota Press.

Deleuze, G. (1990) *The Logic of Sense,* trans. M. Lester, ed. C. V. Boundas. New York: Columbia University Press.

Deleuze, G. (1991a), *Bergsonism,* trans. H. Tomlinson and B. Habberjam. New York: Zone Books.

Deleuze, G. (1991b) *Empiricism and Subjectivity: An Essay on Hume's Theory of Human Nature,* trans. C. V. Boundas. New York: Columbia University Press.

Deleuze, G. (1992) *Expressionism in Philosophy,* trans. M. Joughin. New York: Zone Books.

Deleuze, G. (1993) *The Fold: Leibniz and the Baroque,* trans. T. Conley. London: Athlone Press.

Deleuze, G. (1994) *Difference and Repetition,* trans. P. Patton. New York: Columbia University Press.

Deleuze, G. (1995) *Negotiations 1972–1990,* trans. M. Joughin. New York: Columbia University Press.

Deleuze, G. (1997) *Essays: Critical and Clinical,* trans. D. W. Smith and M. A. Greco. Minneapolis: University of Minnesota Press.

Deleuze, G. and Guattari, F. (1977) *Anti-Oedipus: Capitalism and Schizophrenia,* trans. R. Hurley, M. Seem, and H. R. Lane. New York: Viking Press.

Deleuze, G. and Guattari, F. (1986) *Kafka: Toward a Minor Literature,* trans. D. Polan. Minneapolis: University of Minnesota Press.

Deleuze, G. and Guattari, F. (1987) *A Thousand Plateaus: Capitalism and Schizophrenia,* trans. B. Massumi. Minneapolis: University of Minnesota Press.

Deleuze, G. and Guattari, F. (1994) *What is Philosophy?* trans. H. Tomlinson and G. Burchill. London: Verso.

17 | Jacques Derrida

Roy Boyne

Biographical Details

Jacques Derrida was born near Algiers in 1930. He was educated in Algeria until he was nineteen. His academic record was good, but he did fail his 'Bac' at the first attempt, and subsequently failed the entrance examination for the École Normal Supérieure in Paris on two occasions, before beginning to study there in 1952. Despite an undulating career at the ENS, he finally passed his aggregation in 1956, following this with a year on a scholarship in Harvard, where he married Marguerite Aucoutourier. On his return to France, he did two years' military service as a teacher in Algeria. When this was finished, he resumed his academic career, first as a teacher at the lycée in Le Mans, and then for four years at the Sorbonne, teaching logic. In 1962 his first book, a translation and introduction to Husserl's *Origin of Geometry*, won the Prix Cavaillès. From 1965 he taught the history of philosophy at the ENS, and in 1967 published three major books in the same year, something he did again in 1972, by which time he had regular visiting positions at Yale and Johns Hopkins universities. Through the rest of the 1970s his academic profile increased. In France he was involved in the creation of GREPH (Groupe de Recherches sur l'Enseignment Philosophique), an association founded to defend the teaching of philosophy in schools. In America he was seen as the founder of "deconstruction" and became the key contemporary figure in literary criticism.

Over the last twenty years Derrida's influence has been extended into architecture, art, the administration of philosophy teaching in France, and a range of political issues including racism, antisemitism, nuclear deterrence, and the question of Europe. His radical credentials were strengthened when the Czech state imprisoned him in 1981 for teaching clandestine philosophy seminars in Prague. However, the political implication of his work is still the subject of a serious debate begun in 1987, when it was discovered that the other chief adherent of deconstruction – Paul de Man (1919–83) – had written many articles during World War II for the pro-Nazi Belgian newspaper *Le Soir*. It has not been just the politics of Derrida's work that has been put to the test; the validity of his whole approach is widely disputed. When he was proposed for an honorary degree at Cambridge in 1992, a strong opposition forced a vote. It was in favor of the award by 336 to 204. Those who thought Derrida a charlatan had not won, nor were any of them much in evidence the following year when Toni Morisson, Pierre Bourdieu, Derrida, and others announced the creation of the International Parliament of Writers, based in Strasbourg (until 1998), and formed to combat censorship, to find new types of political engagement, and to affirm the creative relationship between intellectuals and politics. Derrida remains highly committed to this work as activist but also as philosopher, for example raising questions of cosmopolitanism in 1997, and exploring the possibility of a new kind of humanism in his writings on friendship, and in his book on Jean-Luc Nancy. If there is a single model capturing the essence of Jacques Derrida today, it is that of *le philosophe engagé*.

Key Theoretical Contributions

In *Of Grammatology* (1976) Derrida examined the concepts of speech and writing. He explained the traditional view that speech is prime and always comes first, and then in the basic move of deconstruction he demonstrated first that the traditional pairing has always been a matter of subordination of what supposedly comes after to what supposedly is first, and second that it is possible to resist that relationship of subordination and to expose unproven assumptions. He wrote of the Bible that it was received not primarily as a work of writing, that it was "not grammatological but pneumatological" (Derrida 1976: 17). As Derrida went on to say in this text, "The beginning word is understood, in the intimacy of self-presence, as the voice of the other and as commandment." His argument was going to be that there was no pure moment of self-presence, no moment at which an original voice declared itself without intermediary. To assume otherwise, to follow, in other words, the philosophical tradition from Plato to Heidegger, was to abandon social and human responsibility for the horrors done in the name of making the other the same, in the name of forcing all to hear the same voice, which, for Derrida, had never been heard as pure voice and which, in any event, had to be taken on trust or swallowed by force:

> The subordination of the trace to the full presence summed up in the logos, the humbling of writing beneath a speech dreaming its plenitude, such are the gestures required by an onto-theology determining the archeological and eschatological meaning of being ... as life without difference ... Only infinite being can reduce the difference in presence. In that sense, the name of God, at least as it is pronounced within classical rationalism, is the name of indifference itself. (Ibid: 71)

One may object that we are bathed in differences and that quite a few of them hardly appear testament to Derrida's underlying thesis that the violent denial of difference is the secret to the history of the West. One example of this is simply the extraordinary variety of names for every different thing imaginable. But, for Derrida, the process of naming locates what is named in a classificatory system. Names do not simply signify uniqueness or difference; they perpetuate the myth of original transparency in which a duplicated essence is self-labeled for all to see. Perhaps the place where we can see this most clearly is in Derrida's reading of Lévi-Strauss's *Tristes Tropiques*. The Nambikwara of central Brazil did not tell their names to outsiders, but Lévi-Strauss managed to find out most of the names of the tribespeople by befriending the children and playing them off against each other. The children were admonished, and that appeared to be the end of it. Some time later, Lévi-Strauss was asked by the chief for a writing pad, and for some assistance in using it. The Nambikwara had no writing, nor did they do any drawing apart from the odd squiggle scratched in the dirt. Yet the chief knew there were possibilities here for the reassertion of his status and power, and, in a movement of subtle consolidation, he involved Lévi-Strauss in the collusion that he could write.

Derrida reads these two incidents, the artful discovery of the proper names and the collusion with the chief over the simulation of reading and writing, as confirming a foundational prejudice of Western thinking: that there was once a pristine civilization uncontaminated by dissimulation and secrecy; and that this original instance was corrupted by contact with an outside, whether in the case of the enemy who should not know the names used within the tribes or in the case of the anthropologist with his pencils and child psychology. Both examples duplicate the Edenic structure Derrida denies. He denies this notion of a pristine innocence because the potential for its defilement was always already inside, always already a part of the experience of innocence itself. The very facticity of humankind deconstructs the image of a pure God. In a reversal of the ontological argument, that God is first cause, Derrida shows that the first singularity must already have been multiple, and that the first inside must already have been a part of its outside. His demonstration that writing, for the Nambikwara, did not come like a bolt from the blue, that, in other words, the Nambikwara was already a political society, with names to be hidden and a chief with an eye for the consolidation of his power, is an explicative variation on the denial of the original uncontaminated, unmediated voice.

There is, Derrida demonstrated, always a moment of deferral, a delay forever postponing the final moment at which we see the origin, find out the secret, know the structure, meet our God, confront the ideal. He further demonstrated that the idea of a promised land was operative throughout politics, and, in the numerous subtle and obvious ways that literature and art are suffused by values, throughout culture. Thus was the practice of deconstruction born, its spirit being to detect false reliance upon original validity claims in politics and culture, its practice being often to search out binary oppositions, such as between black and white, male and female, East and West, and to challenge their internal hierarchies and blow apart the false claims from one of their sides for exclusive access to some implied moment of presence (the "whiteness" of civilization, the leadership and protection of the male, the rationality of the West). If, however, this is the basic architecture of deconstruction (a term which Derrida does not like, because it seems to imply that there is a fixed method here, so if it has to remain it should be made plural), the elaboration of this basic framework can be quite baroque. Typically it emerges out of close engagement between Derrida and particular texts. The encounter between close, persistent reading and the necessarily subtle critique of the presence claims implicit in the given context sometimes makes Derrida's writing intricate, even labyrinthine.

Major Criticisms

The four major criticisms of Derrida's work are that it is embroidered scholasticism, contemporary sophistry, elitist idealism, and that it is anti-scientific in the sense of being against knowledge.

Michel Foucault replied to Derrida's critical but admiring review of his *L'Histoire de la folie à l'âge classique* that it was an instance of a "historically well-determined little pedagogy." This was not something that he elaborated upon, but he meant that Derrida had picked upon two or three pages in a text of over 600, and had then looked very hard at one of the references, going back to the original Latin of Descartes's *First Meditation* merely to embroider a point of view. The opposition between Foucault and Derrida concerned whether Foucault's project, "to get to know madness itself," was itself mad. Foucault had aspired to escape the clutches of Reason; Derrida thought this to be impossible, since for him madness was a part of reason. The debate, to which Derrida returned in 1994, ten years after Foucault's death, was always undecidable. However, the accusation of minor pedagogy was meretricious. Of course close reading is a part of the French educational tradition; of course academics are both aggressive and defensive about their own and others' work, but Derrida was raising (and yes ornamenting) a basic philosophical issue through his close reading of a few passages in Descartes. It is his favorite trope. We see it illustrated in *Specters of Marx* (1994), in which he makes much of the opening lines of the Communist Manifesto. This play does not prevent cogent insight and analysis from emerging.

Jürgen Habermas (1987: 187) has suggested that "Derrida is particularly interested in standing the primacy of logic over rhetoric, canonized since Aristotle, on its head." Derrida denies this. Habermas does make some interesting points regarding analogies to be drawn between Derrida and Adorno, and concerning the possible connection between Derrida and the anti-Platonic tradition from Dante to Gadamer. But he does not recognize the vast difference between Derrida and, say, Gadamer; nor does he really inquire into the implications of the claim that the priority of logic over rhetoric is sought by Derrida. If Habermas were serious about coming to a view here, at the very least he would have considered Plato's dialogues with the Sophists. Christina Howells's (1999, 69) point that Habermas should not have relied on a secondary source for his understanding of Derrida is unanswerable.

The reception of Derrida's thought among materialists, both feminist and socialist, has been split. The potential of deconstructive critique of the male–female binary has been recognized by many feminist thinkers, such as Johnson, Schor, and Felman. Julia Kristeva has expressed concern that deconstruction has been interpreted too crudely at times, especially in America, while Gayatri Spivak (1993: 51) has wondered whether deconstruction is involved in "legitimizing the polarization between the academy and the real world by disavowing it, and then producing elegant solutions that will never be seriously tested either in large-scale decision-making or among the disenfranchised." This is broadly a view endorsed by Terry Eagleton (Regan 1998: 261): "Deconstruction has always shown the world two faces, the one prudently reformist, the other ecstatically ultra-leftist. Its problem has been that the former style of thought is acceptable but unspectacular; the latter exhilarating, but implausible."

Derrida was not a target of Sokal's and Bricmont's (1998) attack on those French writers, such as Lacan, Deleuze, and Serres, who use scientific terms outside of their home disciplines. Since their book *Intellectual Impostures* was hard to construe as anything other than an assault on the contemporary humanities, Derrida quite properly made a reply. He suspects that they did not bother to read the work of those they attacked, and is quite sure that they never read his work to be sure they were right to exclude him from their critique. Nevertheless, he constructs briefly a set of accusations: he is a relativist and is anti-Enlightenment. "Bien au contraire," replies Derrida, to this phantom critique. Max Dorra, professor of medicine at the Sorbonne, commented alongside Derrida: "The authors who were disingenuously criticized by Sokal and Bricmont all have something in common, each has tried to analyze power, which ultimately means the ability to generate fear." Derrida was not on their list. Perhaps he should have been, but was he too hard a target?

Bibliography

Derrida, J. (1973) *Speech and Phenomena*. Evanston, IL Northwestern University Press.
Derrida, J. (1976) *Of Grammatology*. Baltimore, MD: Johns Hopkins University Press.
Derrida, J. (1978) *Writing and Difference*. London: Routledge.
Derrida, J. (1981a) *Dissemination*. London: Athlone Press.
Derrida, J. (1981b) *Glas*. Paris: Editions Denoël Gonthier.

Derrida, J. (1982) *Margins of Philosophy*. Brighton: Harvester-Wheatsheaf.
Derrida, J. (1987a) *The Post Card*. Chicago: University of Chicago Press.
Derrida, J. (1987b) *The Truth in Painting*. Chicago: University of Chicago Press.
Derrida, J. (1989) *Memoires: For Paul de Man*. New York: Columbia University Press.
Derrida, J. (1994) *Specters of Marx*. London: Routledge.
Derrida, J. (1996) *Archive Fever*. Chicago: University of Chicago Press.
Derrida, J. (1997a) *Cosmopolites de tous les pays, encore un effort!* Paris: Galilée.
Derrida, J. (1997b) *Politics of Friendship*. London: Verso.
Derrida, J. (1997c) "Sokal et Bricmont ne sont pas sérieux." *Le Monde*, November 20.
Derrida, J. (2000) *De Toucher: Jean-Luc Nancy*. Paris: Gallimard.
Dorra, M. (1997) "Metaphores et politique." *Le Monde*, November 20.
Felman, S. (1985) *Writing and Madness*. Ithaca, NY: Cornell University Press.
Foucault, M. (1961) *Histoire de la folie à l'âge classique*. Paris: Plon.
Guberman, R. M. (ed.) (1996) *Julia Kristeva Interviews*. New York: Columbia University Press.
Habermas, J. (1987) *The Philosophical Discourse of Modernity*. Cambridge: Polity Press.
Howells, C. (1999) *Derrida: Deconstruction from Phenomenology to Ethics*. Cambridge: Polity Press.
Johnson, B. (1994) *The Wake of Deconstruction*. Oxford: Blackwell.
Lévi-Strauss, C. (1976) *Tristes Tropiques*. Harmondsworth: Penguin Books.
Michelfelder, D. P. and Palmer, R. E. (eds.) *Dialogue and Deconstruction: The Gadamer–Derrida Encounter*. Albany: State University of New York Press.
Regan, S. (ed.) (1998) *The Eagleton Reader*. Oxford: Blackwell.
Schor, N. (1995) *Bad Objects*. Durham, NC: Duke University Press.
Sokal, A. and Bricmont, J. (1998) *Intellectual Impostures*. London: Routledge.
Spivak, G. C. (1993) *Outside in the Teaching Machine*. London: Routledge.

18 | Norbert Elias

Robert van Krieken

Ideas
Unplanned order □ Habitus □ Figuration □ Interdependence □
Social process □ Involvement/detachment □ Civilizing process □
Decivilization

Major books
The Civilizing Process (2000)
The Court Society (1983)
The Germans (1996)
What is Sociology? (1978)
The Society of Individuals (1991)

Influences
Comte □ Freud □ Marx □ Weber

Biographical Details

The work of Norbert Elias (1897–1990) is central to the development of
contemporary social theory, a powerful example of the possibilities contained within a synthesis of the most dynamic elements of classical sociological thought with an intellectually independent engagement with a
wide range of empirical evidence. His conceptual vocabulary destabilizes
the orthodoxies of social science in a way which enables the reader to
look over and beyond the usual unresolvable debates centered on duali-
ties such as individual/society or state/society.

Born in the then-German (now Polish) town of Breslau, after studying philosophy Elias went on to work with Karl Mannheim at the University of Frankfurt, at the same time that Max Horkheimer and Theodor

Adorno were establishing the Frankfurt Institute for Social Research, where he completed *The Court Society* (1983) in 1933. Driven from Germany by the National Socialists, Elias moved to London via Paris, where he wrote *Über den Prozeß der Zivilisation* (*The Civilizing Process*) in the British Museum between 1934 and 1939. As a historical analysis of the development of human personality structure, Elias saw it as a critique of the academic psychology dominant at the time. The distinctiveness of his ideas kept him out of academic posts in England until the age of 57, when he was appointed to a lectureship in 1954 at the University of Leicester, and where he influenced many of today's leading sociologists. His productivity and real intellectual influence on social theory took off in the 1970s, after his retirement, particularly in the Netherlands and Germany, where students read pirated copies of *The Civilizing Process* (2000) alongside Foucault's *Discipline and Punish*. The influence of Elias's distinctive ideas on social theory continues to grow, particularly for those interested in the history of subjectivity, power, knowledge, violence, state formation, emotions, attitudes towards the body, and sexuality. His analysis of the historical development of emotions and psychological life is particularly important in relation to the connections he established with larger-scale processes such as state formation, civilization, urbanization, globalization, and economic development.

Key Theoretical Contributions

Elias developed his social theory in a relatively modest way, without explicitly presenting himself as a "theorist." He placed more emphasis on the empirical investigation of particular historical and sociological questions, in works such as *The Court Society* and *The Civilizing Process*, because he was concerned to transcend the division between social theory and social research. The approach to social theory which was embedded within his practice as a social researcher, rather than being self-consciously presented as such, was one of drawing on the work of Marx, Weber, and Freud, *inter alia*, in order to elaborate "a comprehensive theory of human society, or, more exactly, a theory of the development of humanity, which could provide an integrating framework of reference for the various specialist social sciences" (Elias 1994: 131).

Elias's social theory (Elias 1978, 1991, 1997) can usefully be seen as being organized around five interconnected conceptual principles. First, although societies are composed of human beings who engage in intentional action, the outcome of the combination of human actions is generally unplanned and unintended. For Elias, what we call "society" consists of the structured interweaving of the diverse activities of various human agents pursuing their own particular goals, resulting in social forms such as "Christianity," "capitalism," "modernity," and particular forms of culture and group identity, without those social forms having been planned or intended by any specific individual or group. The task for sociologists is then to analyze and explain the mechanics of this transformation of intentional human action into unintended patterns of social life, which necessarily takes place over longer or shorter periods of time. For Elias, the goal of such analysis is improved human control over social change, so that "people can only hope to master and make sense of these purposeless, meaningless functional interconnections if they can recognize them as relatively autonomous, distinctive functional interconnections, and investigate them systematically" (Elias 1978: 58).

Second, human individuals can only be understood in their interdependencies with each other, as part of networks of social relations, or what Elias often referred to as "figurations." Rather than seeing individuals as possessing an "autonomous" identity with which they then interact with each other and relate to something we call a "society," Elias argued that we are social to our very core, and only exist in and through our relations with others, developing a socially constructed *habitus* or "second-nature." Central to Elias's articulation of this point was an oft-repeated argument against what he called the *homo clausus* or "closed personality" image of human beings running through much of modern Western philosophy and social and political thought, with its emphasis on autonomy, freedom, and independent agency. He suggested that this picture should be replaced by one of human beings as "open personalities" characterized more by interdependence than autonomy from each other, bound together in social "figurations." Elias introduced the concept of "figuration" in order to place "the problem of human interdependencies into the very heart of sociological theory" (ibid: 134) and to transcend an essentially mistaken opposition between "individual" and "society."

Third, human social life should be understood in terms of relations rather than states or things. For example, instead of power being a "thing" which persons, groups, or institutions possess to a greater or lesser degree, Elias argued that we should think in terms of power *relations*, with ever-changing "balances" or "ratios" of power between individuals and social units. This also made it possible to acknowledge that questions of power are different from questions of "freedom" and "domination," and that all human relationships are essentially relations of power.

Fourth, human societies can only be understood as consisting of long-term processes of development and change, rather than as timeless states or conditions. Elias was convinced that sociologists cannot logically avoid concerning themselves with the diachrony of long-term social processes in order to understand current social relations and structures, and he spoke of the "transformational impetus" (*Wandlungsimpetus*) of all social life, which he saw as "an integral moment of every social structure and their temporary stability as the expression of an impediment to social change" (Elias 1997: 371). An important implication of this is that instead of speaking of rationality, the market, modernity, or postmodernity, Elias would prefer to think in terms of their processual character, of rational*ization*, market*ization*, modern*ization*, or even postmodern*ization*.

Fifth, sociological thought moves constantly between a position of social and emotional involvement in the topics of study, and one of detachment from them. The fact that sociologists study other interdependent human beings means that they are part of their object of scientific study, and thus cannot avoid a measure of involvement in their own research and theorizing. Social scientific knowledge develops within the society it is part of, and not independently of it. At the same time, this involvement is often a barrier to an adequate understanding of social life, especially one which can resolve or transcend any of the persistent problems characterizing human beings' relationships with each other. Elias felt it was important for social scientists to try to transcend the emotion-laden, everyday conceptualization of the human world and develop a "way of seeing" that went beyond current ideologies and mythologies. Indeed, he often referred to sociologists as engaged in the "destruction of myths."

None of these ideas is entirely unique to Elias, but what makes his approach powerful is his synthesis of what is currently spread across a variety of perspectives in social theory. Elias offers a set of sensitizing concepts, an orientation to how one understands and practices social theory, with the promise of drawing many of its various threads together.

It is in *The Civilizing Process* (2000), written in 1939, that one finds the most extensive articulation of Elias's social theory in relation to the history of Western social and psychic life. Elias organized his analysis of this history around Europeans' perception of themselves as particularly "civilized," at the very time that they were descending into horrific barbarism (although he did not yet know its extent), because he felt that the idea and experience of "civilization" lay at the heart of the constitution of the psychic structure and dynamics characteristic of contemporary Western societies.

The argument was that what we experience as "civilization" is constituted by a particular *habitus* or psychic structure which has changed over time and which can only be understood as linked to changes in the

forms taken by broader social relationships. His study of European eti-
quette manuals revealed that from the early Middle Ages onwards, the
standards applied to violence, sexual behavior, bodily functions, eating
habits, table manners, and forms of speech became gradually more sophisticated, with an increasing threshold of shame, embarrassment, and
repugnance. He saw medieval society as characterized by "a lesser degree of social control and constraint of the life of drives" (Elias 2000:
164), and in particular by a greater degree of violence, so that the development of processes of civilization can most usefully be analyzed through
an assessment of the regulation and management of violence and aggression in everyday social life. Elias argued that the restraint imposed by
increasingly differentiated and complex networks of social relations became increasingly internalized and less dependent on its maintenance
by external social institutions, a shift from external, social compulsion
to internal compulsion. This gradual "rationalization" of human conduct, its placement at the service of long-term goals and the increasing
internalization of social constraint was, suggested Elias, closely tied to
the processes of state formation and the development of monopolies of
physical force.

A central problem left unaddressed by this analysis, however, was the
persistence of violence and aggression even when processes of civilization could be seen as relatively advanced, the obvious key example being
German fascism. Elias addressed this question in his later work, much
of which is collected in *The Germans* (1996), where he raised the possibility that civilization and decivilization can occur simultaneously, with
monopolies of force being capable of as extreme violence as situations
where the "means of violence" is more diffusely controlled. He also placed
more emphasis in his later work on the essential precariousness of the
forms of *habitus* generated by processes of civilization, drawing attention to the speed with which established forms of restrained, civilized
conduct can crumble when the surrounding social conditions become
unstable, threatening, and fearful. Nonetheless, for Elias, barbaric human conduct can still only be understood in relation to the social processes by which forms of conduct and feeling we would wish to defend as
civilized have emerged, however tenuously, in human society.

Major Criticisms

The first of the critical responses to Elias's work derives from a fundamental opposition running through much of Western social, cultural,
and political thought, between those who lean towards seeing all human
beings as more or less similar to each other, and those who emphasize

the differences between distinct groups. The latter orientation is divided in turn between a synchronic approach focusing on differences at a particular point in time, and a diachronic perspective concentrating on developments over time, sometimes referred to as "developmentalism."

Elias generally prefers the latter position, studying differences in human *habitus*, conduct, and social structure over time, but of course this brings him into disagreement with those who are more sensitive to the similarities between human beings at different points in time and in different cultural contexts. For example, one of Elias's strongest critics, the German anthropologist Hans-Peter Duerr (1988, 1990), argues that if we agree that human sexual relations are always socially regulated and subjected to some patterned set of rules and norms, then this will universally produce some sort of division between public and private bodily domains, with the private domain constituting the focus of social regulation. For Duerr, the kind of lack of restraint of sexual impulses which Elias seems to observe in the Middle Ages is simply impossible, because the patterned family relations which existed at the time required at least some set of rules governing what one could or could not do in the sexual realm. Since there are no undisputed criteria which might lead us to prefer one approach to the other, the debate is essentially irresolvable and best understood as itself a product of the indeterminacy of the relationship between the universal and the particular, between continuity and change.

Second, Elias's concentration on the connections between state formation and civilizing processes suggests two alternative modes of analysis, the first of which reflects on different aspects of social organization – other than state formation – which might also support processes of civilization. These can include the form taken by family life and religious belief systems, and broaden our view of the "changes in social structure" to include features of social life beyond the formation of particular types of political regimes. The second alternative is to include an examination of the often barbaric or decivilizing dimensions of state formation, indeed the brutality lying at the heart of almost every nation-state: questions concerning colonialism and imperialism, the ways in which Western nation-states have imposed a relationship between their own civilization and the supposedly "barbaric" cultures of subjected peoples, which is itself a brutal and violent one.

Third, Elias's emphasis on the unplanned nature of social change can have the effect of neglecting the organized interventions of powerful social groups into the form and direction of civilizing processes. Most social historians, for example, paint a picture of European history in which diverse groups of lawyers, inquisitors, clergy, judges, entrepreneurs, military leaders, and so on, played an active and constitutive role on shaping history, in addition to being driven in particular directions by abstract social forces. A central concern for those drawing on Elias's social theory is thus an understanding of how to engage with the distinction between civilizing *processes* and civilizing *offensives* (van Krieken 1990).

Bibliography

Duerr, Hans-Peter (1988) *Nacktheit und Scham*. Frankfurt: Suhrkamp.
Duerr, Hans-Peter (1990) *Intimität*. Frankfurt: Suhrkamp.
Elias, N. (1978) *What is Sociology?* London: Hutchinson.
Elias, N. (1983) *The Court Society*. New York: Pantheon.
Elias, N. (1991) *The Society of Individuals*. Oxford: Blackwell.
Elias, N. (1994) *Reflections on a Life*. Cambridge: Polity Press.
Elias, N. (1996) *The Germans*. Oxford: Blackwell.
Elias, N. (1997) "Towards a Theory of Social Processes." *British Journal of Sociology*, 48, 3: 355–83.
Elias, N. (2000) *The Civilizing Process*, revd. edn. Oxford: Blackwell.
van Krieken (1990) "The Organization of the Soul: Elias and Foucault on Discipline and the Self." *Archives Europeénes de Sociologie*, 31, 2: 353–71.

19 | **Michel Foucault**

Gerard Delanty

Ideas
Knowledge as power ☐ Genealogy ☐ Governmentality ☐
Surveillance ☐ Bio-power ☐ Discourse

Major books
Madness and Civilization (1961)
The Order of Things (1966)
Discipline and Punish (1975)
History of Sexuality, 3 vols. (1976, 1984, 1984)

Influences
Bachelard ☐ Bataille ☐ Canguilhem ☐ Cavailles ☐ Dumézil ☐
Freud ☐ Nietzsche

Biographical Details

Michel Foucault (1926–84) was one of the most influential social theorists of the latter part of the twentieth century. Originally trained as a psychiatrist, in early books such as *Birth of the Clinic* (1973a) and *Madness and Civilization* (1965) he very soon turned against the medical profession in his claim that the body was a political object of power and that knowledge about it was always inseparable from relations of power. Foucault was a creative and original thinker whose writings lacked the obscurantism of many of those who were to emulate him. He was influenced by such postwar French thinkers as Dumézil, Cavailles, Canguilhem, and Bachelard, and was also inspired by Nietzsche, Bataille, and Freud. By the time he became Professor of the History of Systems of Thought at the Collège de France in 1970, he had already become one of France's best-known intellectuals. However, it was in the United States that his thought had the greatest impact, inspiring a generation of new thinkers to see the political in the social and above all in the very constitution of the self. Rejecting the utopian and revolutionary promise of knowledge that lay behind Marxism and other Enlightenment ideologies, Foucault turned to Nietzsche and Freud, who in a way replaced Hegel and Marx as the canonical figures in a new approach to modernity centered on the social practices of the self and knowledge. His thought emerged out of a rejection of the prevailing "humanist" philosophies of existentialism, phenomenology, and Marxism that dominated French philosophy in the postwar decades.

Key Theoretical Contributions

Foucault's enduring legacy was his theory of power as a discursive system. Rejecting the conventional view of power in social and political theory as a relation based on action and which may be rooted in legitimate authority or simply in coercion of some kind, Foucault saw power as expressed in what he preferred to call "governmentality," a term he used in a lecture in 1978 (Foucault 1979). This differs from "government" and "governance" in that it is manifest in the micro-structures of everyday life, in the "technology" of social institutions and in the self-governing practices of the individual. This sense of power is one that cannot be reduced to either agency or structure, though it is closer to the latter. For Foucault, power is expressed neither by a social actor (a class or elite for instance), nor by a social structure in the form of legitimate authority, but by the circulation in society of discourses and is underpinned by the abstract apparatus of the state. It is for this reason that Foucault can be located in the context of the "cultural turn" in the social sciences, for he saw discourse as a mediating link between agency and structure. In essence, his conception of power was one that saw power as a culturally shaped discourse which, like Kuhn's paradigms, could not be criticized since it is itself the basis of criticism. But discourses, Foucault was to argue, are also sites of struggles between different kinds of social practices.

Underlying Foucault's writings is a theory of discourse, which was elaborated in the book that established his reputation, *The Order of Things* (1973b), as well as *The Archaeology of Knowledge* (1972a). Discourses are all inclusive language games which are "productive" of knowledge, which does not have a privileged position outside of discourses. Foucault's notion of discourse can also be compared to Wittgenstein's idea of "language games." The implications of this approach that derived from a concern with structure and language led to a rejection of the universality of truth, justice, and equality. Originally this was conceived within the scope of his so-called "archeology of knowledge," the project to uncover how ideas in the human sciences are rooted in historically specific discourses which structured the intellectual field into epistemic frameworks, leading some to claim that Foucault was a structuralist in the sense of Claude Lévi-Strauss. In any case, Foucault soon revised his project, which as announced in his inaugural lecture at the Collège de France in 1970, "The Order of Discourse" (Foucault 1972b) and the classic essay, "Nietzsche, Genealogy and History" (Foucault 1977a), sought to integrate into the structure of discourse social practices. He called his new approach, following Nietzsche, a "genealogy" of power, which was designed as a "history of the present" as opposed to the tendentially structuralist "archeology" and as an alternative to conventional historical writing based on narratives and the quest for an origin. This more deconstructive approach sought to reveal the connections between knowledge and power in a way that would reveal discourses to be potential sites of struggles. A shift can thus be detected in his middle period from discourses as disciplinary rule systems, that is relatively closed epistemic structures, to discourses as more open sites of struggle, but the implications of the genealogical method did not become clear until much later, with power conceived as resistance.

One of his most famous works, *Discipline and Punish* (1977b), opened up a whole new approach to areas as diverse as criminology, ethics, modernity, power, and the self. Probably the single most important influence of the book was the concept of surveillance that it introduced. While in Germany intellectuals such as Habermas saw modernity in terms of the progressive extension of communicative spaces in society as a result of the emergence of social movements and the constitution of the modern public, Foucault saw modernity only as the unfolding of total systems of power such as those linked with the hospital, the asylum, the prison, the workhouse. Recalling the sociology of modernity of the older Frankfurt School and Max Weber's motif of the "iron cage" of modern rationalism, in his early and middle works Foucault chose the dark side of modernity: surveillance of the body and panopticism were to be his motifs of modernity. Modernity for Foucault involved the creation of new technologies of the self, forms of power that were more about what he called "bio-power" than class power, that is forms of power that penetrate into the very constitution of the self and the regulation of the body. The essence of surveillance is that it is invisible and therefore it does not emanate from a particular agent but from a discursive system that is also a system of knowledge. This conception of power as surveillance through knowledge was developed in his history of sexuality, where the genealogical approach is more evident than in *Discipline and Punish*. Sexuality in the modern West, he argued, was given a discursive existence in a technology of surveillance which created desires while seeking to control them.

There is much to indicate that Foucault, especially in his later writings, became increasingly interested in the possibility of a recovery of the subject and that the genealogical approach might extend the "permanent critique" of the Enlightenment to the self and uncover new possibilities for human subjectivity. In *The History of Sexuality* (Foucault 1978, 1985, 1986) and in many of his short pieces and interviews (Foucault 1980), there is a pronounced shift from power to resistance and away from the idea of disciplinary modernity based on panopticism. For a time he was intrigued by the prospect that the non-Western world (Islam or even Japan) might contain the seeds of a new subjectivity. Though frequently seen as a postmodern thinker, he did not always reject the categories of modernity. In the late essay "What is Enlightenment?" he wrote: "I have been seeking to stress that the thread which may connect us with the Enlightenment is not faithfulness to doctrinal elements but, rather, the permanent reactivation of an attitude – that is, of a philosophical ethos that could be described as a permanent critique of our historical era" (Foucault 1997b: 312). This suggests that modernity may contain alternatives within it: "rather than seeking to distinguish the 'modern era' from the 'premodern' or 'postmodern,' I think it would be more useful to try to find out how the attitude of modernity, ever since its formation, has found itself struggling with attitudes of 'counter-modernity'" (ibid: 309–10).

Major Criticisms

Foucault's work has been much debated and it is unlikely that his importance in the history of modern social thought will decline as a result of the obvious problems with his approach. The most common criticism is that in his concern to deconstruct the received wisdom of the human sciences, such as the belief in the universality of knowledge, the emancipatory power of knowledge, and the self-legislating subjectivity, he reduced too much to power. By making power ubiquitous, the concept loses its analytical power and Foucault ends up in the same normative–critical impasse as Adorno and Horkheimer, and indeed one not fundamentally different from Luhmann's theory of autopoesis. Related to this is his view of discourse which for many critics is too structurally conceived. Indeed, there is also a curious functional logic to many of his arguments. Jürgen Habermas, for instance, has criticized Foucault for a view of discourse that does not offer the possibility of communication, and has argued instead for a more open conception of discourse and one that allows for the possibility of critique (see Kelly 1994). For Pierre Bourdieu, too, discourse is conceived too much as a closed system that does not lead to reflexivity within science. For Alain Touraine, by concentrating on the self and the institutional apparatus of power, Foucault ignored the pivotal role of social movements in the making of modernity.

It is clear, of course, that Foucault saw power as entailing resistance, but this was a position that he developed later in his life when the huge international reception of this work forced him to clarify the political possibilities in his history of the present. By the time of his untimely death in 1984 he was certainly embracing a slightly less disciplinary conception of power and with a view of "governmentality" as the site of resistance. However, he never systematized his thought or fully resolved the question of a normative foundation of politics and ethics. Although he clearly did become interested in the possibility of a countermodernity, it was never clear exactly what was the relation of this to his theory of modernity and to modern systems of power and how social practices might express political possibilities. The enduring motif in his work would appear to be the prison rather than social movements.

Finally, the relevance of Foucault's key concepts – the discursive construction of the self – to the social struggles and technologically driven processes of the global and information age may be questioned. In the final analysis his social theory was a critique of the European heritage and in this sense he belongs to the tradition of late modern European thinkers.

Bibliography

Delanty, G. (2000) *Modernity and Postmodernity: Knowledge, Power, the Self*. London: Sage.

Dreyfus, H. and Rabinow, R. (eds) (1982) *Michel Foucault: Beyond Structuralism and Hermeneutics*. Chicago: University of Chicago Press.

Foucault, M. (1965) [1961] *Madness and Civilization: A History of Insanity in the Age of Reason*, trans. R. Howard. New York: Pantheon.

Foucault, M. (1972a) [1969] *The Archaeology of Knowledge*, trans. A. Sheridan Smith. New York: Pantheon.

Foucault, M. (1972b) [1971] "The Order of Discourse," trans. R. Swyer. Appendix to *The Archaeology of Knowledge*, trans. A. Sheridan Smith. New York: Pantheon.

Foucault, M. (1973a) [1963] *Birth of the Clinic: An Archaeology of Medical Perception*. New York: Pantheon.

Foucault, M. (1973b) [1966] *The Order of Things: An Archaeology of the Human Sciences,* trans. A. Sheridan. New York: Vintage.

Foucault, M. (1977a) [1971] "Nietzsche, Genealogy, History." In D. Bouchard (ed.) *Language, Counter-Memory, Practice.* Oxford: Blackwell.

Foucault, M. (1977b) [1975] *Discipline and Punish: The Birth of the Prison,* trans. A. Sheridan. London: Allen Lane.

Foucault, M. (1978) [1976] *The History of Sexuality Vol. 1: An Introduction,* trans. R. Hurley. New York: Vintage.

Foucault, M. (1979) [1978] "Governmentality," trans. P. Pasquino. *Ideology and Consciousness,* 6: 5–12.

Foucault, M. (1980) *Power/Knowledge: Collected Interviews and Other Essays, 1972–1977,* ed. C. Gordon. Brighton: Harvester Press.

Foucault, M. (1985) [1984] *The History of Sexuality Vol. 2: The Uses of Pleasure,* trans. R. Hurley. New York: Vintage.

Foucault, M. (1986) [1984] *The History of Sexuality Vol. 3: The Care of the Self,* trans. R. Holton. New York: Vintage.

Foucault, M. (1988) *Politics, Philosophy, Culture: Interviews and Other Writings, 1977–1984,* ed. L. Kritzman. London: Routledge.

Foucault, M. (1997a) *Michel Foucault: The Essential Works Vol. 1: Ethics.* London: Allen Lane.

Foucault, M. (1997b) "What is Enlightenment?" In *Michel Foucault: The Essential Works Vol. 1: Ethics.* London: Allen Lane.

Gutting, G. (ed.) (1994) *The Cambridge Companion to Foucault.* Cambridge: Cambridge University Press.

Hoy, D. C. (ed.) (1990) *The Foucault Reader.* Cambridge: Polity Press.

Kelly, M. (ed.) (1994). *Critique and Power: Recasting the Foucault/Habermas Debate.* Cambridge, MA: MIT Press.

20 | Hans-Georg Gadamer

David West

Biographical Details

Born in 1900 in Marburg, Gadamer studied philosophy, German literature, history, and art history at the universities of Breslau, Marburg,
and Munich before completing his first doctorate (*Promotion*) with the
neo-Kantians Natorp and Hartmann at Marburg in 1922. In 1923 he
attended lectures by Husserl and Heidegger, completing a second doctorate (*Habilitation*) with Heidegger in 1928. The influence of Husserl's
phenomenology and Heidegger's "ontological hermeneutic" was apparent in his early studies on Plato and Aristotle and his work on aesthetics
(Gadamer 1985). Gadamer was professor at Marburg, Leipzig, Frankfurt, and then Heidelberg, where he has remained. His most influential
work, *Truth and Method*, which was first published in 1960, has been
recognized as "the most important contribution to philosophical

hermeneutics since Heidegger's *Being and Time* (1927)" (Weinsheimer 1985: ix). It has become an important point of reference not only in philosophy, but also in theology, legal and literary studies, art history and criticism, cultural studies, and social theory. During the course of a long and productive career, Gadamer has taught several generations of German scholars and engaged in influential debates with Habermas (see below) and Derrida (Michelfelder and Palmer 1989). He died in 2002.

Key Theoretical Contributions

Gadamer's philosophical hermeneutics grows directly from the philosophy of Heidegger, but shares the later Heidegger's overriding concern with language as the "house of being" (West 1996). Thus, although Gadamer is closely associated with hermeneutics – the theory of interpretation of texts, works of art, historical events, laws, and so on – he develops an ontological rather than merely epistemological hermeneutics. Hermeneutic categories are fundamental not only epistemologically, as Dilthey maintained, to specific cognitive enterprises such as history, aesthetic appreciation, and legal interpretation, but more profoundly to the very ontological nature of self-consciousness and the world as our world. The conjunction of the terms "truth" and "method" in the title of Gadamer's best-known work, *Truth and Method*, is not, therefore, meant to endorse the epistemological concerns of Bacon and Descartes, whose idea of a rigorous scientific *method* was designed to purge knowledge of all distorting subjective influences and so provide it with objective and ahistorical foundations. On the contrary, Gadamer aims to demonstrate the limits of methodical science as against the fundamental human capacity for understanding, which is the ontological basis of human being and truth.

In order to overcome the "dogmatism of method" it is necessary to displace the subject from its pivotal position in the Western philosophical tradition. Gadamer rejects the Cartesian premise of an autonomous and unconditioned subject capable of absolutely certain knowledge, which corresponds to an objectifying scientific knowledge and a manipulative, instrumental stance toward nature. Husserl came close to overcoming the standpoint of subjective consciousness with his concept of the "lifeworld," which refers to the unreflective assumptions, values, and practices that form the intersubjective background of all our thinking and acting. But Husserl ultimately fails to escape the standpoint of the "transcendental" subject of epistemology (Gadamer 1976c: 163ff.). However, understood properly as the unsurpassable and irreducibly historical horizon of all our experience, the notion of the lifeworld has radical implications for both hermeneutics and philosophy.

In the first place, it leads to a critique of the limitations of previous hermeneutics. In their attempts to develop a rigorous theory of interpretation, Schleiermacher and Dilthey had failed to escape the methodical assumptions of modern science. They saw the subjective and historically located point of view of the interpreter as just an obstacle to be overcome on the path to objective understanding (Schleiermacher 1977; Dilthey 1976). For Gadamer, by contrast, the lifeworld is the untranscendable horizon of all understanding. Understanding is always inevitably *for* a historically situated interpreter as much as it is *of* some historically located human expression, and it is inevitable "that in such knowledge the knower's own being comes into play" (Gadamer 1989: 491).

Gadamer's view of the historically situated nature of understanding has radical implications for the Enlightenment's "prejudice against prejudice." It is Gadamer's claim that even the most ambitious rationalism cannot hope to escape from dependence on the "prejudgments" of tradition. As Gadamer provocatively asserts, "there is undoubtedly no understanding that is free of all prejudices" (ibid). However, obedience to authority may be rational if it is based on the free and informed acknowledgment of superior wisdom. Reason aspires to the absolute independence from tradition and prejudice claimed on its behalf by Enlightenment philosophers at the risk of a false objectivism, which appears to "let the 'facts' speak" at the same time as it organizes them in terms of a particular set of questions and concerns. But we can nevertheless learn to "distinguish the true prejudices, by which we *understand*, from the *false* ones, by which we *misunderstand*" (ibid: 298–9). Although "there is undoubtedly no understanding that is free of all prejudices," "the will of our knowledge must be directed toward escaping their thrall" (ibid: 490).

The inescapability of prejudgments has its counterpart in the positive effectiveness of history and tradition. The horizon of understanding that we bring to the study of historical expressions has itself been influenced by tradition. Our tradition is not simply an object to be known, it is also what has made us into the particular "subjects" who attempt to understand it. The interval between a historical expression and its contemporary interpretation is enriched by the labors of previous interpreters, whose insights (and even mistakes) contribute to our understanding. In this sense, Gadamer speaks of the "history of effect" (*Wirkungsgeschichte*) or, in other words, the way historical human expressions are continually effective in the present (ibid: 300–1). In this sense, too, interpretation is an instance of the practice of "application," a notion that has traditionally played an important role in both legal judgment and biblical exegesis. In the case of a law, its application must both be attentive to its "original meaning" and "take account of the change in circumstances and hence define afresh the normative function of the law" (ibid: 327). Similarly, interpretation "applies" the original text within a tradition that has, in the meantime, moved on.

Further, because it always occurs from the perspective of a historically situated interpretive horizon, understanding is irreducibly relational. So although there can certainly be better or worse, and even incorrect interpretations, there can be no uniquely true and certainly no final interpretation. The productivity of tradition implies that meaning is strictly "inexhaustible." Nor can the productivity of a work be circumscribed by the original intentions of its author, which similarly depend on a horizon of meaning transcending the author's subjectivity. Language speaks through individual subjects as much as they speak through it.

But if meaning is relational and inexhaustible, how can Gadamer claim that understanding is nevertheless the basis of truth? Drawing on an older tradition of European humanism, Gadamer conceives understanding as an instance of what Aristotle calls *phronesis* or "practical wisdom," which is the capacity most directly manifested in moral and aesthetic judgment (Beiner 1983). Like interpretation, judgment is unmethodical but not, for that reason, merely arbitrary. In the end, Gadamer is confident that "what the tool of method does not achieve must – and really can – be achieved by a discipline of questioning and inquiring, a discipline that guarantees truth" (Gadamer 1989: 491). What is more, in the productive dialogue between interpretation and meaning, between present and past, both history and tradition continue to be active and effective in the present. Understanding, as the universal ontological ground of human being-in-the-world, is thus fundamental to the ongoing creation and recreation of a distinctively human culture and life.

Major Criticisms

Gadamer's positive evaluation of tradition and prejudice has been criticized as essentially conservative (Warnke 1987: 134–8). But it can be argued that Gadamer does not so much reject the Enlightenment's commitment to critical rationality as question its favored view of reason as something absolutely other than, and opposed to, both tradition and authority (Gadamer 1989: 279). Critics have also questioned whether Gadamer successfully steers the difficult course between the reductive objectivism of methodical science and a relativist abdication of truth (Warnke 1987: 171–3; Weinsheimer 1985: 40ff., Seung 1982). But Gadamer's relational view of understanding does not rule out genuine critique and mutual understanding between horizons or cultures. We can escape the "monadic isolation" of our particular horizons of meaning, albeit never absolutely or once and for all (Linge 1976: xxxvi–xxxvii.). Both relativism and conservatism are implied in Habermas's critical engagement with Gadamer's "claim of universality" for hermeneutics. For Habermas, "hermeneutic consciousness remains incomplete as long as it does not include a reflection upon the limits of hermeneutic understanding" (Hekman 1986: 130–1). Through its exclusive concern with the meanings of utterances, texts, and symbols, hermeneutic understanding is allegedly ill-equipped to uncover ideological forms of consciousness – forms of communication "distorted" by the power of dominant social groups (Habermas 1970a, 1970b; Holub 1991). Against Habermas, Gadamer has maintained that critique of ideology, though possible, only deludes itself when it lays claim to objective and timeless foundations (Gadamer 1970).

Bibliography

Beiner, R. (1983) *Political Judgment*. London: Methuen.
Bubner, R. (1981) *Modern German Philosophy*. Cambridge: Cambridge University Press.
Dilthey, W. (1976) *Dilthey: Selected Writings,* ed. H. P. Rickman. Cambridge: Cambridge University Press.
Gadamer, H.-G. (1970) "On the Scope and Function of Hermeneutical Reflection." *Continuum*, 8: 77–95.
Gadamer, H.-G. (1976a) *Hegel's Dialectic: Five Hermeneutic Studies,* trans. P. C. Smith. New Haven, CT: Yale University Press.
Gadamer, H.-G. (1976b) *Philosophical Hermeneutics,* ed. D. E. Linge. Berkeley: University of California Press.
Gadamer, H.-G. (1980) *Dialogue and Dialectic: Eight Hermeneutical Studies on Plato,* trans. P. C. Smith. New Haven, CT: Yale University Press.
Gadamer, H.-G. (1981a) "Heidegger and the History of Philosophy." *Monist,* 64: 434–44.
Gadamer, H.-G. (1981b) *Reason in the Age of Science,* trans. F. G. Lawrence. Cambridge, MA: MIT Press.
Gadamer, H.-G. (1985) *Philosophical Apprenticeships,* trans. R. R. Sullivan. Cambridge, MA: MIT Press.
Gadamer, H.-G. (1986a) *The Idea of the Good in Platonic Aristotelian Philosophy,* trans. P. C. Smith. New Haven, CT: Yale University Press.
Gadamer, H.-G. (1989) [1960] *Wahrheit und Methode,* 5th German edn. Tübingen. Trans. by J. Weinsheimer and D. Marshall as *Truth and Method*. New York: Crossroad Publishing.
Habermas, J. (1970a) "On Systematically Distorted Communication." *Inquiry,*

13: 205–18.

Habermas, J. (1970b) "Summation and Response." *Continuum*, 8: 123–33.

Hekman, S. J. (1986) *Hermeneutics and the Sociology of Knowledge.* Cambridge: Polity Press.

Holub, R. C. (1991) *Jürgen Habermas: Critic in the Public Sphere.* London: Routledge.

Linge, D. E. (1976) "Introduction." In H.-G. Gadamer, *Philosophical Hermeneutics.* Berkeley: University of California Press.

Michelfelder, D. P. and Palmer, R. E. (eds.) (1989) *Dialogue and Deconstruction: The Gadamer–Derrida Encounter.* Albany: State University of New York Press.

Palmer, R. E. (1969) *Hermeneutics: Interpretation Theory in Schleiermacher, Dilthey, Heidegger, and Gadamer.* Evanston, IL: Northwestern University Press.

Roberts, D. (ed.) (1995) *Reconstructing Theory: Gadamer, Habermas, Luhmann.* Melbourne: Melbourne University Press.

Schleiermacher, F. E. D. (1977) *Hermeneutics: The Handwritten Manuscripts,* ed. H. Kimmerle, trans. J. Duke and J. Forstman. Missoula, MT: Scholars Press.

Seung, T. K. (1982) *Structuralism and Hermeneutics.* New York: Columbia University Press.

Silverman, H. J. (ed.) (1991) *Gadamer and Hermeneutics.* New York: Routledge.

Wachterhauser, B. R. (ed.) (1994) *Hermeneutics and Truth.* Evanston, IL: Northwestern University Press.

Warnke, G. (1987) *Gadamer: Hermeneutics, Tradition and Reason.* Cambridge: Polity Press.

Weinsheimer, J. C. (1985) *Gadamer's Hermeneutics: A Reading of Truth and Method.* New Haven, CT: Yale University Press.

West, D. (1996) *An Introduction to Continental Philosophy.* Cambridge: Polity Press.

Winch, P. (1958) *The Idea of a Social Science and its Relationship to Philosophy.* London: Routledge and Kegan Paul.

21 | **Anthony Giddens**

Anthony Elliott

Ideas
Structuration □ Duality of structure □ Reflexivity

Major books
New Rules of Sociological Method (1976)
The Constitution of Society (1984)
The Consequences of Modernity (1990)
Modernity and Self-Identity (1991)
The Third Way (1998)

Influences
Durkheim □ Goffman □ Marx □ Weber □ Wittgenstein

Biographical Details

According to many, Anthony Giddens is Britain's preeminent social theorist. The influence of Giddens's work in sociology is certainly comparable to that of Parsons, Foucault, or Habermas. Like these social theorists, he has fashioned, over many years, a dense and extremely subtle theoretical scaffolding for the interpretation of human action and institutional processes in the social sciences and humanities. In doing so, he has drawn from an eclectic array of theoretical traditions in the social sciences – including hermeneutics, ethnomethodology, systems theory, psychoanalysis, structuralism, and poststructuralism. Out of these diverse conceptual traditions, Giddens has developed a novel sociological approach that he terms "structuration theory," a theoretical analysis of the relationship between self and society, with particular emphasis upon processes of social reproduction and institutional transformation.

Giddens, born in London in 1938, spent the better part of his academic career at the Faculty of Social and Political Sciences, University of Cambridge. During this time, he wrote an extraordinary number of sociological tracts, including his bestselling textbook *Capitalism and Modern Social Theory* (1971), *The Class Structure of the Advanced Societies* (1973), *Central Problems in Social Theory* (1979), *A Contemporary Critique of Historical Materialism* (1981), *The Nation-State and Violence* (1986), and *Politics, Sociology and Social Theory* (1995). In 1996 Giddens left Cambridge University to take up the post of Director of the London School of Economics. Since this time his work has become much more explicitly political, as he has sought to reconnect debates in social theory to public policy and the development of a radical political agenda beyond orthodox divisions of left and right. A major contributor to the global third way discussion, his more recent books – including *Beyond Left and Right* (1994), *The Third Way* (1998), and *The Global Third Way Debate* (2001) – have had a significant impact upon debate about the future of progressive politics worldwide. In what follows, I shall confine my discussion to the analysis of Giddens's theoretical contributions to sociology and modern social thought, paying attention to both the strengths and limitations of his general social theory.

Key Theoretical Contributions

Of central importance for grasping the contemporary transformation of the social sciences, Giddens thinks, is the relation between human action and social structure. In a series of pathbreaking books, principally *New Rules of Sociological Method* (1976) and *The Constitution of Society* (1984), Giddens outlines a dynamic model of the relation between agent and system, action and structure, individual and society. He argues it is necessary for social theory to provide an account of the conditions and consequences of human action as directly embroiled with social structure. To do so, Giddens suggests that action and structure should be seen as complementary terms of a duality, the "duality of structure": social structures, he says, are both medium *and* outcome of the practices that constitute those structures. That is to say, social systems are viewed by Giddens as simultaneously enabling and constraining. The structuring properties of social systems, he suggests, at once render human action possible and, through the performance of action, serve to reproduce the structural properties of society. For Giddens, the key task for social theory is to grasp how action is structured in everyday contexts of social life, while simultaneously recognizing that the structural elements of society are reproduced by the performance of action. In suggesting that there is a highly dynamic and creative relation between action and structure, Giddens borrows the term "structuration" from the French. The starting point of Giddens's analysis is not society as given or fixed, but rather the active, creative flow of social life. In contrast to theoretical approaches that downgrade the importance of human agents, Giddens argues that human agents, in the performance of action, draw from social structures in order to carry out social interaction – and in so doing contribute to the reproduction of structures and institutions. As Giddens (1984: 26) formulates this, "structure has no existence independent of the knowledge that agents have about what they do in their day-to-day activities."

To talk of the "structuring properties" of social systems, as Giddens does, is to adopt a radical, indeed novel, view of the ways in which social structures work in relation to individual subjects. Giddens does not view structures so much as things that exist in themselves as, to use his terminology, a "virtual order" of transformative relations that exhibit themselves only in instantiated social practices and memory traces. When Giddens writes of this virtual order of structures his analysis sometimes sounds reminiscent of a poststructuralist critique of language – that is to say, as a structuring of presences against a backdrop of absences. What distinguishes his theory of structuration from poststructuralist thought, however, is a strong conception of human agency. For Giddens, subjects necessarily know a great deal about the social world in which they recursively organize their practices; such practices, he says, are socially embedded as virtual order properties of structures. This mutual dependence of structure and agency is what Giddens calls the "recursive character" of social life, in which self-reflexivity and self-critique are defining features.

Subjective experience and engagement with the social is primarily preconscious or unconscious rather than cognitive, Giddens thinks. In contrast to what agents are able to say about their own action (what he calls "discursive consciousness"), Giddens argues that most human activities are known about by agents in a way that cannot be readily articulated. Such practical stocks of knowledge – what Giddens terms "practical consciousness" – are central to the realization of social actions and intersubjective settings. Yet below the domain of practical consciousness lurks something more anonymous: the unconscious. Giddens argues that the unconscious is a core subjective feature in the reproduction of social life, especially for grasping disruptions of social reproduction at moments of institutional stress or crisis. He makes considerable use of psychoanalytical theory in order to theorize the unconscious dislocations between self and society, drawing not only from Freud and Lacan, but also from Erikson and Winnicott.

During the 1990s Giddens became increasingly preoccupied with the nature of self-identity, particularly the question of the self in social analysis. His books *The Consequences of Modernity* (1990), *Modernity and Self-Identity* (1991), and *The Transformation of Intimacy* (1992) have strongly influenced debates in recent social theory. The issue of the self as a knowledgeable agent, and especially the concept of self-reflexivity, are especially relevant in this context. The concept of "reflexivity" is of immense significance for grasping the production of personal and social life, thinks Giddens. Reflexivity can be defined, he suggests, as a self-defining process that depends upon monitoring of, and reflection upon, psychological and social information about possible trajectories of life. Such information about self and world is not simply incidental to contemporary cultural life; it is actually constitutive of what people do and how they do it. As Giddens (1990: 38) develops this point, "the reflexivity of modern social life consists in the fact that social practices are constantly examined and reformed in the light of incoming information about those very practices, thus constitutively altering their character." In one sense, what is underscored here concerns the richness of the sense-making process, primarily the mixings of certainty and anxiety that allow an individual to *read* cultural life and its textured flow for social action. This imperative to read cultural signs with some degree of sophistication is perhaps an index of our postmodern, speed-driven information age, evident in everything from serious social criticism (in which commentary refers to previous commentary, which in turn is premised upon prior commentary) to the latest trends in pop music, which routinely invoke parodies of style and genre. In another sense, reflexivity stretches beyond the cultural and subjective, deeply rooted as it is in institutional social life. From mapping the demographic characteristics of cities to monitoring the flight paths of aircraft, the intrusion of expert reflexive systems in daily life is pivotal to the world of modernity.

Major Criticisms

Giddens's sociological writings, as well as his reflections on culture and politics, have been sharply criticized for a variety of reasons. Many sociologists remain unhappy with his claim that structuration theory transcends the traditional opposition between subjectivism and objectivism in the social sciences. Margaret Archer (1982, 1990), for example, argues that it is undesirable to amalgamate agency with structure. Her argument is that it is crucial for sociologists to treat agency and structure as analytically distinct in order to analyze core methodological and substantive problems in the social sciences. In particular, Archer criticizes Giddens's claim that structures have no existence independent of the knowledge that individuals have about what they do in day-to-day life. Similar analytical problems have been raised by Thompson (1989), who questioned Giddens's notion of structural constraint in particular.

Notwithstanding the influence and interest of Giddens's work on the self for social theorists, so too critics have responded with a sense of disbelief to the claim that the self is a self-mastering, self-monitoring project. For Giddens's critics, the reflexive project of self-making and self-actualization exhibits a distinctively individualist bent, in a social theory that reduces struggles over power and politics to mere personal interest in change. The core concern here is that Giddens's theory of the reflexive self fits too neatly with the liberal ideology of individualism – the notion that the sovereign individual self lies at the heart of society. It is equally arguable, however, that such criticism is misguided, since Giddens is at pains to underscore the increasing interconnection between personal life and globalizing social influences. His account of the relation between self and society is highly subtle and complex, and is far removed from the "monadic" conception of the individual person advanced by many liberal political theorists.

Still other critics remain troubled by Giddens's failure to accord embodiment a central subjective place in his social theory (see Turner 1992). Craib (1992: 171) argues that Giddens's failure to appreciate the unconscious dynamics of subjectivity and intersubjectivity limits the strengths of his social theory; other critics are concerned that Giddens's appropriation of psychoanalysis circumscribes too narrowly the functioning of the unconscious within social processes (see Elliott 1994, 1996).

Bibliography

Archer, M. (1982) "Morphogenesis vs. Structuration." *British Journal of Sociology*, 33: 455–83.
Archer, M. (1990) "Human Agency and Social Structure." In J. Clark, C. Modgil, and F. Modgil (eds.) *Anthony Giddens*. New York: Falmer Press.
Craib, I. (1992) *Anthony Giddens*. London: Routledge.
Elliott, A. (1994) *Psychoanalytic Theory: An Introduction*. Oxford: Blackwell.
Elliott, A. (1996) *Subject to Ourselves: Social Theory, Psychoanalysis and Postmodernity*. Cambridge: Polity Press.
Giddens, A. (1971) *Capitalism and Modern Social Theory*. Cambridge: Cambridge University Press.
Giddens, A. (1973) *The Class Structure of the Advance Societies*. London: Hutchinson.
Giddens, A. (1976) *New Rules of Sociological Methods*. London: Hutchinson; New York: Basic Books.

Giddens, A. (1979) *Central Problems in Social Theory*. London: Macmillan; Berkeley: University of California Press.

Giddens, A. (1981) *A Contemporary Critique of Historical Materialism*. London: Macmillan; Berkeley: University of California Press.

Giddens, A. (1984) *The Constitution of Society: Outline of the Theory of Structuration*. Cambridge: Polity Press; Berkeley: University of California Press.

Giddens, A. (1986) *The Nation-State and Violence*. Cambridge: Polity Press.

Giddens, A. (1990) *The Consequences of Modernity*. Cambridge: Polity Press; Palo Alto, CA: Stanford University Press.

Giddens, A. (1991) *Modernity and Self-Identity*. Cambridge: Polity Press; Palo Alto, CA: Stanford University Press.

Giddens, A. (1992) *The Transformation of Intimacy*. Cambridge: Polity Press; Palo Alto, CA: Stanford University Press

Giddens, A. (1994) *Beyond Left and Right*. Cambridge: Polity Press; Palo Alto, CA: Stanford University Press

Giddens, A. (1995) *Politics, Sociology and Social Theory*. Cambridge: Polity Press; Palo Alto, CA: Stanford University Press.

Giddens, A. (1998) *The Third Way*. Cambridge: Polity Press.

Giddens, A. (2001) *The Global Third Way Debate*. Cambridge: Polity Press.

Thompson, J. B. (1989) "The Theory of Structuration." In D. Herrald and J. B. Thompson (eds.) *Social Theory of Modern Society*. Cambridge: Cambridge University Press.

Turner, B. S. (1992) *Regulating Bodies*. London: Routledge.

22 | Erving Goffman

Yves Winkin

Ideas
Social order/interaction order □ Impression management □ Total institution □ Social organization of experience □ Stigma

Major books
The Presentation of Self in Everyday Life (1959)
Asylums: Essays on the Social Situation of Mental Patients and Other Inmates (1961)
Stigma: Notes on the Management of Spoiled Identity (1963)
Interaction Ritual: Essays on Face to Face Behavior (1967)
Relations in Public: Micro-Studies of the Public Order (1971)
Frame Analysis: An Essay on the Organization of Experience (1974)
Gender Advertisements (1979)
Forms of Talk (1981)

Influences
Durkheim □ Freud □ Mead □ Radcliffe-Brown □ Simmel

Biographical Details

Erving Goffman (1922–82) was born in Dauphin, Manitoba. He was the son of a department store owner who came to Canada in 1917 to escape the pogroms in the Ukraine. Erving Goffman attended St John's Technical High School in Winnipeg before studying chemistry for three years at the University of Manitoba. He then spent some time at the National Film Board in Ottawa where he assimilated the visual culture of the documentary filmmakers working under John Grierson's spell. He finally obtained his first training as a social scientist at the University of Toronto, reading Durkheim's *Suicide* (in French) under C. W.

M. Hart and learning the social significance of body movements from Birdwhistell.

Goffman got his Ph.D. in Sociology from the University of Chicago in 1953, after four strained years of courses (1945–9), two uneasy years of fieldwork in Baltasound, in the Shetland island of Unst, and one delightful year of thesis writing in Paris with his wife-to-be, Angelica Choate, who happened to be a very rich heiress from the Boston aristocracy.

In 1955 Goffman was doing fieldwork again, this time in the huge mental hospital of St Elizabeth's, right above Washington, DC. For about a year he shared the patients' everyday life, from meals to tennis sessions, although he did not spend every night in the wards. The data he collected reverberated with his personal life: his wife was starting to show signs of mental disorders that were to lead to her suicide in 1964.

From 1957 to 1967 Goffman taught at the University of California, Berkeley. This was a period of intense publishing: *The Presentation of Self in Everyday Life* in 1959, *Encounters* and *Asylums* in 1961, *Behavior in Public Places* and *Stigma* in 1963, *Interaction Ritual* in 1967. *Frame Analysis* was initiated and much fieldwork was done, this time in the casinos of Reno and Las Vegas.

Goffman ultimately resettled at the University of Pennsylvania, Philadelphia, where he was allowed to teach only when he felt like it. He kept publishing at high speed: *Strategic Interaction* in 1969, *Relations in Public* in 1971, *Frame Analysis* in 1974, *Gender Advertisements* in 1979, *Forms of Talk* in 1981. The book on casinos may have been partially written, but it never came out. Goffman died of cancer in November 1982.

Key Theoretical Contributions

Goffman contributed several hundred notions which disappeared as quickly as they popped up. But a few major ideas kept coming back from one book to the next. Let's single them out.

Goffman's first major contribution is certainly his introduction of the interaction in the realm of sociology. The study of interaction was traditionally the business of social psychologists, who considered it as the moment when two persons bang into each other (emotionally more than physically, that is). Goffman saw interaction as a ritual, which had meaning well beyond the persons involved. From the days of his doctoral dissertation to his final paper (Goffman 1983), Goffman stressed that the "interaction order," as he called it, is a kind of social order. To disrupt an interaction is to disrupt society. Freely borrowing from Durkheim's *The Elementary Forms of the Religious Life* (1954 [1912]),

Goffman (1967) argued that, rather like religious ceremonies, interactions give us a sense of our social belonging and a sense of our sacredness as persons. To show one's "involvement" in interaction (smiling, nodding, looking at the other in the eyes) is an act of societal worshiping and binding. Goffman's capacity to conceive of interaction as a miniature society is certainly a major coup in the history of sociology.

Goffman is probably best known for his notion of "total institution," which he defined in *Asylums* as "a place of residence and work where a large number of like-situated individuals, cut off from the wider society for an appreciable period of time, together lead an enclosed, formally administered round of life" (Goffman 1961b: xiii). This definition applies not only to mental hospitals but to a whole class of "social establishments," ranging from geriatric homes to jails, from boarding schools to monasteries. The power of Goffman's notion lies in this capacity to point out properties shared by institutions that first seem far apart (for example, orphanages and concentration camps). Students of complex organizations throughout the world have used *Asylums* to see beyond appearances: what are the forces at work behind the apparently benign routines of residential living?

This leads us to a third major contribution, which is as much political as theoretical. Goffman was often described as ethically aloof, if not cynically disengaged. It can be argued that, to the contrary, he was morally outraged, and that he devoted four major pieces of work to the defense of losers in society.

His doctoral dissertation (1953) is indeed a study of "communication conduct in an island community," but it can also be seen as a demonstration of the capacity of the "inlanders" of the Shetland Islands to live a full life, socially and culturally, away from the "mainlanders" (from Scotland and England), who tended to consider them as a bunch of marginal people. This is at least Goffman's own argument, in a letter to his main informant, who inquired about the results of the study he helped document (quoted in Winkin 2000).

Asylums is an explicit indictment of the large mental hospitals that developed after World War II throughout the United States. Through the notion of total institution, mental hospitals are not only set in juxtaposition to concentration camps – they *are* a kind of concentration camp. Goffman's prose is never boisterous; he just keeps offering data and suggesting lines of analysis. But his apparent detachment makes his indignation even louder. This is a masterful demonstration of the political power of theorizing.

The same contained rage is at work in *Stigma* (1963b), which is not based on fieldwork but on a close reading of many autobiographical pieces written by so-called handicapped people. Goffman's argument goes beyond the usual statement that "beauty [the handicap] is in the eye of the beholder." He wants to demonstrate that the stigmatized individual bears the social weight of his role through his "good adjustment." As Goffman puts it: "It requires that the stigmatized individual cheerfully and unselfconsciously accept himself as essentially the same as normals, while at the same time he voluntarily withholds himself from those situations in which normals would find it difficult to give lip service to their similar acceptance of him" (ibid: 126). No moaning – just a terribly lucid vision of reality.

The same attitude can be found in *Gender Advertisements* (1979), his picture-based study of the ways female bodies are displayed in advertising. He did not address the usual issue of pornographic exploitation, but the rather subtle "arrangement between the sexes" (Goffman 1977) that lead men to be shown in parental, protective attitudes *vis-à-vis* women, who are shown acting as excited or ecstatic children. Goffman points out how often women are pictured smiling absently, lying on the floor, or caressing their hair. Beyond the behavioral details lies a vision of society based on the necessary subordination of women: social order lies on their "good adjustment." But while mentally and sometimes physically handicapped people are set aside, women are structurally stuck, like fat people and other slightly "faulty" (Goffman's term) persons who can still perform in public. The violence of Goffman's analysis is sometimes hard to bear.

These four studies of domination show that Goffman was far from a "symbolic interactionist": for him, society cannot be reduced to myriads of interactions. He is in fact much closer to Bourdieu, whose notion of "symbolic violence" complements nicely Goffman's own theoretical apparatus.

From a methodological point of view, Goffman's contribution is quite original. He combined his classical Chicago fieldwork training with a rare literary gift. Lloyd Warner and Everett Hughes wanted their students to immerse themselves like anthropologists in a chosen milieu. Goffman spent years of his life in small communities, be they villages, hospitals, or casinos. He relied massively on participant observation (rather than interviews). Goffman, however, went beyond writing plain ethnographic reports like many of his colleagues: he dared to use literary strategies to convey his vision of the social world. His reliance on "style" was grating to many colleagues, but his work quickly reached audiences beyond academia. By 1980 *Presentation of Self* had already sold over half a million copies in English (Ditton 1980: 1).

Major Criticisms

Erving Goffman is presently considered by commentators as "the most influential American sociologist of the twentieth century" (Fine, Manning, and Smith 2000: ix). Papers and books of exegesis keep piling up, twenty years after his death. This is a rather surprising fate for a sociologist whose books were considered by many as too essayistic, too cynical, or too keen to please the new middle class.

The traditional criticism leveled against his work was that it amalgamated data from different sources (fieldwork observations, literature, newspapers, etc.) for the sake of beefing up new ideas. Goffman was seen as a brilliant writer, but as a poor social scientist, since he offered no well-bound, empirical monographs, gave few methodological clues for his work to be double-checked by others, and seemed to care less about his theoretical lineage. He was thus slotted into the "lunatic fringe of sociology" (Rose 1966).

A more philosophically oriented criticism addressed the issue of Goffman's vision of the individual in society, a vision in which people seem to be constantly manipulative and deceitful as they engage in operations of impression management. In books such as *Strategic Interaction* (1969) Goffman even used the vocabulary of spymasters and Cold War diplomats to analyze face-to-face interactions. Moral philosophers such as Alistair MacIntyre felt very uncomfortable about a position that "dissolves the individual into his role-playing performances" (MacIntyre 1969).

Sociologists tried to sociologize Goffman's work as an example of middle-class sociology. Since Goffman focused on interactions without apparently giving much explanatory weight to social classes or social structures, like "macro-sociologists" all do, he was seen as an agent of the new bourgeoisie which wants to believe that one can be liberated from social determinisms through sheer individual efforts and maneuvers. Goffman's readership outside academia was explained by his "liberal" ideology (Boltanski 1973; Gouldner 1970).

Goffman never responded to his critics, except once, when two colleagues published a devastating review of *Frame Analysis* (1974), the 586-page book dearest to him because it cost him ten years of strenuous effort. According to Denzin and Keller (1981) the book was simply misguided structuralism: old fashioned, to put it crassly. Goffman's outraged reply (1981b) was basically this: "you just don't know what you're talking about" – like many commentators who did not consider the overall economy of Goffman's *oeuvre*.

Bibliography

Boltanski, L. (1973) "Erving Goffman et le temps du soupçon." *Information sur les sciences sociales*, 12, 3: 127–47.

146   YVES WINKIN

Burns, T. (1992) *Erving Goffman*. London: Routledge.
Ditton, J. (ed.) (1980) *The View from Goffman*. London: Macmillan.
Denzin, N. K. and Keller, C. M. (1981) *"Frame Analysis* Reconsidered." *Contemporary Sociology*, 10, 1: 52–60.
Drew, P. and Wootton, A. (eds.) (1988) *Erving Goffman: Exploring the Interaction Order*. Cambridge: Polity Press.
Durkheim, E. (1954) *The Elementary Forms of the Religious Life*. New York: Free Press. (First published in French 1912).
Fine, G. A., Manning, P., and Smith, G. W. (eds.) (2000) *Erving Goffman*. London: Sage.
Goffman, E. (1953) *Communication Conduct in an Island Community*. Chicago: University of Chicago Ph.D. dissertation.
Goffman, E. (1959) *The Presentation of Self in Everyday Life*. New York: Doubleday Anchor.
Goffman, E. (1961a) *Encounters: Two Studies in the Sociology of Interaction*. Indianapolis, IN: Bobbs-Merrill.
Goffman, E. (1961b) *Asylums: Essays on the Social Situation of Mental Patients and Other Inmates*. New York: Doubleday Anchor.
Goffman, E. (1963a) *Behavior in Public Places: Notes on the Social Organization of Gatherings*. Glencoe, IL: Free Press.
Goffman, E. (1963b) *Stigma: Notes on the Management of Spoiled Identity*. Englewood Cliffs, NJ: Prentice-Hall.
Goffman, E. (1967) *Interaction Ritual: Essays on Face to Face Behavior*. New York: Doubleday Anchor.
Goffman, E. (1969) *Strategic Interaction*. Philadelphia: University of Pennsylvania Press.
Goffman, E. (1971) *Relations in Public: Micro-Studies of the Public Order*. New York: Basic Books.
Goffman, E. (1974) *Frame Analysis: An Essay on the Organization of Experience*. New York: Harper and Row.
Goffman, E. (1977) "The Arrangement Between the Sexes." *Theory and Society*, 4, 3: 301–31.
Goffman, E. (1979) *Gender Advertisements*. New York: Harper and Row.
Goffman, E. (1981a) *Forms of Talk*. Philadelphia: University of Pennsylvania Press.
Goffman, E. (1981b) "A Reply to Denzin and Keller." *Contemporary Sociology*, 10, 1: 60–8.
Goffman, E. (1983) "The Interaction Order." *American Sociological Review*, 48, 1: 1–17.
Gouldner, A. W. (1970) *The Coming Crisis of Western Sociology*. London: Heinemann.
Lemert, C. and Branaman A. (eds.) (1997) *The Goffman Reader*. Oxford: Blackwell.
MacIntyre, A. (1969) "The Self as Work of Art." *New Statesman*, March 28: 447–8.
Manning, P. (1992) *Erving Goffman and Modern Sociology*. Cambridge: Polity Press.

Riggins, S. (ed.) (1990) *Beyond Goffman: Studies on Communication, Institution, and Social Interaction*. Berlin: Mouton de Gruyter.

Rose, J. D. (1966) *Erving Goffman's The Presentation of Self in Everyday Life: A Critical Commentary*. New York: American RDM Corporation (A Study Master Publication).

Smith, G. W. (ed.) (1999) *Goffman and Social Organization: Studies in a Sociological Legacy*. London: Routledge.

Winkin, Y. (2000) "Baltasound as the Symbolic Capital of Social Interaction." In G. A. Fine, P. Manning, and G. W. Smith (eds.) *Erving Goffman*. London: Sage.

23 | Jürgen Habermas

William Outhwaite

Ideas
Communicative action □ Discourse ethics □ Public sphere □
Postmetaphysical thinking

Major books
The Structural Transformation of the Public Sphere (1962)
Theory and Practice (1963)
Knowledge and Human Interests (1968)
Legitimation Crisis (1973)
Theory of Communicative Action (1981)
Moral Consciousness and Communicative Action (1983)
The Philosophical Discourse of Modernity (1985)
Postmetaphysical Thinking (1988)
Justification and Application (1991)
Between Facts and Norms (1992)
The Inclusion of the Other (1996)

Influences
Adorno □ Apel □ Hegel □ Horkheimer □ Kant □ Marx

Biographical Details

Jürgen Habermas (b. 1929), who retired in 1994 from his post as Professor of Philosophy and Sociology at the University of Frankfurt, is the leading representative of the second generation of the neo-Marxist Critical Theorists often known as the Frankfurt School. Habermas, who studied under Theodor Adorno and Max Horkheimer after their return to Frankfurt from exile in the USA, has pursued the kind of interdisciplinary critical social theory practiced before World War II in Horkheimer's

Institute of Social Research. From the time of *The Structural Transformation of the Public Sphere* (1962) he has argued against technocratic social science and policy and for a communicative or dialogical approach to moral and political issues. His critiques of positivism in the 1960s cleared the way for his communicative and developmental model put forward in *Theory of Communicative Action* (1981) and subsequently applied to moral questions in *Moral Consciousness and Communicative Action* (1983) and law and politics in *Between Facts and Norms* (1992). He has also analyzed contemporary societies in *Legitimation Crisis* (1973) and many volumes of theoretical and political writings. He has intervened in a number of major public debates in Germany, notably in the protest movements of 1968, in which he played a prominent role, the "Historians' Dispute" of the mid-1980s over Germany's relation to its Nazi past, and the ongoing debates since 1989 about the place of a reunited Germany in a united Europe.

Key Theoretical Contributions

Habermas's mature theory, as he has developed it from the early 1970s, can best be understood as what he would call a "reconstruction" of what is presupposed and implied by human communication, cooperation, and debate. In terms of the orthodox academic disciplines which his work respects but also transcends, there is a theory of communication (linguistics), a theory of communicative action (sociology), and a theory (both descriptive and normative) of morality, politics (including political communication), and law. At the back of all this are substantial elements of a philosophy of science (including, though not confined to, a critique of positivistic social science) and an account of the development of human societies – and in particular of Western modernity – which culminates in a diagnosis of what he sees as the central political problems confronting the advanced capitalist democracies and the modern world as a whole.

Habermas's basic idea is that any serious use of language to make statements about the world, as opposed, for example, to exclamations or the issuing of orders, presupposes the claims that what we say makes sense and is true, that we are sincere in saying it, and that we have the right to say it. These presuppositions can be questioned by our hearers or readers. Only a rational agreement which excluded no one and no relevant evidence or argument would provide, in the last resort, a justification of the claims we routinely make and presuppose in our assertions.

This idea gives us, Habermas claims, a theory of truth, anticipated by the American pragmatist philosopher C. S. Peirce, as what we would ultimately come to rationally agree about. Moreover, if Habermas is right that moral judgments also have cognitive content and are not mere expressions of taste or disguised prescriptions, it also provides a theory of truth for issues of morality and of legitimate political authority. Moral norms are justified if they are what we would still uphold at the end of an ideal process of argumentation.

The critical analysis of language use (universal pragmatics) can thus, Habermas believes, be expanded into a broader theory of communicative action, defined as action oriented by and toward mutual agreement. In social theoretical terms, this can be contrasted with the models of instrumental or strategic, self-interested action (the model of economic "man" which also largely dominates rational choice theory), normatively regulated action (the model, familiar from functionalism, in which we orient our action to a shared value system), or dramaturgical action, described by Goffman, Garfinkel, and others, in which our actions are analyzed as a performance, designed to optimize our public image or self-image. All these types of action, Habermas claims, can be shown to be parasitic upon communicative action, which incorporates and goes beyond each of them (Habermas 1981, vol.1: 82–101). In the modern world, he argues, people cannot just appeal to authority or tradition but must act communicatively. The theory of communicative action, then, underpins a communication theory of morality, law, and democracy, and it is these aspects which have dominated Habermas's most recent work.

Theory of Communicative Action (1981) traces the conflict between, on the one hand, the rationalization of worldviews in early modernity, expressed for example in secularization and formal law and in the erosion of appeals to traditional authority, and, on the other hand, the restriction of this newly attained sphere, open in principle to rational debate, as market and bureaucratic structures come to dominate the modern world. This is where Habermas comes closest to the dominant motifs in critical theory between the world wars, though he diverges from these more radical perspectives in his acceptance of a role for market economies and for the democratically institutionalized and legitimated rule of law (which he is now concerned to theorize in contexts which go beyond the nation-state towards a "world civil society").

Major Criticisms

Habermas's work has been influential in a whole range of fields, and has become one of the principal reference points for much discussion both in social theory and, for example, moral philosophy, legal theory, and theories of international relations. Historians and theorists of culture have also increasingly been influenced by his conception of the public sphere and other elements of his thought (see Calhoun 1992). Habermas is of course too Marxist, speculative, utopian, or "theoretical" for more orthodox social scientists, and not Marxist enough for more orthodox Marxists, such as those in France and the English-speaking countries who have often favored more structuralist variants of Marxism. A related line of criticism, represented by Gillian Rose and Jay Bernstein, is that he has remained too much in debt to Kant, to his friend Karl-Otto Apel's powerful version of neo-Kantianism and, more recently, to John Rawls's liberal theory of justice.

More particularly, Habermas is weak in the areas of economics and culture, which earlier critical theory had attempted to bring together – no doubt somewhat too fast and easily, as Axel Honneth (1985) has argued. Habermas's attempt to fill out the critical dimension of social and political theory restores the center that was missing from much of the work of the first generation of critical theorists, but in a way which leaves the analysis of global political economy and contemporary cultural processes, and the crucial interrelations between them, to others. To say that Habermas has not done this, however, is not to say that it cannot be done within a recognizably Habermasian framework, and a good deal of recent work in international relations theory has taken this direction. His own work and that of others using a Habermasian approach has also been particularly illuminating in relation to recent discussion of the post-1989 world; thinkers concerned with, for example, the political consequences of globalization for our conceptions of ethics, democracy, citizenship, and (post-)national identity have drawn significantly on Habermas's insights.

Bibliography

Apel, K.-O. (1980) [1972] *Towards a Transformation of Philosophy*, abridged edn. London: Routledge and Kegan Paul.
Bernstein, J. M. (1995) *Recovering Ethical Life: Jürgen Habermas and the Future of Critical Theory*. London: Routledge.
Calhoun, C. (ed.) (1992) *Habermas and the Public Sphere*. Cambridge, MA: MIT Press.
Dews, P. (ed.) (1992) *Habermas. Autonomy and Solidarity*, 2nd edn. London: Verso.
—— (ed.) 1999 *Habermas: A Critical Reader*. Oxford: Blackwell.
Habermas, J. (1962) *Strukturwandel der Öffentlichkeit*. Neuwied/Berlin: Luchterhand. 2nd edn. Frankfurt: Suhrkamp, 1989. Trans. T. Burger, *The Structural Transformation of the Public Sphere*. Cambridge: Polity Press, 1989.
Habermas, J. (1963) *Theorie und Praxis*. Neuwied/Berlin: Luchterhand. Trans.

J. Viertel, *Theory and Practice*. London: Heinemann, 1974.

Habermas, J. (1968a) *Technik und Wissenschaft als Ideologie*. Frankfurt: Suhrkamp. Part trans. J. Shapiro, *Toward a Rational Society*. London: Heinemann, 1971.

Habermas, J. (1968b) *Erkenntnis und Interesse*. Frankfurt: Suhrkamp. Trans. J. Shapiro, *Knowledge and Human Interests*. London: Heinemann, 1971.

Habermas, J. (1971a) *Philosophisch-Politische Profile*. Frankfurt: Suhrkamp. Part trans. F. G. Lawrence, *Philosophical–Political Profiles*. London: Heinemann, 1983.

Habermas, J. (1971b) *Zur Logik der Sozialwissenschaften*, 2nd edn. Frankfurt: Suhrkamp. Trans. S. W. Nicholsen and J. A. Stark, *On the Logic of the Social Sciences*. Cambridge, MA: MIT Press, 1988.

Habermas, J. (1973a) *Kultur und Kritik*. Frankfurt: Suhrkamp.

Habermas, J. (1973b) *Legitimationsprobleme im Spätkapitalismus*. Frankfurt: Suhrkamp. Trans. T. McCarthy, *Legitimation Crisis*. London: Heinemann, 1976.

Habermas, J. (1976) *Zur Rekonstruktion des historischen Materialismus*. Frankfurt: Suhrkamp. Part trans. F. G. Lawrence, *Communication and the Evolution of Society*. Boston: Beacon Press, 1979.

Habermas, J. (1981) *Theorie des kommunikativen Handelns*, 2 vols. Frankfurt: Suhrkamp. Trans. T. McCarthy, *Theory of Communicative Action*. London: Heinemann, 1984; Cambridge: Polity Press, 1987.

Habermas, J. (1983) *Moralbewußtsein und kommunikatives Handeln*. Frankfurt: Suhrkamp. Trans. C. Lenhardt and S. W. Nicholsen, *Moral Consciousness and Communicative Action*. Cambridge, MA: MIT Press.

Habermas, J. (1984) *Vorstudien and Ergänzungen zur Theorie des Kommunikativen Handelns*. Frankfurt: Suhrkamp.

Habermas, J. (1985a) "Modernity: An Incomplete Project." In *Postmodern Culture*, ed. H. Foster. London: Pluto Press.

Habermas, J. (1985b) *Die neue Unübersichtlichkeit*. Frankfurt: Suhrkamp. Trans. S. W. Nicholsen, *The New Conservatism*. Cambridge: Polity Press, 1989.

Habermas, J. (1985c) *Der Philosophische Diskurs der Moderne*. Frankfurt: Suhrkamp. Trans. F. G. Lawrence, *The Philosophical Discourse of Modernity*. Cambridge, MA: MIT Press, 1987.

Habermas, J. (1988a) "Law and Morality." *The Tanner Lectures on Human Values*, 8: 217–19.

Habermas, J. (1988b) *Nachmetaphysisches Denken*. Frankfurt: Suhrkamp. Trans. W. M. Hohengarten, *Postmetaphysical Thinking*. Cambridge: Polity Press, 1992.

Habermas, J. (1990) *Die nachholende Revolution*. Frankfurt: Suhrkamp.

Habermas, J.(1991a) *Erläuterungen zur Diskursethik*. Frankfurt: Suhrkamp. Trans. C. Cronin, *Justification and Application*. Cambridge, MA: MIT Press, 1993.

Habermas, J. (1991b) *Vergangenheit als Zukunft*, ed. M. Heller. Zürich: Pendo; 2nd edn. Munich: Piper, 1993. Trans. M. Pensky, *The Past as Future*. Lincoln: University of Nebraska Press, 1994.

Habermas, J. (1992a) *Faktizität und Geltung*. Frankfurt: Suhrkamp. Trans. W.

Rehg, *Between Facts and Norms*. Cambridge: Polity Press, 1996.

Habermas, J. (1992b) *Texte und Kontexte*. Frankfurt: Suhrkamp.

Habermas, J. (1996) *Die Einbeziehung des Anderen*. Frankfurt: Suhrkamp. Trans. and ed. Ciaran Cronin and Pablo De Greiff as *The Inclusion of the Other*. Cambridge, MA: MIT Press, 1998.

Habermas, J. (1998a) *Die Postnationale Konstellation. Politische Essays*. Frankfurt: Suhrkamp. Trans. and ed. Max Pensky, *The Postnational Constellation*. Cambridge: Polity Press, 2001.

Habermas, J. (1998b) *On the Pragmatics of Communication*, ed. M. Cooke. Cambridge: Polity Press.

Habermas, J., von Friedeburg, L., Oehler, C., and Weltz, F. (1961) *Student und Politik*. Neuwied/Berlin: Luchterhand.

Holub, R. C. (1991) *Jürgen Habermas: Critic in the Public Sphere*. London: Routledge.

Honneth, A. (1985) *Kritik der Macht*. Frankfurt, 1985. Trans. K. Baynes, *Critique of Power*. Cambridge, MA: MIT Press, 1992.

Honneth, A. and Joas, H. (eds.) (1988) *Kommunikatives Handeln*. Frankfurt: Suhrkamp. Trans. J. Gaines and D. L. Jones, *Communicative Action*. Cambridge: Polity Press, 1991.

Honneth, A. et al. (eds.) (1989) *Zwischenbetrachtungen. Im Prozess der Aufklärung*. Frankfurt: Suhrkamp. Trans. W. Rehg, *Philosophical Interventions in the Unfinished Project of the Enlightenment*. Cambridge, MA: MIT Press, 1992; trans. B. Fultner, *Cultural–Political Interventions in the Unfinished Project of the Enlightenment*. Cambridge, MA: MIT Press, 1992.

Müller-Doohm, S. (ed.) (2000). *Das Interesse der Vernunft*. Rückblicke auf das Werk von Jürgen Habermas seit 'Erkenntnis und Interesse'. Frankfurt: Suhrkamp.

Outhwaite, W. (1994) *Habermas: A Critical Introduction*. Cambridge: Polity Press.

Outhwaite, W. (ed.) (1996) *The Habermas Reader*. Cambridge: Polity Press.

Ray, L. (1993) *Rethinking Critical Theory*. London: Sage.

Rose, G. (1981) *Hegel Contra Sociology*. London: Athlone Press.

Thompson, J. B. and Held, D. (eds.) (1982) *Habermas: Critical Debates*. London: Macmillan.

White, S. K. (ed.) (1994) *The Cambridge Companion to Habermas*. Cambridge: Cambridge University Press.

24 | **Stuart Hall**

Michael Kenny

> *Ideas*
> Hegemony □ Ideology □ Culture □ Identity
>
> *Major books*
> *Resistance Through Rituals: Youth Subcultures in Post-war Britain* (ed. with T. Jefferson) (1976)
> *Policing the Crisis: Mugging, the State, and Law and Order* (with C. Critcher, T. Jefferson, J. Clarke, and B. Roberts) (1978)
> *The Politics of Thatcherism* (ed. with M. Jacques) (1983)
> *The Hard Road to Renewal: Thatcherism and the Crisis of the Left* (1988)
> *New Times* (ed. with M. Jacques) (1989)
>
> *Influences*
> Foucault □ Gramsci □ Marx □ Althusser

Biographical Details

Stuart Hall (b. 1932) has been one of Britain's most prominent and charismatic "public intellectuals" since the 1950s. He arrived from Jamaica in 1951, becoming a Rhodes Scholar at Oxford University (Chen 1996). Soon after, he emerged as a central figure in the fledgling New Left movement that developed in England and Scotland from 1956 to 1961, and was installed as the first editor of the journal that arose from this current, *New Left Review* (Hall 1989; Kenny 1995). Hall resigned this position amid the decline of this early phase of the New Left and later joined the Centre for Contemporary Cultural Studies (CCCS) at Birmingham University, where he was Director from 1968 to 1979. In 1979 he was appointed to a Professorship in Sociology at the Open University. In subsequent years his ideas were introduced to a wide audience, through his own political writings on "Thatcherism," his compelling public lectures, and his many composed and thoughtful performances on various media. As an intellectual figure Hall resembles the model of intellectual practice laid out by the Marxist theoretician Antonio Gramsci: an "organic" intellectual always ready to cross the divide between politics and the academy. Hall has, for instance, forged a number of important relationships with, and been a promoter of, black artists and cultural initiatives. Equally, he has combined his intellectual labors with involvement in a succession of political–intellectual projects, including his writings for the influential magazine *Marxism Today* in the 1980s (Gilroy, Grossberg, and McRobbie 2000).

Key Theoretical Contributions

Hall has contributed enormously to the reformulation of the moral and political thinking of the political left in Britain, and elsewhere, over the last twenty years. He remains a widely respected and much cited intellectual figure. Widely regarded as one of the founding "fathers" of cultural studies, his writings have also exerted enormous influence within the fields of sociology and social theory. He has achieved a readership beyond the academy as well, and is perhaps best known in public life as the inventor of the label "Thatcherism" in the early days of the first Thatcher government (1979–83).

Hall's political and intellectual thinking developed in discrete phases of his intellectual career: in a series of collective projects at the CCCS in the 1970s (Hall and Jefferson 1976; Hall et al. 1978); in a number of widely read essays in *Marxism Today* throughout the 1980s (Hall 1988a); and, latterly, in a number of contributions to emergent intellectual debates about cultural analysis, social change, and ethnic identity (Hall in Morley and Chen 1996: 411–75). Yet the sensibilities he displayed during these phases of his writing career were prefigured by some of his lesser-known essays from the late 1950s and early 1960s, particularly those written for the journals of the fledgling New Left movement. These pieces (Hall 1958, 1959, 1960; Kenny 1995: 54–68) intermingle reflections on the limitations of the base–superstructure model which dominated Marxist interpretation of the social and cultural worlds, with thoughtful sociological essays on the cultural changes sweeping across Britain in the 1950s, in particular the emergence of a generation of young people alienated from conventional cultural life.

Following the demise of this "early" New Left movement, Hall produced a series of essays in which he reviewed the legacy of Marxism in the fields of cultural and ideological analysis. In "The Problem of Ideology: Marxism Without Guarantees" (Hall 1983) he unpicked the presumption that there exists a natural or necessary correspondence between social classes and ideological perspectives. He particularly stressed that the collective consciousness, and indeed the identity, of the subaltern classes had to be "constructed" through active political and ideological work; neither would emerge in a pure revolutionary form at the behest of the socioeconomic situation. There emerged from his engagement with the Marxist tradition a non-essentialist understanding of political and social agency in which social identities were viewed as the sites of multiple and often contradictory struggles (Grossberg 1996: 157).

During his time at the CCCS Hall was involved in collective projects undertaken with colleagues and students (Hall 1980a). Underpinning these endeavors was a collective engagement with the writings of a number of Marxist theorists in the West European tradition, notably Louis Althusser and Antonio Gramsci. Hall himself was deeply influenced by his readings from Gramsci's *oeuvre*. Many of the political ideas and theoretical categories in the latter's fragmentary writings recur in Hall's own thinking after this period (Hall 1988a: 161–74). Within the CCCS he and various colleagues began to suggest that the political instability of the late 1960s and early 1970s amounted to a crisis of "hegemony" (a key Gramscian term) in which the balance of the relations of class forces had been upset and the state was increasingly drawn towards the coercive, rather than consensual, end of its repertoire. The authors detected a new authoritarian consensus as the polity began to drift towards a "law and order society" in response to relative economic decline and novel forms of social conflict. The text that arose from these deliberations, *Policing the Crisis* (Hall et al. 1978), is a theoretically eclectic and politically charged examination of the interwoven discourses about crime, youth delinquency, and race within British public life in this period.

Hall was perhaps the first commentator to grasp the significance of the gathering of a new alliance of forces on the right of the political spectrum in the mid-1970s and pinpointed the bid for intellectual and moral "hegemony" that this fermentation involved. In a powerful analysis of "the great moving right show" (Hall and Jacques 1983: 19–39) which characterized British politics at this juncture, he observed how this "New" Right was gaining ideological momentum and legitimacy as the worldwide recession exacerbated the weaknesses of Britain's economic and social life. These ideas underpinned his pioneering and highly prescient interpretation of the watershed moment in British political life represented by the election to office of the Conservative Party, under Mrs Thatcher, in 1979.

It was his analysis of "Thatcherism" that brought Hall's thinking to a wide audience, and which established him as a controversial and important presence on Britain's intellectual scene (Hall 1988a). From the start, he regarded the politics of the revamped Conservative Party as an attempt to construct a new "hegemony" within British political life, and hence to legitimate new kinds of solutions to the problems attendant upon relative economic decline and social fragmentation. Hall stressed both the breadth and depth of the discursive repertoire that the bid for Thatcherite hegemony involved. Whereas other commentators typically regarded Thatcher's interventions on issues of race, national identity, and crime as rhetorical froth, Hall interpreted such emphases as deliberate efforts to bolster and rearticulate the "common sense" of the people; these were attempts to connect deeply rooted prejudice and sentiment to a Thatcherite perspective. He also emphasized the depth of this hegemonic politics, in particular the ways in which the symbolic construction of new "subjects" and identification of new enemies enabled the legitimation of policy moves and underpinned continuing electoral success. Particular groups – "welfare scroungers" and militant trade unionists for example – were demonized in the hard-boiled vernacular deployed by Thatcher and her allies, and such identities were positioned as "enemies within" the body politic, responsible for the moral and economic decline of the nation. In the face of this new moral and political vision, as well as the potent social coalition assembled behind it, the left looked bewildered and irrelevant. Hall's mission in these years was to enhance within the communities of the left a deeper understanding of the significance of the politics of Thatcherism. He also sought to reorientate the political imagination of the Labour Party to engage with the realities of Conservative hegemony (ibid: 175–268).

Most disturbing of all, for Hall, was the refusal of many socialists to accept that Thatcherism had successfully appealed to and orchestrated the consciousness of sections of the working class. He described this process through the notion of an "authoritarian populism" (ibid: 123–49). This involved the legitimation of a stronger, more coercive state apparatus while Thatcherites simultaneously presented themselves as in sympathy with the interests of the "people" against the power of entrenched political and social elites. Such an ideological strategy was nowhere better revealed than during the crisis occasioned by the occupation of the Malvinas/Falkland Islands and the British government's bellicose response in 1983 (ibid: 68–74). The populist character of Thatcherism was evident in other domains as well. Hall proved adept at illuminating the processes whereby substantive economic doctrines were inscribed within popular "common sense" through the adoption of the language of everyday experience and various moralistic imperatives. At the heart of this populism was a potent combination of aspects of the tradition of Burkean Toryism, with an aggressively revived neoliberalism.

Though the world of politics has continually informed his intellectual reflections, in his other writings of this period Hall was more concerned with the analysis of cultural phenomena. Several of these essays have become established within the central canon of the fledgling discipline of cultural studies. As with his political theorizing, Hall developed ways of "reading" the cultural against the backdrop of Marxist thought, but he leavened this heritage with his fertile and critical appropriation of the ideas of Michel Foucault (Morley and Chen 1996: 25–130). Cultural practices, he suggested, should be understood not as "objects whose meaning and identity can be guaranteed by their origin or their intrinsic essences," but as "signifying practices" (Hall 1997; Grossberg 1996: 157). The analysis of culture should involve the interpretation of the cultural–ideological field within which the struggle over meanings occurs. Such struggles always take place within a field of relations established through prior struggles for domination and which always show evidence of re-sistance. In understanding how cultural practices come to possess cer-tain meanings, and not others, the concept of ideology was invaluable. It is through ideology that particular sets of meanings are yoked together to construct a systematic chain of meanings. By seeking to present its prior assumptions as "natural," ideology works to render its own exist-ence barely visible (Hall 1982; Larrain in Morley and Chen 1996: 47–70). The task of the analyst of cultural texts and products, therefore, is to illustrate the discursive operations whereby ideological values are pro-duced in texts, but also to attend to the multiple ways in which these are "received" by human agents. His description of this process, rendered as the double movement of "encoding" and "decoding" in an influential essay on the interpretation of television, has achieved a central place within the field of cultural studies (Hall 1980a: 128–38). It follows from his analysis that the ideological content of, for instance, a television pro-gram can never be guaranteed in an absolute way, since it depends both upon the cultural–ideological field in which a program is made and upon that which positions the subject who receives it. This interpretive stance represented a significant departure from approaches to contemporary culture associated both with other leading theorists of the mass media and also advocates of the thesis that a coherent dominant ideology is a necessary condition for the domination of the capitalist economy.

Major Criticisms

Perhaps the most controversial of Hall's ideas are those that have a di-rectly political bearing. This is not surprising, since Hall set out to shock and persuade left intellectuals and activists into rethinking some of their most basic presumptions and cherished shibboleths (Hall 1988b). Not surprisingly, his ideas were received with skepticism and hostility in many quarters and he has been accused of various "sins" by his critics, particularly the capitulation to intellectual fashion and the justification of the wholesale abandonment of socialist principle. Neither of these claims stands up to scrutiny, but some important ambiguities about his political ideas remain, and are worth closer consideration:

- The suggestion that in his deployment of "hegemony" Hall was guilty of overlooking Gramsci's commitment to the decisive nucleus of economic relations, making his analyses insufficiently sensitive to the role of social and economic determinants in contemporary politics.
- The argument that his interpretation of Thatcherism falsely imputed to this phenomenon a coherence that it never possessed. In particular, political historians and analysts question the impression bequeathed by Hall's work that the ideological discourses of Thatcherism were equally significant across the operations of the government. On the contrary, some claim that Thatcherite policy really amounted to a mish-mash of continuity, confusion, and incremental change.
- The accusation that Hall and some of his collaborators were insufficiently clear on the vital question of whether the "new times" altering the landscape of modern Britain were either independent from or the consequence of Thatcherism. An associated criticism is that in his account of "new times" Hall offered an economically reductionist account of change by presuming that a new "mode of production" (post-Fordism) necessitated *certain kinds* of political and ideological adaptation (Hall and Jacques 1989).

Hall has replied to all of these criticisms, and is adamant that they are misrepresentations of his ideas. It certainly does not follow from his account of hegemony that substantial sections of the British public should have converted wholesale to Thatcherite beliefs – an erroneous but often repeated criticism. Nor is it true that he seeks to displace economics with ideology in his reading of political developments: his defense here is that he has sought to "bend the stick" towards ideology against the recurrent preference for economistic analysis on the political left.

Hall's usage of the notion of hegemony might be open to a rather different sort of criticism. One by-product of it is the assertion that the left is required to construct a "counter-hegemonic" politics before it can displace Thatcherite "common sense." This is a challenging and perceptive argument. Yet it is open to question whether such a concept permits a sufficiently "political" engagement with politics. In the domain of politics, ideas experience a thousand mediations and filters – through personalities, factionalism, institutional cultures, and many other factors. Following Hall's deep disillusionment with the "New Labour" government elected in 1997, and his criticisms of its failure to launch such a "counter-hegemony," one is left wondering whether this perspective really is sufficiently engaged with the contradictory realities of contemporary political life (a discipline that Hall himself continually urged on the left during the 1980s). For all its failures of courage and imagination, it is clear that the New Labour administration has not simply perpetuated the hegemonic politics of Thatcherism. Whatever this government amounts to in ideological terms, it is not obvious that the rather "heroic" conception of politics implied by Hall's usage of the terms "hegemony" and "counter-hegemony" is always appropriate. Such points aside, Hall's writings exhibit a welter of intelligent and imaginative observation of the changing political scene. They may well come to be regarded as particularly significant for the justification that he provides for the retention of the concept of ideology in what many regard as "post-ideological" times.

Bibliography

Chen, H.-K. (1996) "The Formation of a Diasporic Intellectual: An Interview with Stuart Hall." In D. Morley and H.-K.Chen (eds.) *Stuart Hall: Critical Dialogues in Cultural Studies*. London: Routledge.

Davies, I. (1995) *Cultural Studies and Beyond: Fragments of Empire*. London: Routledge.

Gilroy, P., Grossberg, L., and McRobbie, A. (eds.) (2000) *Without Guarantees: In Honour of Stuart Hall*. London: Verso.

Grossberg, L. (1996) "History, Politics and Postmodernism: Stuart Hall and Cultural Studies." In D. Morley and H.-K.Chen (eds.) *Stuart Hall: Critical Dialogues in Cultural Studies*. London: Routledge.

Hall, S. (1958) "A Sense of Classlessness." *Universities and Left Review*, 5: 26–32.

Hall, S. (1959) "Absolute Beginnings." *Universities and Left Review*, 7: 16–25.

Hall, S. (1960) "The Supply of Demand." In E. P. Thompson (ed.) *Out of Apathy*. London: Stevens.

Hall, S. (1980a) "Encoding/Decoding." In S. Hall, D. Hobson, A. Lowe, and P. Willis (eds.) *Culture, Media, Language: Working Papers in Cultural Studies*. London: Hutchinson.

Hall, S. (1980b) "Cultural Studies and the Centre." In S. Hall, D. Hobson, A. Lowe, and P. Willis (eds.) *Culture, Media, Language: Working Papers in Cultural Studies*. London: Hutchinson.

Hall, S. (1982) "The Rediscovery of 'Ideology': The Return of the Repressed in

Media Studies." In M. Gurevitch et al. (eds.) *Culture, Society and the Media*. New York: Methuen.

Hall, S. (1983) "The Problem of Ideology: Marxism Without Guarantees." In B. Matthews (ed.) *Marx: A Hundred Years On*. London: Lawrence and Wishart.

Hall, S. (1988a) *The Hard Road to Renewal: Thatcherism and the Crisis of the Left*. London: Verso.

Hall, S. (1988b) "The Toad in the Garden: Thatcherism Amongst the Theorists." In C. Nelson and L. Grossberg (eds.) *Marxism and the Interpretation of Culture*. Urbana: University of Illinois Press.

Hall, S. (1989) "The 'First' New Left: Life and Times." In Oxford University Socialist Group (ed.) *Out of Apathy: Voices of the New Left Thirty Years On*. London: Verso.

Hall, S. (ed.) (1997) *Representation: Cultural Representations and Signifying Practices*. London: Sage; Milton Keynes: Open University Press.

Hall, S. and Jacques, M. (eds.) (1983) *The Politics of Thatcherism*. London: Lawrence and Wishart.

Hall, S. and Jacques, M. (eds.) (1989) *New Times*. London: Lawrence and Wishart.

Hall, S. and Jefferson, T. (eds.) (1976) *Resistance Through Rituals: Youth Subcultures in Post-war Britain*. London: Hutchinson.

Hall, S., Critcher, C., Jefferson, T., Clarke, J., and Roberts, B. (eds.) (1978) *Policing the Crisis: Mugging, the State, and Law and Order*. London: Macmillan.

Kenny, M. (1995) *The First New Left: British Intellectuals after Stalin*. London: Lawrence and Wishart.

Morley, D. and Chen, K.-H. (eds.) (1996) *Stuart Hall: Critical Dialogues in Cultural Studies*. London: Routledge.

25 | **Max Horkheimer**

Larry Ray

Ideas
Critical theory □ Ideology critique □ Eclipse of reason □ Science and technology as oppressive □ Dialectic of enlightenment

Major books
Dämmerung (under the alias Heinrich Regius) (1934)
Dialectic of Enlightenment (with Theodor Adorno) (1944)
Eclipse of Reason (1947)
Critical Theory (1972)
Critique of Instrumental Reason (1974)

Influences
Dilthey □ Hegelian Marxism □ Judaism □ Kant □ Psychoanalysis □ Schopenhauer □ Weber

---

Biographical Details

Max Horkheimer (1895–1973) was from 1930 the second and most influential Director of the Institute of Social Research in Frankfurt. Together with Theodor Adorno, Herbert Marcuse, Walter Benjamin, Leo Löwenthal, Otto Kirchheimer, Frederick Pollock, and Franz Neumann he developed "Critical theory," which was to become one of the most influential social theories of the twentieth century.

Horkheimer was born into an Orthodox Jewish family in Bavaria. Having been conscripted for a brief period in the army in 1917, Horkheimer began in 1919 to study psychology and philosophy in Munich. After the fall of the Munich Soviet Republic it was dangerous for identified militants such as Horkheimer to remain, and he moved to Frankfurt where he studied under Cornelius, the initiator of Gestalt psychology. Horkheimer studied with Husserl and in Freiburg met Heidegger. While working on his *Habilitation* (on Kant's *Critique of Judgement*) he met Pollock and Adorno, both of whom were to work with Horkheimer in the Institute. During this period he knew Georg Lukács, whose influence on their work, especially through the concept of reification, is now often underrated. Lukács, Horkheimer, and Adorno were members of the tight networks of Central European theoretical and cultural Marxists in the Weimar period.

Following Karl Grunberg's departure, Horkheimer became Director of the Frankfurt Institute, which under his directorship gradually moved from being an orthodox Marxist institute to a more heterodox center for critical social research. After the Nazi coup in 1933 the Institute and its members began a peripatetic and dispersed existence, moving to Geneva, Paris, and then New York. During this time the highly abstract Hegelian Marxism of earlier critical theory engaged increasingly with empirical social research. The need to understand Nazism, and especially the Holocaust, prompted Horkheimer and Adorno to write one of the most brilliant, though deeply pessimistic tracts of critical theory, *The Dialectic of Enlightenment* in 1944. This brought into play not simply, or primarily, a Marxist analysis of the descent of civilization into barbarism, but a critique of the domination of nature through technology, positivism, the psychodynamic bases of authoritarianism and antisemitism, and the "culture industry."

After the war, in 1949, Horkheimer, along with Adorno, accepted invitations to return to Frankfurt, where the Institute was reestablished within Frankfurt University. In 1953 Adorno became Director of the Institute for Social Research, and Horkheimer became less prominent in its activities. During the 1950s Horkheimer increasingly turned away from even a residual commitment to Marxism. His critique of "instrumental reason" was in part inspired by pessimistic readings of Weber that stressed the notion of the future within an "iron cage" of rationality (Chalcraft 1994). His critique was further influenced by a Schopenhaurian pessimism, for which the human condition would never be improved, although escape from the world and from the will for gratification was possible through aesthetic experience. The later Horkheimer also drew increasingly on theological arguments as the expression of humanity's insatiable longing for justice. He became politically conservative, opposing for example the appointment of Jürgen Habermas to the Institute on the grounds that the latter was too radical (Wiggersaus 1994: 257).

The later Horkheimer's position was complex, however. Although he rejected critical theory's belief in the immanent possibility of a "good society," his critique of instrumental reason retained a utopian moment.

In a totally administered world, a non-oppressive alternative remains possible, not because of the presence of anti-hegemonic forces, but because of the openness of Being of the human subject. Horkheimer's mature work does not abandon critique of ideology and resistance to the logic of capitalism, even though this critique loses appeal to a historical agent of transformation, such as the proletariat. This turn is informed not only by a belief that the revolutionary potential that inspired Marx was exhausted by the mid-twentieth century (Jay 1974: 61). It was based also on a critique of the arrogance of the revolutionary tradition that itself becomes oppressive (Horkheimer 1985b: 274). One way out of the iron cage of instrumental reason might be via counter-education that was influential in the philosophy of Critical Pedagogy developed by thinkers such as Paulo Freire. However, when interest in critical theory underwent resurgence in the late 1960s, it was from his earlier, more explicitly Marxist works that, much to his dismay, the young radicals drew inspiration.

Key Theoretical Contributions

The origins of the term "critical theory" are unclear, but it can be traced with confidence as far back as Horkheimer's essay "Traditional and Critical Theory" (1937), which contrasts the approaches of traditional and critical theory. Traditional theory is grounded in Cartesian duality between knowing subject and external objects and is modeled on the criteria of knowledge in the mathematical natural sciences. Traditional theory reifies the world, by failing to recognize that what might appear to be external and immutable facticity is historically produced in conditions of exploitation and struggle. If this is so, then historically produced conditions are subject to transformation through critique and action. One object of this critique, that was to become increasingly significant for critical theory, was positivist epistemology. Two aspects of this were particularly important. First, there was the division of labor within scientific activity which "takes place alongside all the other activities of a society but in no immediately clear connection with them" (Horkheimer 1976: 121). Here the real social function of science as a social location embedded in the structures of bourgeois society is not made manifest. Secondly, traditional theory reduces knowledge *per se* to the confines of that which can be reproduced in mathematical models. However, this is not just a *Geisteswissenschaften* critique of the impoverishment of positivist methods, for the exponents of the cultural sciences themselves (notably Wilhelm Dilthey) were caught within traditional theory because of their contemplative and undialectical approach to knowledge.

Critical theory, by contrast, is a form of praxis. It is an essential element in the historical effort to create a world that satisfies people's needs. It would therefore engage with the social conditions within which people lived and in which their concepts and actions were formed. To this end, it would be interdisciplinary and reach out for a "total" understanding of knowledge and history. The concept of "social totality" refers to the "history of man [sic] himself, to his *Bildung*, his cultural formation and development" (Adorno and Horkheimer 1973: 25). Horkheimer was still enough of a Marxist at this stage to argue that Marx's critique of political economy represented the paradigm for renewed critical theory. However, critical theory resisted positivistic conceptions of "scientific socialism" associated (differently) with both the Second International and Soviet Marxism. Critical cheory would develop an immanent critique of bourgeois society through which "ideology-critique" attempted to locate the "utopian content" of dominant systems of thought. The principles of justice, equality, democracy, and freedom on which bourgeois society is supposedly based anticipate a genuinely emancipated future. Further, the categories of critique do not derive simply from contemplative reflection on existing society. On the contrary, "the meaning of Marxist categories of class, exploitation, surplus value, profit, pauperization and breakdown is not to be sought in contemporary society but in its transformation into a proper (*richtigen*) society (Horkheimer 1972: 167).

This optimistic radicalism gradually faded when confronted by war, exile, and the horrors of Nazism and Stalinism. In 1940 Horkheimer could still invoke the "trailblazing" tradition of workers' councils going back to 1871, which was to imminently sweep aside the authoritarian state (Horkheimer 1973). But earlier, in *Dämmerung*, Horkheimer had suggested that there were "subtle apparatuses" (education and mass media) working to protect capitalism against revolutionary consciousness. In 1936 (in "Egoism and the Freedom Movement") Horkheimer engaged with psychoanalysis to grasp the underlying dynamics of populism and authoritarianism. He made three claims in particular. First, revolutionary populism combines defense of tradition with innovation; thus charismatic leaders assault the powers that be in the name of restoring antiquity. Secondly, the bourgeois order entails instinctual renunciation, since the egotism of the market conflicts with the desire for "happiness," associated with which is deep anger towards the perceived enjoyment of others. Thirdly, this is the basis for a sado-masochistic bond between authoritarian leaders and their followers, since the former harness repressed rage and allow its vicarious enjoyment through brutality towards enemies within, notably the Jews (Horkheimer 1982–3). These themes are further developed in *Dialectic of Enlightenment* and

Eclipse of Reason, which address directly the descent of European civilization into barbarism. In *Eclipse of Reason* Horkheimer linked positivist and instrumental reason with the rise of fascism. He distinguished between "subjective," manipulative, instrumental reason (*Verstand*) and the "objective" reason (*Vernunft*). The latter penetrates beyond appearances to address ultimate choices in morality, politics, and religion, while the former focuses only on matters of technical efficiency. But since positivistic reason rules that all discussion of ethical and political choices is metaphysical and non-rational, as mere preferences, all ethical positions are equally meaningless. Thus if irrational nationalism or fascism oust self-interest in people's minds, reason (as *Verstand*) must become their servant too; no moralist can object, for no choice can be condemned as wrong. Reason commits suicide (Horkheimer 1974b). This theme is developed in *Dialectic of Enlightenment* into a wide-ranging critique of the "self-destruction of enlightenment." Adorno's and Horkheimer's thesis was that the prime cause of the retreat from enlightenment into mythology is not to be found in Nazi mythologies but in "enlightenment" itself (Adorno and Horkheimer 1973: xvi). The domination and manipulation of nature, rather than freeing humankind from myth, turns into its reverse as it gives birth to the calculating ego, which was epitomized by the character of Odysseus. Their reinterpretation of the classical Homeric character as the prototype of the bourgeois individual is one of the most engaging passages of these rich essays. The domination of nature, and of woman, by the male rational ego is ultimately a failure and this apparently civilized form of life faces the "revolt of nature." The repressed otherness of nature and violence returns in ways that positivistic reason, which fails to understand history or ethics, is unable to resist.

Major Criticisms

Critical theory has been highly influential in many areas of social theory. But Horkheimer's thought is located within the context of mid-twentieth century Marxism and from a later perspective loses some or indeed much of its relevance. The failure of the proletariat to deliver the promised revolutionary transition is hardly any longer a central concern. Most social theory has long since acknowledged that there is no grand subject of historical change and that the process of emancipation, if it happens at all, does so through gradual incremental shifts in culture, ethics, structures, and practices. On the other hand the need to balance economistic reductionism with analysis of culture and psychology is now so widely shared that while Horkheimer's work here is of relevance, it is no longer controversial.

Horkheimer, like Adorno, was attached to the "philosophy of con-sciousness," for example the problem of the influence of popular culture on consciousness and the decline of class consciousness. Thus part of the project of critical theory was to keep alive, in the face of total admin-istration, the possibility of an alternative consciousness. The subsequent growth of linguistic and structural theoretical approaches cast doubt on the centrality of the consciousness of actors as opposed to structures of communication and discourse as key objects of theorization. The "lin-guistic turn" in critical theory represented by Jürgen Habermas has re-formulated many of these problems beyond recognition.

With Horkheimer, in many ways more than with Adorno, critical theory encountered some intractable problems. One of these was find-ing any foundation for theory critique. If critique was not to be based on mere opinion (which would lapse back into the positivist fallacy) then what ethical or social foundation might exist, in the absence too of the historical mission of the proletariat? One might invoke Objective Rea-son as the standpoint of critique, but on what basis might this be grounded? Again, early critical theory's concern with the triumph of instrumental reason assumes that modern societies are becoming pro-gressively de-differentiated, when they have actually (as Weber noted) become highly differentiated, for example into state/economy, public/private spheres, multiple cultural value spheres, and dimensions of per-sonality, society, and culture. Horkheimer, then, could not distinguish between the different logics of rationalization within these various spheres and the possibility that there might also, along with the extension of instrumental control, be processes of emancipation and freedom from traditional authorities. He was finally, as Habermas (1985) has argued, "careless of achievements of Western modernity" (such as democratic institutions) that provide opportunities for a more emancipated future.

Bibliography

Adorno, T and Horkheimer, M. (1972) *Aspects of Sociology*. London: Heinemann.
Adorno, T. and Horkheimer, M. (1973) [1944] *Dialectic of Enlightenment*. Lon-don: New Left Books
Chalcraft, D. (1994) "Bringing the Text Back In: On Ways of Reading the Iron Cage Metaphor in the Two Editions of *The Protestant Ethic*." In L. J. Ray and M. Reed (eds.) *Organizing Modernity: New Weberian Perspectives on Work, Organization and Society*. London: Routledge.
Habermas, J. (1985) *Philosophical Discourse of Modernity*. Cambridge: Polity Press.

Horkheimer, M. (1972) *Critical Theory: Selected Essays*. New York: Herder and Herder.

Horkheimer, M. (1973) "The Authoritarian State." *Telos,* 15: 3–20.

Horkheimer, M. (1974a) *Critique of Instrumental Reason*. New York: Seabury Press.

Horkheimer, M. (1974b) [1947] *Eclipse of Reason*. New York: Seabury Press.

Horkheimer, M. (1974c) *Notizen 1950 bis 1969 und Dämmerung*. Frankfurt: Verlag.

Horkheimer, M. (1976) "Traditional and Critical Theory." In P. Connerton, *Critical Sociology*. Harmondsworth: Penguin Books.

Horkheimer, M. (1982–3) "Egoism and the Freedom Movement (1936)." *Telos,* 54: 10–60.

Horkheimer, M. (1985) *Max Horkheimer, Gesammelte Schriften* 13. Frankfurt am Main: Fischer Verlag.

Jay, M. (1974) *The Dialectical Imagination*. London: Heinemann.

Tar, Z. (1977) *The Frankfurt School: The Critical Theories of Max Horkheimer and Theodor Adorno*. New York: Wiley.

Wiggersaus, R. (1994) *The Frankfurt School*. Cambridge: Polity Press.

26 | Luce Irigaray

Kwok Wei Leng

Ideas
Specula(riza)tion □ Hom(m)osexualité □ Masculine imaginary □
Symptomatic listening □ Mimicry □ Parler-femme □ Feminine
genealogies □ Sexual difference

Major books
Speculum of the Other Woman (1985)
This Sex Which is Not One (1985)
The Irigaray Reader (1991)
An Ethics of Sexual Difference (1993)
Sexes and Genealogies (1993)
Je, Tu, Nous (1993)
Thinking the Difference (1994)
I Love to You (1996)
Democracy Begins Between Two (2000)
To be Two (2000)

Influences
Derrida □ Freud □ Hegel □ Heidegger □ Lacan □ Levinas □
Nietzsche

Biographical Details

Luce Irigaray (b. 1930) is Director of Research in Philosophy at the
Centre National de la Recherche Scientifique, Paris, where she has held
a research post since 1964.[*] Born in Belgium but a French national for

---

[*] Irigaray's year of birth remains a mystery. Margaret Whitford (1991), author of the
first book-length study on Irigaray, puts it at 1932. Tina Chanter, author of a subsequent

many years, Irigaray's training was initially undertaken at Louvain and focused on Paul Valéry. After earning her first doctorate in linguistics, Irigaray earned a second doctorate in philosophy at the University of Paris VIII (Vincennes). One of her first major publications, *Speculum: De l'autre femme*, was based on her second doctoral thesis, and in her book she produced a spectacular reading of the underlying sexual premises of Western thought from Freud (back) to Plato. As Irigaray admits, "I had much trouble on account of *Speculum*. I was excluded from the university, and afterward in France I couldn't get a teaching appointment" (Irigaray 1995a: 113). No official reason was ever offered for her dismissal. It has, however, been suggested that Jacques Lacan's reorganization of the Department of Psychoanalysis at Vincennes, which excluded Irigaray, reflected his personal displeasure at the feminist critique of the father(s) of psychoanalysis contained in her book (Burke, Schor, and Whitford 1994: 40).

Lacan aside, the positive impact of Irigaray's work in France and beyond cannot be underestimated. She is the author of many books, several of which have appeared in English. As well as being a major French thinker and political activist, Irigaray's influence has spread throughout Europe, especially Italy and the Netherlands. In the Anglo-American context she is a central figure in key debates that have shaped the contours of academic feminism for over two decades, including the essentialism/anti-essentialism discussions; the figuration of French feminisms in the US feminist imaginary; the poststructuralism versus feminism arguments; the fluctuating fortunes of psychoanalysis in feminism; and the various theoretical advancements on the sex/gender system (corporeal feminisms, queer theory).

Central to these debates is Irigaray's conceptualization of sexual difference as the single most important question of our age. Many commentators consider Irigaray to be *the* theorist of sexual difference.

In addition to her formal qualifications Irigaray is trained as a psychoanalyst but no longer engages in private practice. Although she recognizes the interdisciplinary appeal of her work (literary studies, cultural studies, women's studies, social theory), Irigaray sees her writing above all as philosophical texts, with a "theoretical filiation" to the tradition of Western thought (Irigaray 1995a: 113).

---

study, puts it at 1930 (Craig 1998). In my contribution to the *Encyclopedia of Feminist Theories* I followed Whitford's lead (Code 2000). Leaving aside for the moment the question of why such biographical details matter, I am siding with Chanter this time around.

Key Theoretical Contributions

Irigaray divides her work into three periods. The first is the most criti-cal one, where she presents a critique of the "auto-mono-centrism" of the Western subject – the masculine subject of culture, history, politics, and philosophy as the "master discourse" (Irigaray 1985a: 149). This phase includes *Speculum of the Other Woman* (1985), *This Sex Which is Not One* (1985), and *An Ethics of Sexual Difference* (1993). The second phase focuses on the "mediations" that might permit a feminine subjec-tivity not bound to the eternal return of the masculine subject. Here, Irigaray attempts to bring to life a subject not yet breathing in the realm of discourse and culture; and this phase includes *Sexes and Genealogies* (1993) and *Je, Tu, Nous* (1993), as well as elements of the texts that comprise phase one. The third phase is experimental and also creative, and seeks to develop new models for relationships between sexuate be-ings; that is, without submitting any one sexual subject to the other(s). Irigaray describes this phase as "the construction of an intersubjectivity respecting sexual difference" and adds that it reflects the properly ethi-cal moment in her work (Irigaray 1995a: 96). In this phase, she includes books such as *I Love to You* (1996) and *To be Two* (2000).

Speculum of the Other Woman is best known for Irigaray's method of turning philosophy against itself to show what it says (or more precisely does not say) about sexual difference – the technique, borrowed from psychoanalysis, of symptomatic listening. The book's thesis is that throughout the history of Western thought, representation and discourse have been appropriated by a singular subject and defined by its param-eters. That subject is the masculine One, and within His purview the universe looks just like Him and the "feminine" a mere function or copy of the self-Same (a diversion, a deflection, a reduction, a subtraction, a deficit, a lack, a nothing). Thus, philosophical speculation is at once specularizing (a mirroring back of the Self, with reference to Lacan's infant sunk in imaginary misrecognitions) and specular (invoking the ghostly presence of an absence coded as "feminine") – each captured beautifully in Irigaray's concept of specula(riza)tion. Far from offering anything on sexual difference, philosophy instead speaks volumes about a universal sexual *in*difference and *hom(m)osexualité* (desire for the Same).

That Irigaray takes Freud himself as exemplary of the "mono-subjective, monosexualized, patriarchal, and phallocratic" horizon that is philosophy makes the technique of symptomatic listening and the ar-gument in *Speculum* all the more compelling (Irigaray 1995b: 12). Within the history of ideas, Freud stands at the pinnacle of a certain undoing of

Western thought. The Freudian discovery of the unconscious, together with its conception of the subject divided from itself, strikes a blow against the metaphysical system of the West (certainty, closure, truth). Yet Irigaray reveals how Freud is caught in an "old dream of symmetry." Freud defines sexual difference with reference to the masculine term, supporting his demonstration through analogy, comparison, symmetry, and opposition (as in "the differences between the sexes are completely eclipsed by agreements" or "the little girl is a little man"). And in defaulting to a standardization of sexuality presented as "truth," Freud's text offers itself up for analysis. Thus, Irigaray plays analyst to Freud by interpreting his "blind spot": by bringing to the surface what is metaphysically latent in his system, namely, the desire that secures the "closure" and "unity" of his thought.

Irigaray completes *Speculum* by traveling back through the history of Western thought, ending with Plato but stopping along the way (in a reversal of the reversal in the middle section of the book) with Aristotle, Descartes, Kant, and Hegel. Only by disrupting philosophy can culture (its grammar, its syntax, its symbolic structures) be shifted – and Irigaray regards herself preeminently as a theorist of social change. To her mind, philosophy is "the discourse on discourses," the one that lays down the law to the others (Irigaray 1985a: 149).

Having interpreted the philosopher's desire, Irigaray next attempts to move out of the all-powerful model of the One to a model in which two are truly different – her second phase. This means affirming certain characteristics (morphologies) of the feminine subject thus far deprived of self-affection and self-representation. But there are warning bells everywhere. It is not simply a matter of turning negatives into positives: of installing oneself within lack, for instance, even as one denounces it. Nor is it a matter of replacing the masculine with the feminine as standard for sexual difference, for this would only repeat the desire for the Same. Rather, one needs to mime one's assigned role deliberately without being absorbed by the exercise and without being seduced by the notion of a collective "consciousness raising" that might lead to a historical reversal of things (ibid: 161).

Mimicry, then, is a strategy adopted by Irigaray that recognizes the limits of its own effects as well as the tradition within which it is staged. There is no simple way of stepping outside of the masculine horizon, just a going back inside the "philosopher's house" by way of a radical citationality of the shards, fragments, remnants, and wastes that silently support it. So Irigaray assumes culture's symptoms not in order to produce a theory of woman, but to provoke the absurdities upon which culture rests.

If woman is the mirror by which the philosopher ensures his own image, for instance, then she is also that same mirror which keeps suspended "in an unreflected blaze of its brilliance" those elements that do not themselves reflect: its backing, its dazzlements, its resource as reflective material (ibid: 154). To reshape the mirror as concave (a speculum) rather than as flat would bring through what is ignored in the philosopher's specula(riza)tions, so caught up as he is in his desire for the Same (hence the title of Irigaray's book, *Speculum of the Other Woman*). Similarly, if woman is the "nothing" through which the philosopher gains subjective presence, then she is also quite literally no/thing, no (one singular) thing: that is, multiple, plural, more than one, precisely not One. To listen with another ear to the philosopher's claim of a "nothing" in woman is thereby to hear a different language of a self that remains unheard in Western thought (hence the title of another book, *This Sex Which is Not One*).

The question is how to devise methods to bring these excesses to the fore, such that the masculine no longer determines everything and the philosophical machinery is suspended for long enough for something of the feminine to be "seen" or "heard." Irigaray's poetic explorations of female sexuality carried through the metaphor of two lips (neither one nor two) may be considered within this overall strategy, designed "to cast phallocentrism loose from its moorings" and thus permit a glimpse of feminine subjectivity not determined by the One (Irigaray 1985a: 80). The lips are therefore not calling on biology or anatomy to define woman once and for all. They are rather attempting to find a way through the philosophical system exactly by being evocative – figuratively yet literally a *parler femme* ("speaking (as) woman").

One other approach considered during the second phase, and discussed at length in *Sexes and Genealogies* and *Je, Tu, Nous*, is the restoration of feminine genealogies, or daughter–mother relations. For Irigaray, Western culture is founded not on patricide (as Freud would have us believe), but matricide. In the Oedipus complex, the father forbids the bodily encounter with the mother, who is henceforth tolerated as a "non-active" bystander in the child's individuation. And while the son, motivated by the threat of castration, will re-find his relation to the origin by taking a woman/mother of his own, the daughter will never represent her relation to the origin, destined as she is to become a replacement for the mother in "the discourse-law-desire" of man. Man's place is thus to inhabit the world and woman's "place" is in exile, a state of *déréliction*. This is not so much a relation between the sexes as a masculine law of substitution (one woman for another). In *Sexes and Genealogies* Irigaray therefore suggests that we do not continue to kill the mother and exile the daughter, and instead invent the words and sentences (a grammar and syntax) that might speak the relationship between the mother's body and the daughter's. This way, Irigaray makes the horizontal relations between the sexes contingent upon the vertical relations between women.

Relations between the sexes is, of course, the focus of Irigaray's third phase, where she seeks to create a universe, the first kind in history, of sexuate beings: the *je-elle* ("I-she") and the *je-il* ("I-he"). Saying "I-she" or "I-he" makes visible that the subject is two. It constitutes a decisive political and philosophical moment in which the singular is finally abandoned in favor of two beings and a new dialectic between subjectivity and objectivity. In *Democracy Begins Between Two* Irigaray explains: "It is not only a question of the right to be different-from ... but of the right and duty to be diverse-between. Thus, not: 'I'm different from you,' but: 'we differ amongst ourselves,' which implies a continual give-and-take in establishing boundaries and relationships, without the one having greater authority over the other" (Irigaray 2000a: 14).

For Irigaray, this gesture is the necessary foundation for a new ontology and ethics: "the other is recognized as other and not as the same: bigger or smaller than I, or at best my equal" (Irigaray 1995b: 19). In this sense, Irigaray stands radically apart from the French philosopher she is often compared to, Simone de Beauvoir. Where de Beauvoir refuses to be the other, Irigaray demands to be radically other, for it is only in staging this other that we can exit from our current horizon.

Major Criticisms

The story of Irigaray and her critics is almost as famous as Irigaray herself, especially in the Anglo-American feminist context. Criticisms initially clustered around the essentialist charge: Irigaray's metaphor of the two lips and her reading of psychoanalysis in *Speculum* and *This Sex Which is Not One* as the primary targets of biological essentialism and psychic essentialism respectively (Moi 1985; Rose 1986). But as critics like Jane Gallop emerged to defend Irigaray against the varieties of essentialism pitched at her, she "morphed" into a curious figure tagged to both sides of the debate (Gallop 1988). By the 1990s the essentialism/anti-essentialism divide had itself "de-hystericized," thus paving the way for a reconsideration of Irigaray's philosophical interventions beyond the early translations (Schor 1994).

In the meantime, Irigaray had become a key figure in what critics in the US characterized as New French Feminisms, fueling reflections on the supposed differences between the philosophically and psychoanalytically inspired French version of feminism and the more pragmatic US kind (Marks and de Courtivron 1981; Moi 1985). After numerous transatlantic crossings (Jardine 1985) discussions evolved more broadly into the pleasures and pains of poststructuralism versus feminism (Alcoff 1988). Critics also began to point out the homogenizing tendencies of labels like "French feminism," with the holy trinity of Irigaray, Julia Kristeva, and Hélène Cixous as parts taken for the whole. As Christine Delphy (1995) has lamented, the term "French feminisms" is an invention of Anglo-American feminists that flattens the field. Then again, when set within an international frame beyond the Atlantic – the West versus the Rest – any heterogeneity of "French" or "Anglo-American" starts to look pretty superficial (Spivak 1988).

Irigaray's insistence on sexual difference as the fundamental parameter of the sociocultural order, with sexual orientation or sexual choice as "secondary" (Irigaray 1995a: 112), has additionally earned her a controversial place in lesbian politics (Jargose 1994). Her emphasis on the woman–man couple has nonetheless inspired Judith Butler, the reigning "Queen" of gender trouble (Rubin 1994: 97), to elaborate the heterosexualization of identification and desire that governs the norms of both gender and sex (Butler 1990). Thus, the dissolution of the sex/gender distinction, already considerably advanced in feminism through Irigaray's assertion of sexual difference (Gatens 1991), has been pushed even further in surprisingly queer ways.

Just like the two lips, "Irigaray Studies" is therefore more than just one, and it has without a doubt left a lasting impression on the shifting sands of feminism.

Bibliography

Alcoff, L. (1988) "Cultural Feminism Versus Poststructuralism." *Signs*, 13, 3: 405–36.

Burke, C., Schor, N., and Whitford, M. (eds.) (1994) *Engaging With Irigaray*. New York: Columbia University Press.

Butler, J. (1990) *Gender Trouble: Feminism and the Subversion of Identity*. New York: Routledge.

Chanter, T. (1995) *Ethics of Eros: Irigaray's Rewriting of the Philosophers*. New York: Routledge.

Code, L. (ed.) (2000) *Encyclopedia of Feminist Theories*. New York: Routledge.

Craig, E. (ed.) (1998) *Encyclopedia of Philosophy*. New York: Routledge.

Delphy, C. (1995) "The Invention of French Feminism: An Essential Move." *Yale French Studies*, 87: 190–221.

Gallop, J. (1988) *Thinking Through the Body*. New York: Columbia University Press.

Gatens, M. (1991) *Feminism and Philosophy: Perspectives on Difference and Equal-*

ity. Cambridge: Polity Press.

Irigaray, L. (1985a) *Speculum of the Other Woman*, trans. G. C. Gill. Ithaca, NY: Cornell University Press.

Irigaray, L. (1985b) *This Sex Which is Not One*, trans. C. Porter and C. Burke. Ithaca, NY: Cornell University Press.

Irigaray, L. (1991) *The Irigaray Reader*, ed. M. Whitford. Oxford: Blackwell.

Irigaray, L. (1993a) *An Ethics of Sexual Difference*, trans. C. Burke and G. C. Gill, Ithaca, NY: Cornell University Press.

Irigaray, L. (1993b) *Je, Tu, Nous: Toward a Culture of Difference*, trans. A. Martin. New York: Routledge.

Irigaray, L. (1993c) *Sexes and Genealogies*, trans. G. C. Gill. New York: Columbia University Press.

Irigaray, L. (1994) *Thinking the Difference: For a Peaceful Revolution*, trans. K. Montin. New York: Routledge.

Irigaray, L. (1995a) "'Je – Luce Irigaray': A Meeting With Luce Irigaray" by E. Hirsch and G. A. Olson. *Hypatia*, 10, 2: 93–114.

Irigaray, L. (1995b) "The Question of the Other." *Yale French Studies*, 87: 7–19.

Irigaray, L. (1996) *I Love to You*, trans. A. Martin. New York: Routledge.

Irigaray, L. (2000a) *Democracy Begins Between Two*, trans. K. Anderson. London: Athlone Press.

Irigaray, L. (2000b) *To be Two*, trans. M. M. Rhodes and M. F. Cocito-Monoc. London: Athlone Press.

Jardine. A. A. (1985) *Gynesis: Configurations of Woman and Modernity*. Ithaca, NY: Cornell University Press.

Jargose. A. (1994) *Lesbian Utopics*. New York: Routledge.

Marks, E. and de Courtivron, I. (1981) *New French Feminisms: An Anthology*. Brighton: Harvester Press.

Moi, T. (1985) *Sexual/Textual Politics*. London: Routledge.

Rose, J. (1986) *Sexuality in the Field of Vision*. London: Verso.

Rubin. G. (1994) "Sexual Traffic." With Judith Butler. *differences*, 6, 2/3: 62–99.

Schor, N. (1994) "This Essentialism Which is Not One." In C. Burke, N. Schor, and M. Whitford (eds.) *Engaging With Irigaray*. New York: Columbia University Press.

Spivak, G. C. (1988) *In Other Worlds: Essays in Cultural Politics*. New York: Routledge.

Whitford, M. (1991) *Luce Irigaray: Philosophy in the Feminine*. London: Routledge.

Wright, E. (ed.) (1992) *Feminism and Psychoanalysis: A Critical Dictionary*. Oxford: Blackwell.

27 | **Fredric Jameson**

Andrew Milner

Ideas
Political unconscious □ Cultural logic □ Cognitive mapping

Major books
Marxism and Form (1971)
The Prison-House of Language (1974)
The Political Unconscious (1981)
Late Marxism (1990)
Postmodernism (1991)
Brecht and Method (1998)

Influences
Adorno □ Brecht □ Lukács □ Sartre

Biographical Details

Fredric Jameson was born in Cleveland, Ohio, in 1934. He was educated as an undergraduate at the Quaker-influenced Haverford College
in Pennsylvania, and as a postgraduate at Yale, where he studied under
Auerbach. He traveled to Germany as a graduate student on a Fullbright
Fellowship. His doctoral thesis on Sartre was later published as his first
book, *Sartre: The Origins of a Style* (1961). Neither thesis nor book were
especially "Marxist," but Jameson was attracted to the New Left counter-culture during "the 1960s," which he would later date as ending in
1974 (Jamesom 1988b: 184). This led, in turn, to a growing interest in
Marxist ideas. His initial reputation as a Marxist critic was established
by two books published in the early 1970s, *Marxism and Form* (1971)
and *The Prison-House of Language* (1974). But his most influential work
of literary criticism was almost certainly *The Political Unconscious* (1981),

which prompted Hayden White to describe him as "the best socially oriented critic of our time." The early 1990s witnessed two books almost in tandem, *Late Marxism* (1990) and *Postmodernism, or the Cultural Logic of Late Capitalism* (1991). Thereafter, he has continued to work on postmodernism, the cinema and, more recently, Brecht. Jameson has taught French and Comparative Literature at Harvard University, the University of California, San Diego, Yale University, and the University of California at Santa Cruz. In 1986 he moved to Duke University at Durham, North Carolina, where he is currently Distinguished Professor of Comparative Literature. He has written widely on both elite and popular cultural forms and is as much at home in cultural studies as in comparative literature.

Key Theoretical Contributions

Jameson has characterized his work in terms of a "vocation" to explain and popularize the "Marxist intellectual tradition" (Jameson 1988a: xxvi). The term "Marxist" here clearly refers to Hegelian "Western Marxism," as distinct from more orthodox communist "scientific" Marxism. This interest in Western European "Theory" was conditioned simultaneously by a political engagement with the internationalism of the New Left and by a disciplinary commitment to comparative literature, understood as the study of Goethe's *Weltliteratur*. Both *Marxism and Form* and *The Prison-House of Language* were substantially preoccupied with French theory. Over time, however, German theorists came to occupy an increasingly prominent place, expecially Lukács, Adorno, and Brecht. For Jameson, the key concept in Hegelian dialectics, which distinguishes Western from Soviet Marxism, is what Lukács termed "totality," Sartre "totalization": "There is no content, for dialectical thought, but total content" (Jameson 1971: 306).

The Political Unconscious is Jameson's most Lukácsian work and also, perhaps, his most theoretically original. Here he develops the systematic outline of a "totalizing" critical method deeply indebted to Lukács. Precisely because it is totalizing, dialectical Marxism is the "untranscendable horizon," capable of subsuming all other apparently incompatible critical methods, by "at once canceling and preserving them" (Jameson 1981: 10). Jameson argues that the objects of inquiry for cultural analysis can be located at three analytically distinct levels: "text," "ideologeme," and "ideology of form." Each of these has its socio-historical corollary in an equivalent "semantic horizon," respectively: "political history," or the sequence of events; "society"; and global "history," or the sequence of modes of production (ibid: 75–6). By ideologeme Jameson means the kind of collective discourse in relation to which texts function as little more than "individual *parole* or utterance." Since society can be characterized primarily in terms of class struggle, the ideologeme can be defined as "the smallest intelligible unit of the essentially antagonistic collective discourses of social classes" (ibid: 76). So for Jameson, as for Lukács, class becomes a key analytical tool. Witness, for example, his analysis of the medieval romance as providing an imaginary resolution to the emergent contradicition between positional ethics and noble class solidarity in twelfth-century Europe (ibid: 110–19).

Class analysis of this kind gives rise to a "double hermeneutic," simultaneously embracing both the negative hermeneutic of ideology critique and the positive hermeneutic of a non-instrumental conception of culture. For Jameson, class consciousness is thus simultaneously a matter of both ideology and utopia: all class consciousness, including even the most exclusive forms of ruling-class consciousness, "is in its very nature Utopian" (ibid: 289). Utopianism is a recurring theme in Jameson, from the initial encounter with Bloch, through later discussions of science fiction and other popular cultural forms, to the recent essay on Brecht (Jameson 1971: 120–58; 1982; 1991: 154–80; 1998a: 139–40).

The range of Jameson's cultural reference, from architecture to video, from conceptual art to dystopian cinema, is at its most impressive in the work on postmodernism. Jameson posits a historical periodization according to which there have been three main stages in the history of capitalism, each accompanied by a characteristic "cultural dominant." So aesthetic realism was the cultural dominant of nineteenth-century "market capitalism," modernism of early twentieth-century "monopoly capitalism," postmodernism of contemporary multinational "late capitalism" (Jameson 1991: 35–6). Late capitalism is capital in its purest form, "a prodigious expansion of capital into hitherto uncommodified areas" (ibid: 36); postmodernism is a commodity culture, distinguishable from the earlier modernisms as much by its "resonant affirmation" of the market as by any distinctive style (ibid: 305). The postmodern is thus a "field of stylistic and discursive heterogeneity without a norm" (ibid: 17). One important aspect of this process is what Jameson terms the "waning of historicity," whereby the past as referent is gradually "bracketed," so as eventually to leave nothing but texts and intertextuality (ibid: 18–21).

Jameson argues that the transition from monopoly to late capitalism has entailed a radical transformation in the nature of contemporary class structures (ibid: 319). So the "truth" of postmodernism is in its peculiar fidelity to the lie which is late capitalism. The preconditions for the

emergence of class consciousness are effectively postponed, not indefi-
nitely, but for the duration of this "transitional" period, in which the
"new global economy has not yet allowed its classes to form in any stable
way, let alone to acquire genuine class consciousness" (ibid: 348). In
these circumstances, radical politics become group politics, the preserve
of new social movements, whose characteristic narratives lack the alle-
gorical capacity to map the system (ibid: 349). Postmodern politics thus
entail a "ceaseless alternation" between identity and difference, which
itself attests to a kind of cultural "blockage" that obstructs further development (Jameson 1994: 65–6, 70).

Jameson's *Postmodernism* was published within a year of *Late Marxism*, his deeply appreciative treatment of Adorno. In retrospect, it is
clear how closely the two are connected. For Jameson, postmodernism
is primarily a periodizing category: he is ready to concede its local theoretical value, but only on the conditon that Marxism "must necessarily
become true again" (Jameson 1988b: 208). There is thus an almost inescapable logic in the resort to Adorno "to restore the sense of something
grim and impending within the polluted sunshine of the shopping mall"
(Jameson 1990: 248). Since the emergence of class consciousness has for
the moment been structurally preempted, the capacity to map or model
"the system" either disappears altogether or must temporarily lie elsewhere. That elsewhere is located somewhere between critical theory itself and a hypothetically postmodern political art.

This is Jameson's solution to the temporary absence of class consciousness from postmodern late capitalism: to posit the need for an
"aesthetic of cognitive mapping," through which to learn how to represent "the truth of postmodernism," that is, "the world space of multinational capital" (Jameson 1991: 54). Cognitive mapping, he explains,
is in reality a "code word" for class consciousness "of a new and hitherto undreamed of kind," which has not yet come into being. Hence,
the sense of his own work as the anticipation in theory of what may
eventually become class consciousness. The rhetorical strategy thus
invoked is clearly reminiscent of the Frankfurt School. Adorno and
Horkheimer had initially imagined their own critical theory as cognate
with a proletarian opposition to facism. But over time such emancipatory potential increasingly inhered in the immanent logic of critical
theory itself, as the attempt to discover, within the empirical, the tendency that points beyond it. As Jameson himself notes, this led Adorno
to a kind of "temperamental and cantankerous quietism" that would
prove a disabling liability at moments of popular politicization (Jameson
1990: 249). But "in the postmodern" this self-same Adorno becomes
"a joyous counter-poison and a corrosive solvent to apply to the surface of 'what is'" (ibid).

Major Criticisms

Jameson's work has been criticized by other Marxists as too Hegelian and "over-totalizing," an argument which leads to the conclusion that his method is so generously synthetic as to occlude its distinctively Marxist characteristics. Conversely, some feminists have argued that his work is too preoccupied with class, at the expense of race and gender. This argument can be linked to the charge that Jameson's view of postmodern culture is one-sidedly hostile, much like Lukács's of modernism. Both arguments are more properly addressed, however, to general questions of theory and method than to Jameson's own specific contributions.

Nonetheless, the increasingly Adornian cast of Jameson's Marxism clearly does expose it to the charge of latent quietism. Marxism of this kind functions by way of a great refusal, both of the system and of the ideologies that legitimate it. There is a certain grandeur to such intransigent resistance to the lures of commodity culture. But it tends to proceed virtually unaccompanied by any developed sense of the empirical realities of what Marxists and others might actually do. Jameson's recent interest in Brecht can be read, in part, as an attempt to rectify this state of affairs, especially in its concern for Brecht's "usefulness," if not in the postmodern, then certainly "right now" (Jameson 1998a: 1).

Bibliography

Anderson, P. (1998) *The Origins of Postmodernity*. London: Verso.
Burnham, C. (1995) *The Jamesonian Unconscious: The Aesthetics of Marxist Theory*. Durham, NC: Duke University Press.
Dowling, W. C. (1984) *Jameson, Althusser, Marx: An Introduction to the Political Unconscious*. Ithaca, NY: Cornell University Press.
Homer, S. (1998) *Fredric Jameson: Marxism, Hermeneutics, Postmodernism*. New York: Routledge.
Jameson, F. (1961) *Sartre: The Origins of a Style*. New Haven, CT: Yale University Press.
Jameson, F. (1971) *Marxism and Form: Twentieth Century Dialectical Theories of Literature*. Princeton, NJ: Princeton University Press.
Jameson, F. (1974) *The Prison-House of Language: A Critical Account of Structuralism and Russian Formalism*. Princeton, NJ: Princeton University Press.
Jameson, F. (1979) *Fables of Aggression: Wyndham Lewis, The Modernist as Fascist*. Berkeley: University of California Press.
Jameson, F. (1981) *The Political Unconscious: Narrative as a Socially Symbolic Act*. London: Methuen.

Jameson, F. (1982) "Progress v. Utopia; or, Can We Imagine the Future?" *Science Fiction Studies*, 9, 2.

Jameson, F. (1988a) *The Ideologies of Theory: Essays 1971–1986*, Vol. 1: *Situations of Theory*. London: Routledge.

Jameson, F. (1988b) *The Ideologies of Theory: Essays 1971–1986, Vol. 2: The Syntax of History*. London: Routledge.

Jameson, F. (1990) *Late Marxism: Adorno, or the Persistence of the Dialectic*. London: Verso.

Jameson, F. (1991) *Postmodernism, or The Cultural Logic of Late Capitalism*. Durham, NC: Duke University Press.

Jameson, F. (1992a) *The Geopolitical Aesthetic: Cinema and Space in the World System*. Bloomington: Indiana University Press.

Jameson, F. (1992b) *Signatures of the Visible*. London: Routledge.

Jameson, F. (1994) *The Seeds of Time*. New York: Columbia University Press.

Jameson, F. (1998a) *Brecht and Method*. London: Verso.

Jameson, F. (1998b) *The Cultural Turn: Selected Writings on the Postmodern, 1983–1998*. London: Verso.

Kellner, D. (ed.) (1989) *Postmodernism/Jameson/Critique*. Washington, DC: Maisonneuve Press.

Wise, C. (1995) *The Marxian Hermeneutics of Fredric Jameson*. New York: Lang.

28 | **Julia Kristeva**

John Lechte

Ideas

Dialogical word □ Ambivalence □ Poetic language □ The
semiotic □ The subject-in-process □ *Signifiance* □ Abjection □
Transubstantiation □ Revolt

Major books

Séméiotiké: recherches une sémanalyse (1969)
Le Texte du roman (1970)
About Chinese Women (1974)
Desire in Language (1980)
Powers of Horror (1982)
Revolution in Poetic Language (1984)
Tales of Love (1987)
Black Sun (1989)
Strangers to Ourselves (1991)
Time and Sense (1996)
La Révolte intime (1997)
Le Génie féminine: Hannah Arendt (1999)
Sense and Non-sense of Revolt (2000)

Influences

Bakhtin □ Barthes □ Bataille □ Benveniste □ Freud □ Hegel □
Husserl □ Joyce □ Lacan □ Mallarmé □ Proust □ Saussure

Biographical Details

Julia Kristeva, born in Bulgaria in 1941, came to Paris as a bursary student in the Christmas of 1965. She immediately became immersed in the elite of Parisian intellectual life, attending Roland Barthes's seminar, and joining the editorial board of *Tel Quel*, the then avant-garde literary journal edited by her husband to be, Philippe Sollers. Over the next thirty years the woman from Sophia would become a leading literary theorist, psychoanalyst, intellectual, and novelist.

For Kristeva, being a foreigner in France has heightened her sense that hostility to foreigners, like that which surfaced in the 1980s with the rise of the National Front, is doubly misplaced, firstly because in a racist society all are losers, and secondly because ultimately, foreignness, following Freud, is the uncanny otherness that is already in each of us (see Kristeva 1991).

On the other hand, Kristeva has said that sectarian ethnicity is loathsome, and that she has a deep respect for the French Enlightenment tradition and its formal processes for integrating foreigners into French society. Here, even de Gaulle does not look so bad, albeit in retrospect (Kristeva 1993: 65–76). Is this Kristeva unconsciously putting herself in favor for some public recognition? In any case she did receive recognition for her work in 1997 when she was inducted into the French *Légion d'honneur*.

Key Theoretical Contributions

Following Bakhtin, Kristeva's early work compares the homogeneous epic, myth, folktale, and religious apologue (all studied by early structuralism) with the novel, which first marks itself as modern by the heterogeneous structure of its narrative. Although it took centuries for the novel to reach the pinnacle set by Dostoyevsky or Joyce, rudiments of a more "polyphonic" text emerged in the middle of the fifteenth century. Two terms in particular assume importance in Kristeva's work at this time. These are "dialogue" and "ambivalence." Both will play a role in the effort to formalize "poetic language."

By "dialogue" Kristeva means that a literary work is structurally plural. As Bakhtin had shown in his study of Dostoyevsky, each voice in the dialogical novel has equal narrative and poetic force; there is no single overriding, monological narration which comes to subsume all the rest, as there still is in some of Tolstoy.

By "ambivalence" is meant a phenomenon or concept that is one *and* other simultaneously. Ambivalence thus challenges the either/or, digital logic of rationalist science, which rigidly upholds the law of contradiction. Ambivalence is "both ... and," and so evokes analogue processes. Carnival, too, has such a structure, and becomes a concrete incarnation of ambivalence, where the rulers become the people and the people become rulers, even if only for a day.

In the wake of interest in avant-garde writing à la Mallarmé and Joyce, Kristeva in the late 1960s pursued a project aiming to formalize the sounds and rhythms that are poetic language. Characterizing conventional scientific logic as being essentially binary, or bivalent – "0-1" (false/true) – Kristeva then attempted to symbolize the unobservable, ambivalent logic of poetic language as "0-2." As others have noted, the presence of "0" in this supposed mark of ambivalence is a problem, because it is precisely "0" that marks binary systems as digital, whereas poetic language is analogical (without zero). Kristeva herself seems to have recognized this, for the "0-2" has never again appeared in her work.

Even if this attempt to formalize the affective aspect of language was misplaced, it drew attention to the importance of giving poetic language an equal prominence with communicative language (i.e., prose). Indeed, science (including information science) can go blindly on without ever having to acknowledge the specific rigor of poetic or subjective processes, if no means exist for speaking *about* poetic language.

In an attempt show how the rhythm and song of language relates to late nineteenth- and early twentieth-century society, Kristeva's *doctorat d'état*, published as *La Révolution du langage poétique* (1974) (abridged in English as *Revolution in Poetic Language*, 1984), examined the work of Mallarmé and Lautréamont through a framework informed in particular by Hegel, Husserl, Freud, and Lévi-Strauss. The aim was to look both at the constitution of society (Freud says it began with a murder) and subjectivity as expressed in poetic language (the affective dimension). One result of this mammoth work (both in terms of theoretical ambition and length) was the production of a number of key concepts which have made Kristeva's name so prominent as a social theorist. These include the semiotic, the subject-in-process, and *signifiance*. Each of these terms points to the drive, or affective level of language. As analogical, they evoke the sound, rhythm, repetition, inflection, and intonation of the voice. The semiotic can be observed both in the infant's holophrastic utterances, as well as in the musicality of the avant-garde poet's language. The semiotic is fluid, not static; it is the body speaking, but it is not the body; it can be experienced in the timbre of words, not in their semantics; it is evocative of the feminine and the mother. As a consequence of the latter, Kristeva's work in general, and the notion of the semiotic in particular, has been of great interest to feminists. For the semiotic challenges the hegemony of the digital rationalism of science and conventional linguistics, as it also challenges the dominance of the Law in political life. The Law gives rise to parties and to the bureaucracy, which tends to crush subjectivity and individuality. Indeed, the semiotic shows that conventional politics of the right and the left are caught in a partial straitjacket of binary social arrangements. "Music in letters is the counterpart of the parliamentary oration," Kristeva says with a nod to Mallarmé (Kristeva 1974: 402). The semiotic ("the music in letters"), then, is the poetic shock that can lead to the opening up of new political forms.

If the subject and subjectivity from Descartes to Husserl have been conceptualized as the punctual, already posited, static subject of Western modernity, the semiotic (manifest in something as close to us as a child's pre-linguistic babble) calls to presence what that tradition represses: the musical basis of words and the movement of painted images. Few thinkers before or since have had the courage to link, via the working of affect, the poet and the child. This, to be sure, is Kristeva's greatest achievement.

During the 1980s Kristeva published three psychoanalytically informed studies on, respectively, abjection (Kristeva 1982), love (Kristeva 1987), and melancholia (Kristeva 1989). Each work is a modification of Lacanian psychoanalytic theory, which privileges the symbolic over the drive aspect of psychic life. By "symbolic" is meant everything that is law-like and rule-based: language in general, the legal system (the formal basis of society and politics), representation, and the sciences. Interestingly, Freud and Lacan were not musical. Whether this influenced their theories directly is unknown. What is known is that the semiotic in Kristeva's sense is not part of the Lacanian theoretical universe. Hence, when Kristeva proceeds to describe a subject that begins to form itself prior to the mirror stage (prior to the subject–object division) and the acquisition of articulate language, it does not fit the Lacanian scheme of things. In *Powers of Horror* (1982) this subject emerges in light of what it rejects: things that instil horror most of all. To think that desire, implying the loss of the Mother as object, is the key to the formation of the subject, is to neglect the formative aspect of what, in non-Western cultures, is the system of taboos and rituals, a system that is not based in desire, but on negative elements which instil fear because they are polluting. Desire is there to be sure; but it is put back in its place.

With love, Kristeva notes that there is *agape* love as well as love based in the symbolic (romantic love). *Agape* love is there almost from before we are born in the figure of Freud's "Father of individual prehistory." This is God's love which precedes us, a love that also opens up a minimal, loving separation from the mother. Here is a separation that is barely one. Love also gives rise to the psyche as an open system which thrives on the incorporation into it of otherness (difference).

Extreme melancholia is marked, at one level, by an absence of affect in words and language and a consequent withdrawal from the symbolic. The melancholic person experiences words as empty and abstract because they are only words. Affect must thus be reinjected into symbolic processes. This occurs, Kristeva suggests, when the (perceived) source of suffering itself is translated into a symbolic form. Difficult as this might be, the sufferer must endeavor to *represent* the hell of torment, so that there can be, says Kristeva, a "resurrection in signs" (as Holbein showed with his *Corpse of Christ in the Tomb*, 1521). In this very process a new constitution of the self can arise.

Through her study of Proust, Kristeva (1996) addresses what she sees as the postmodern impoverishment of the imaginary faculty, and thus of experience. At its fullest the imaginary enables the self and the world, affect and words, body and the senses, to merge with each other. Thus Proust's novel does not simply recapture time in memory; it enables one to relive time in memory through the imaginary. There is, it is said, a "transubstantiation." Thus, when the imaginary reaches its full potential, words and things can fuse in a new way, and the self can be restructured.

In the courses she gave at the end of the 1990s, as well as in her novels, Kristeva has tried to address what she sees as the atrophying of psychic space brought about by the "society of the spectacle." The phrase is taken from the title of Guy Debord's 1967 work, which criticizes the way that everything that was once "directly lived has moved away into a representation." The society of the spectacle brings with it a plethora of standardized virtual forms and the loss of a capacity to create personal fantasies (that is, to create a new self in a spirit of revolt). The imaginary becomes a standardized "thing," Kristeva bemoans, and society becomes nihilist because no one is questioning existing values any more.

Old-style transgressions (often violent) are not necessary for revolt, for it can also be realized in an infinite array of more or less intimate assertions of individual difference: in art, literature, and in psychoanalysis (Kristeva says that her police novel *Possessions* (1998) is her intimate revolt). Or, indeed, revolt can now simply be a different way of living one's life, as Kristeva's current project, centered on the notion of feminine genius, intends to show.

Major Criticisms

Because Kristeva does not subscribe to separatist feminism, she has been criticized for her failure to be an outspoken advocate of a feminist culture. More substantially, perhaps, thinkers like Judith Butler (1990) have challenged what they see as Kristeva's privileging of heterosexuality over homosexuality, while Kelly Oliver (1998: 87) argues that despite the "imaginary, loving father," Kristeva is in fact still the captive of Lacan's stern, symbolic father.

From another angle, following her claim to be a "cosmopolitan," and her positive reappraisal of de Gaulle, Kristeva has sometimes been cast as someone who is too close to establishment power when it comes to the politics of culture. A tension exists between her being a supporter of French Enlightenment ideals while yet evincing a sympathy for those so-called *français de souche* who have a hostility to foreigners.

More philosophically, Richard Beardsworth (1995) has argued that Kristeva's theory of the semiotic, which cannot be formalized, is in fact given a *logic* of its own. Similarly, the same critic argues, the subject-in-process, based in the semiotic, also has a logic attributed to it. In short, in the very act of theorizing the semiotic, Kristeva would seem to betray it; for theory is part of the symbolic order, the very opposite of the semiotic.

Kristeva could however retort that the distinction, semiotic–symbolic, is analytical only and that, in reality, the semiotic flows into the symbolic, implying ambivalence.

Bibliography

Beardsworth, R. (1995) *"Tel Quel's* Écriture: Avant-Garde Logic and Time." *Paragraph,* 18, 2: 248–72.
Butler, J. (1990) *Gender Trouble: Feminism and the Subversion of Identity.* New York: Routledge.
Debord, G. (1994) [1967] *Society of the Spectacle,* trans. D. Nicholson-Smith. New York: Zone Books.
Kristeva, J. (1969) *Séméiotiké: recherches pour une sémanalyse.* Paris: Éditions du Seuil.
Kristeva, J. (1970) *Le Texte du roman. Approche sémiologique d'une structure discursive transformationelle.* The Hague: Mouton.
Kristeva, J. (1974) *La Révolution du langage poétique.* Paris: Éditions du Seuil.
Kristeva, J. (1980) *Desire in Language: A Semiotic Approach to Literature and Art,* trans. T. S. Gora, A. Jardine, and L. S. Roudiez. Oxford: Blackwell.
Kristeva, J. (1982) [1980] *Powers of Horror: An Essay on Abjection,* trans. L. S. Roudiez. New York: Columbia University Press.
Kristeva, J. (1984) *Revolution in Poetic Language,* trans. M. Waller. Columbia: Columbia University Press.
Kristeva, J. (1986) [1974] *About Chinese Women,* trans. A. Barrows. New York: Marion Boyars.

Kristeva, J. (1987) [1983] *Tales of Love,* trans. L. S. Roudiez. New York: Columbia University Press.

Kristeva, J. (1989) [1987] *Black Sun: Depression and Melancholia,* trans. L. S. Roudiez. New York: Columbia University Press.

Kristeva, J. (1991) [1988] *Strangers to Ourselves,* trans. L. S. Roudiez. New York: Columbia University Press.

Kristeva, J. (1993) *Nations Without Nationalism,* trans. L. S. Roudiez. New York: Columbia University Press.

Kristeva, J. (1996) [1994] *Time and Sense: Proust and the Experience of Literature,* trans. R. Guberman. New York: Columbia University Press.

Kristeva, J. (1997) *La Révolte intime: pouvoir et limites de la psychanalyse II.* Paris: Fayard.

Kristeva, J. (1998) [1996] *Possessions,* trans. B. Bray. New York: Columbia University Press.

Kristeva, J. (1999) *Le Genie féminine: Hannah Arendt.* Paris: Fayard.

Kristeva, J. (2000) [1996] *Sense and Non-sense of Revolt,* trans. J. Herman. New York: Columbia University Press.

Oliver, K. (1998) "The Crisis of Meaning." In J. Lechte and M. Zournazi (eds.) *After the Revolution: On Kristeva.* Sydney: Artspace.

29 | Jacques Lacan

Stephen Frosh

Ideas
Language and the unconscious □ Imaginary □ Symbolic □
Real □ Mirror phase □ Desire □ Lack □ Phallus

Major books
Écrits (1966)
The Seminars (various)
Quasi una fantasia (1994)

Influences
Freud □ Hegel □ Lévi-Strauss □ Saussure

Biographical Details

Jacques Lacan (1901–81) was one of the most significant psychoanalysts of the post-Freudian era, with an influence on social and cultural studies in excess of his influence on psychoanalysis itself. He practiced psychiatry and psychoanalysis in Paris for most of his career, including the period of the Nazi occupation, during which he worked in a military hospital. He was very colorfully at the center of numerous intra-institutional squabbles, spawning admirers and dissenters in all his activities.

Lacan earned his medical degree in 1932 with a doctoral dissertation on paranoia. In 1934 he joined the Société Psychanalytique de Paris (SPP), becoming a full member in 1938. The first version of his "mirror phase" theory was presented in 1936 to the International Psychoanalytic Association (IPA); his more developed account of the theory was given in 1949. In 1953 Lacan became president of the SPP, but his practice of giving variable-length sessions had already provoked dissent and for this and other reasons the SPP split. Lacan resigned from the SPP to join the new Société Française de Psychanalyse (SFP), a move which resulted in his membership of the IPA being rescinded. Lacan retaliated with his grand(iose) paper, "The function and field of speech and language in psychoanalysis," commonly known as the "Rome Discourse," which perhaps truly marked his ascension as the one who would lead the "return to Freud." In November 1953 Lacan began his first public seminar in the Hôpital Sainte-Anne, a seminar which continued on an annual basis for twenty-seven years and which became the primary site for the articulation of Lacanian psychoanalysis.

At various times the SFP applied for affiliation to the IPA and it became clear that the main stumbling block preventing its acceptance was the hostility of the IPA to Lacan. In 1963 the IPA recommended acceptance of the application on condition that Lacan and two others were removed from the list of training analysts and that Lacan's training activities be banned forever. Lacan resigned and in 1964 founded the École Freudienne de Paris (EFP), having also moved his seminar to the École Normale Supérieure. With the publication in 1966 of a selection of his (mainly spoken) papers under the ironic title *Écrits*, Lacan became a celebrity; his support for the May 1968 student protests consolidated this position. The first publication of any of his seminars was not until 1973 (an edited transcript of his 1964 Seminar XI, *The Four Fundamental Concepts of Psychoanalysis*). By 1980 internal tensions in the EFP led Lacan to disband it for what he claimed was its deviation from Freudian principles. He died in 1981, in between schisms.

Key Theoretical Contributions

Lacanian theory is both a comprehensive attempt to locate psychoanalysis as a rigorous and critical domain of knowledge, and a subversive exploration of the structure of unconscious activity. It centers around a group of concerns with language, fantasy, and representation, perhaps best summarized as an attempt to explore the way the unconscious makes unsustainable any notion of the "mature," "healthy," or integrated ego – or indeed of any autonomous and free identity.

Language

Lacan's "return to Freud" is most famously through the medium of structural linguistics. At its heart is a repudiation of traditional representation theories of language in favor of a dynamic account of the productivity or effectivity of language. This is to some extent a commonplace in psychoanalysis: if the "talking cure" is to work, language must have effects – it must produce something new. However, Lacan takes this further through an account of what it means to be a subject of language, saturated with loss. If I project myself into language, nominating myself as the personal pronoun "I," I am already risking the loss of something else, at the boundaries or beyond language. Language calls us into being as human, social subjects; it positions us in discourse and hence can be seen as causal; it "structures" the unconscious.

Desire

Lacan evokes an empty subject, constituted through lack and marked by the impossibility of fulfillment or of recognition of the actuality of the other. Desire is a difference, forged out of the distinction between need and demand, between what is required by the human subject, what becomes translated into communicable symbols, and what is left over, as an ache or gap between the hope and its realization. "Demand" is the fantasy that the other can completely give itself up to the subject; but the actual impossibility of this means that demand is left unfulfilled, reflecting back on the subject as lack of recognition, as something still to be desired. It is in this gap between need and demand, between what can be fulfilled and what is impossible, that desire arises: "Thus desire is neither the appetite for satisfaction, nor the demand for love, but the difference resulting from the subtraction of the first from the second, the very phenomenon of their splitting" (Lacan 1958: 81).

As complete love is impossible, as each subject is split by the operations of language and the unconscious, so every human subject finds her or himself looking for proofs of love, and standing in as the cause of the other's desire; that is, each subject strives to arouse in the other recognition of the necessity of the subject's existence.

The Imaginary and the mirror

The Imaginary is characterized by the narcissistic relation with the image, in which the fantasy is that wholeness and integrity can be achieved. The emblem here is the pre-Oedipal relation between infant and mother, replicated in analysis when the subject fantasizes that the analyst is the one who "actually" knows, with whom oneness is possible, and who can treasure and hold the subject and make them whole. The dominant motif for the Imaginary is the mirror phase, taken as a point of traumatic, jubilant entry. In Lacan's (1949) exposition, he captures something of the sense of being "misrecognized," which is possibly characteristic of contemporary culture. In contrast to Winnicott, who uses the idea of mirroring to convey the importance of a developmental process in which the child sees themself accurately and thoughtfully reflected back by a concerned mother, Lacan emphasizes the impossibility of identity as related to a "true" self. In his view, the ego comes from outside and is used to create an armor or shell supporting the psyche, which is otherwise experienced as in fragments.

Lacan emphasizes the *exteriority* of this process: that which appears to us as our "self" is in fact given from the outside as a refuge, an ideal ego, a narcissistically invested image. This makes the structure of human knowledge and ego functioning delusional, and Lacan reads this as a paranoid sensation. The negativity and persecutory associations of the paranoiac are to do in part with the aggressivity of the drives, threatening to burst the image apart – a notion akin to those worked on by Klein in her description of paranoid-schizoid functioning. But it is also connected with the haunting of this satisfying image of the integrated self by the specter or memory of something else; somewhere inside, each of us knows that we are not really whole, that this seeming-self is a bare cover for something disturbing. In the mirror stage the terrible struggle to hold the forces of dissolution at bay is repressed in the face of a manic optimism that "identity" will solve the problem, fixing what is fluid in us as a meaning expressible in an easy sentence: "I am this and not that."

The Symbolic and the castration complex

The imaginary wholeness promised by the mirror is shattered by the move to the symbolic order of experience in which the structures of language interfere with the image-making process, revealing that it is already organized by a law indifferent to the emotions and desires of the individual subject. The moment of entry to this order is the castration complex. This introduces a third term into the Imaginary self–other unity, disrupting this but also enabling the subject to take up a position in language; essentially, this means being placed in the circuit of human communication. Without accession to the Symbolic, there is only narcissism and the Imaginary: "foreclosure" of this kind produces psychosis. Nevertheless, giving up the fantasy of oneness is painful and never fully accomplished: the Imaginary is central to much of human consciousness.

As in the classical Oedipus complex, the Lacanian Symbolic is instituted through a prohibition: the law against incest, here coded as the paternal "non"; the subject thus enters the Symbolic on the basis of division and absence. Again as in Freud's theory, the central player here, what

Lacan calls the "primary signifier," is the phallus. The Lacanian phallus is neither a physical organ nor a specific fantasy, but it is a signifier with a particular function: it guarantees the existence of symbolic meaning. It is generative and connecting, possessed of an aura of procreation and sexual linkage. On the other hand, it also specifically signifies a cancellation; it is, therefore, not to be thought of as something positive and full of potency, but as a kind of negativity: "The phallus can only play its role as veiled, that is, as in itself the sign of the latency with which everything is struck as soon as it is raised to the function of signifier" (Lacan 1958: 82).

The phallus cannot be taken literally; it only works if it is not seen, its message being that there is no center to power, just the emanation of some remarkable effects. The phallus is a function, something that happens and makes things happen; it is often related to in the Imaginary register as a fantasy, like the fantasy of mastery, but no one can have it because it is not a thing to be had.

The Symbolic order is thus the province of language and sexual difference, marked by the splitting of the subject and the creation of subjectivity around lack. The Imaginary holds the promise of integration, the Symbolic is there to announce that there can never be complete wholeness, for desire slips in everywhere, pursuing what it has lost. Love is an aching after something, not a finding; psychoanalysis attests to this.

The Real

This is the third Lacanian order, bubbling away under the other two. The Real is not a biological given or site of mysticism, but an order of experience, that which cannot be put into words, that dissolution or abyss from which the subject flees into the arms of symbolization. At certain times it breaks through to link us with everything we have left out; this is what Žižek (1991) refers to as "the answer of the Real." But much of the time it pulses away as a threat, as that which can demolish all our attempts at identity construction.

Major Criticisms

The flamboyantly phallocentric and exhibitionist, not to say narcissistic mode in which Lacan's theorizing was cast, coupled with a rather relentless fascination with the abstractions of structuralist theories, have produced an enormous variety of criticisms. Some of these have been concerned with contradictions in the theory itself, for example around the way it threatens to slip either into the essentialism it abhors or into such a relentless structuralism that no content at all is allowed the human subject. In particular, it can be argued that Lacan's insistence on the constructive primacy of language leads to a form of pessimistic determinism (the subject is fully determined by culture) and can also be used to legitimize oppressive practices or the patriarchy which it seems to deconstruct. Lacan's emphasis on the arbitrary nature of sexual division is an important attraction for feminist theory, because it provides the tools with which to challenge the biologistic reasoning that so often is used to legitimize sexist practices. But his identification of the Law of the Father with the whole of culture undermines this gain. This is seen most clearly in the discussion of the nature and functions of the phallus. It seems to be the Lacanian argument that the *arbitrary* linking of phallus and penis is what is primarily responsible for the ridiculousness of the claims that men make to dominance, but the dominance of the phallus cannot itself be challenged because of its structuring role in the construction of the human subject. As Gallop (1982) argues, this fails to acknowledge the conditions of power that actually surround human relationships. The fact that it is the penis which gives shape to the image of power is not totally arbitrary; rather, it reflects pervasive social arrangements which are built on underlying relations of force. This is part of a general critique of Lacan for using a structuralist paradigm that gives his theory a tendency to "collapse into an account of a universal, albeit contradictory, subject who is not situated historically, who is tied and bound by preexisting language, and is incapable of change because of it" (Henriques et al. 1984: 217).

The loss of *agency* in Lacanian theory also has significant implications. Lacan evokes an empty subject, constituted through lack and marked by the impossibility of fulfillment or of recognition of the actuality of the other. This seems to offer little prospect for a reconfigured subjecthood out of which new political and psychological realities could be born.

Restoring agency or, in Benjamin's (1998) intersubjectivist terms, "authorship" to the subject may be an important step in articulating the possibilities for people to grasp their futures differently – just as it is an important step in examining the difference between those ways of structuring society which impose paranoid splits on subjects, and those which do not, or do not to the same extent.

Bibliography

Benjamin, J. (1998) *Shadow of the Other: Intersubjectivity and Gender in Psychoanalysis*. New York: Routledge.

Bowie, M. (1991) *Lacan*. London: Fontana.

Clément, C. (1983) *The Lives and Legends of Jacques Lacan*. New York: Columbia University Press.

Evans, D. (1996) *An Introductory Dictionary of Lacanian Psychoanalysis*. London: Routledge.

Felman, S. (1987) *Jacques Lacan and the Adventure of Insight*. Cambridge, MA: Harvard University Press.

Frosh, S. (1994) *Sexual Difference*. London: Routledge.

Gallop, J. (1982) *Feminism and Psychoanalysis*. London: Macmillan.

Gallop. J. (1985) *Reading Lacan*. Ithaca, NY: Cornell University Press.

Grosz, E. (1990) *Jacques Lacan: A Feminist Introduction*. London: Routledge.

Henriques, J., Hollway, W., Urwin, C., Venn, C., and Walkerdine, V. (1984) *Changing the Subject*. London: Methuen.

Irigaray, L. (1985) [1977] *This Sex Which is Not One*. Ithaca, NY: Cornell University Press.

Lacan, J. (1949) "The Mirror Stage as Formative of the Function of the I as Revealed in Psychoanalytic Experience." In J. Lacan, *Écrits: A Selection*. London: Tavistock, 1977.

Lacan, J. (1953) "The Function and Field of Speech and Language in Psychoanalysis." In J. Lacan, *Écrits: A Selection*. London: Tavistock, 1977.

Lacan, J. (1955–6) *The Seminars of Jacques Lacan, Book 2*. Cambridge: Cambridge University Press, 1988.

Lacan, J. (1958) "The Meaning of the Phallus." In J. Mitchell and J. Rose (eds.) *Feminine Sexuality*. London: Macmillan, 1982.

Lacan, J. (1959–60) *The Ethics of Psychoanalysis*. London: Routledge, 1992.

Lacan, J. (1964) "Guiding Remarks for a Congress on Feminine Sexuality." In J. Mitchell and J. Rose (eds.) *Feminine Sexuality*. London: Macmillan, 1982.

Lacan, J. (1973) *The Four Fundamental Concepts of Psycho-Analysis*. London: Hogarth Press, 1977.

Lacan, J. (1975) *The Seminars of Jacques Lacan: Book 1 (1953–4)* Cambridge: Cambridge University Press, 1988.

Mitchell, J. (1982) "Introduction – I." In J. Mitchell and J. Rose (eds.) *Feminine Sexuality*. London: Macmillan.

Roudinesco, E. (1990) *Jacques Lacan and Co*. Chicago: University of Chicago Press.

Rustin, M. (1995) "Lacan, Klein and Politics: The Positive and Negative in Psychoanalytic Thought." In A. Elliott and S. Frosh (eds.) *Psychoanalysis in Contexts*. London: Routledge.

Zizek, S. (1991) *Looking Awry*. Cambridge, MA: MIT Press.

30 | Claude Lévi-Strauss

Zygmunt Bauman

Ideas
Culture □ Structuration □ Opposition □
Signifier and Signified □ Linguistics □ Synchrony vs. diachrony

Major books
Les Structures elémentaris de la parenté (1949)
Tristes Tropiques (1955)
Structural Anthropology (1974, 1983)

Influences
Geology □ Jakobson □ Marxism □ Psychoanalysis □ Saussure □
Trubetzkoy

Biographical Details

Born November 28, 1908 in Brussels, Claude Lévi-Strauss studied philosophy and law at the University of Paris from 1927 to 1932 . From 1934 to 1937 he taught sociology in São Paulo while conducting field research among the Indian tribes of the Brazilian interior. In 1941–5 he worked at the New School for Social Research in New York. After the war he returned to France and taught between 1950 and 1974 at the École Pratique des Hautes Études; he was called in 1959 to the Chair of Social Anthropology at the Collège de France.

From the 1960s on, Lévi-Strauss has been the major influence behind the "structuralist revolution" in social anthropology and a wide range of social sciences and humanities (sociology, literary and religious studies, media studies, linguistics, and philosophy). His work set the scene for the establishment of broadly understood cultural studies by casting culture as, first and foremost, a system of communication and shifting the focus of research and interpretation of culture from the traditional pre-occupation with self-sustained and functionally self-sufficient total systems to the ongoing, ubiquitous, and dispersed activity of structuration: the production of meanings through manipulations of significant differences and of the structural relations between elements.

Key Theoretical Contributions

The first major exercise in what was soon to become a comprehensive cognitive frame and methodology for the new style of cultural research was *Les Structures elémentaris de la parenté* (1949), the outcome of a thorough rethinking of the orthodox representations of kinship systems, and their reinterpretation as an interplay of significant (cognitive, evaluative as well as behavioral) oppositions – a work of unconscious human mind. In 1955 *Tristes Tropiques* followed, the literary account of Lévi-Strauss's experience gained during his fieldwork in the Brazilian rain forest; whether praised or condemned by the reviewers, this book was recognized as the manifesto of the entirely new concept of human studies.

In *Triste Tropiques* Lévi-Strauss spelled out the reasons which prompted him to challenge the received anthropological wisdom. The young Parisian graduate embarked on his expedition indoctrinated in what to expect to find and what to seek in the Amazonian jungle: "I wished to reach the ultimate limit of wilderness," he confessed. He finally arrived at what seemed to be such a limit: the natives immaculate in the "wildness," never seen before by a "civilized eye." They were tantalizingly close, ready to tell everything an anthropologist could dream to know about their pristine customs and beliefs – but there was no language in which they could do so. "They were so near like a reflection in the mirror, I could touch them, but not understand ... I got, simultaneously, my reward and my punishment."

Since at least Bronislaw Malinowski's time (that is, for half a century or more), to be an anthropologist meant first of all having passed the test of a "field study": to spend a number of months or years in the company of far-away islanders, bush nomads, or mountain tribes as isolated as possible from outside contacts, and describe in as much detail as possible their ostensibly "pure" customs, kinship system, rites, cosmic beliefs, myths, creeds, and daily routines. An expedition to a far-away land populated by culturally distant people was the obligatory *rite-de-passage* to the profession, but also an initiation into the role of conduct defining the specifically anthropological nature of inquiry: when confronting carriers of "another culture" one should take care to keep one's intellectual distance while struggling for maximal physical proximity. When "in the field," anthropologists should strive to erase from their mind all that their own culture taught them to think, and to suspend all judgments which their own values inclined them to pass – while immersing themselves "naively" in the dealings and thoughts of the "natives": best of all, try to turn themselves, for a time, into the "natives whom they studied." What Lévi-Strauss proposed was nothing less than to reverse that rule and thus the very nature of anthropological inquiry; while keeping a physical distance from the "natives," remove the anathema from intellectual proximity and use the means put at our disposal by modern science to crack the code of our shared human "unconscious" working in the "savage" as much as in the "civilized" mind.

For cultural studies, Lévi-Strauss's innovation had an effect as seminal as the abolition of the "rotten borough" constituencies for the maturation of modern democracy. To propose the abolition of privileged and invariably secluded places from which the inner mechanism of culture could be gleaned and the work of culture described, meant to open up new and vast, potentially infinite expanses of collective human experience to the study of culture. For the first time anthropology offered the practitioners of other humanities something more than an assortment of first-hand reports of the ways and means of exotic and obscure peoples against which to set the distinctives of their own "civilized" experience; namely, a method to arrive at cultural generalization, not by following the strategy of "butterfly collectors" (as Edmund Leach, the British follower of Lévi-Strauss, caustically described the search for universals as pursued by the orthodox anthropology), but through an insight into the mechanism of "structuration" common to all humans. Such insight could be obtained by all students of culture watching at close quarters single fragments and aspects of the manifold human existence and doing it from admittedly local standpoints, from their (cultural as well professional) home. Lévi-Strauss's anthropology gave the whole spectrum of humanities a chance of genuine cumulativeness of the kind which so far only the sciences of nature had boasted. Studies of literature and arts, fashions and taste, myths and ideologies, eating habits and conversation patterns could now talk to each other, exchange and compare their findings, and help each other in unraveling the mysteries of human cultural potential and practice.

In a meeting held on January 25, 1999 to celebrate his ninetieth birthday and the publication of a special issue of the journal *Critique* dedicated to his life-work, Claude Lévi-Strauss invoked Montaigne's musings about the cruelty of old age: well before they die, human beings start to disappear part by part and death takes away but a fraction of what they used to be in the fullness of their powers. This is not how I feel, said Lévi-Strauss: Montaigne failed to note that, like in a hologram, each remaining part, however minuscule, "preserves the complete image and represents the whole." Being old, said Lévi-Strauss, feels like being a worn-out or broken hologram, but hologram all the same. The "hologram metaphor" that Lévi-Strauss applied to his life experience grasps also the gist of his lifelong scholarly strategy, which (to use the old dream of the Romantics as another metaphor) aims "to see the universe in a drop of water": to seek and find the universal traits of "being-in-and-through-culture" in every fragment of human thought and action. It was such a strategy that was consistently pursued by Lévi-Strauss throughout a whole series of widely influential studies (*Anthropologie structurale*, 1961, 1973; *Le Pensée sauvage*, 1962; *Le Totemisme aujourd'hui*, 1962) and finally in Lévi-Strauss's *magnum opus* – the four-volume inquiry (published between 1964 and 1971) into the mechanism of "culture and structuration" documented through the analysis of eating habits, culinary arts, and table manners.

Lévi-Strauss's approach to culture as an activity of structuration was inspired by structural linguistics (in his view the most scientifically advanced branch of the humanities), and particularly the works of Roman Jakobson, Nicolas Trubetzkoy, and Ferdinand de Saussure. Taking a lead from the study of language was in Lévi-Strauss's view not just well justified, but long overdue, for before it could perform its other functions which heretofore stood at the center of the anthropologist's attention (i.e., servicing the social order or satisfying individual needs), culture had to fulfill the requirements set for all communicative systems, of which the fullest and purest embodiment is language: it is in language that the features of the communicative system may be seen in their purest and uncompromised form. In developing the science of culture, one should therefore follow the findings of structural linguistics and the strategies of the structural analysis of language and obey the following principles:

1   The shift of focus of investigation from conscious phenomena (articulated beliefs, commonly accepted definitions) to the unconscious infrastructure: networks of metaphorical or paradigmatic (functionally equivalent) and metonymical or syntagmatic (contiguous) relations between phenomena; and from *parole* (speech) to language, that is to a system of oppositions and the rules of their combination and permutation, which determines the (practically infinite) range of legitimate, meaningful expressions.

2   Seek the meaning, "the semantic load," of cultural tokens and usages in the relation they enter into with other tokens and usages; remember that meaning is deposited not in a single sign, nor in the connection between the *signifiant* (the sensually accessible form) and the *signified* (its referent), but in the oppositions between signs. Mean-

ing is a function of paradigmatic and syntagmatic relations between signs which combine into a network of differences; it is solely through "commutation" (this is, the structural equivalence) between opposi-tions at the level of signs and the differentiations at the level of cul-turally organized reality that the elements of culture acquire (create) meanings.

3 Just as one cannot learn the meaning of words from their etymology, one cannot learn the meaning of cultural tokens and usages from their history. Semantic analysis must be *synchronic* rather than *dia-chronic* (the idea later developed in the "structural semantics" of Alan Greimas): whatever their past references, signs are meaningful in as far as they are contemporaneously engaged in the relations of oppo-sition/equivalence or continguity with other signs coexisting within the system.

4 Just as meaning cannot be derived from the origins and history of a sign, it cannot be drawn from the similarity or any "natural" precultural connection between the sign and its referent. Cultural signs, just like the words of language, are "unmotivated": arbitrary, neither causally nor in any other way determined. There is no un-breakable, once-and-for-all established link between the "signifier" and a specific "signified" and no links exhaust the signifying poten-tial of the sign. The discriminating activity of the unconscious mind follows its own logic and weaves its own network of significations, subsequently superimposed upon the natural divisions of empirical reality and adding to them a dense web of artificial distinctions.

5 Just as all languages are products of the same linguistic capacity com-mon to all human beings (Noam Chomsky called that capacity *gen-erative grammar*, pointing out that thanks to this universal, inborn ability of the human mind a practically infinite number of coherent languages can be formed), so any cultural system at the empirical, sensual level is a concretization of the mental property universal to the human species; one of the many possible permutations in a ma-trix of essential or basic oppositions. An often quoted example of the many applications of Lévi-Strauss's cognitive strategy is his thor-oughly original analysis of kinship systems which, however distinct from each other, are but different patterns woven of the same three invariable relations of consanguinity (siblings), affinity (spouses), and descent (parents–children).

Lévi-Strauss named Marxism, psychoanalysis, and geology as his "three mistresses." What unites these apparently disparate and unconnected fields of scholarship is the distinction they all make between "surface" and "depth" and the effort they take to reconstruct the invisible structure of the second while starting from the empirically accessible data exposed at the first; they all view "surface phenomena" as traces, leftovers, sedimentations, or relics left by "depth processes," and then proceed to model the subterranean forces which can account for their shape and meaning. It is this strategy that became the trademark of Lévi-Strauss's own science of culture: what one can read out of an inventory of cultural usages is the logic of unconscious mind ("modern" and "primitive" alike) in its relentless meaning-constructing activity. Myths, for instance, which James Frazer saw as "word magic" and inchoate attempts to "explain the inexplicable," and which Malinowski treated as "charters of justification for conduct in the present-day situations" and thought to be understandable only in connection with the currently practiced rituals and routines, Lévi-Strauss perceived as, above all, logical models which allow human mind to avoid contradictions; myths, like totems and innumerable other cultural creations, are first and foremost "good for thinking."

In Lévi-Strauss's studies, "culture" stands for the silent activity of unconscious mind that renders the world intelligible by *structuring* it, thereby making it into a legible message. Structuration, in turn, deploys discrimination, inclusion and exclusion, separation and connection as its major stratagems. Structuration is an ongoing process which can be revealed in every dimension and any aspect of human relations. There is no such thing as *the* structure of society or a cultural system as a whole; there is only an unremitting play of differences in every field of social life.

Major Criticisms

According to John Fekete (1984), Lévi-Strauss's "combinative, categorizing unconscious" could be counted among the few ideas which, for the humanities, were "an analogue to the paradigm shifts of modern biology and quantum physics": "as decisive as the shift to the model of the genetic code or Schrödinger's equations." Gyorgy Markus spelled out what the "paradigmatic shift" entailed: namely, "the *antisubjectivist* turn and the *linguistic* turn" – Lévi-Strauss's "structuralism" was an audacious attempt to transcend earlier paradigms of mechanical causality and historical evolution "by finding invariable, structural interconnection that would constitute the constant and 'natural' basis and presupposition of all historical change." Susan Sonntag (1963) introduced Lévi-Strauss to her American readers as "the man who has created anthropology as a total occupation"; intellectually, "a hero of our times."

A prominent role in developing and complementing Lévi-Strauss's essential insights has been played by the British anthropologists Edmund Leach and Mary Douglas. Both focused on the endemic lack of overlap between the logic of structuration and the complexity of experience which resists neat divisions: as a rule, oppositions leave out a wide range of phenomena which do not fit into either of the opposed categories or spread over both sides of the opposition. Such phenomena form an area of (cognitive) ambiguity and (behavioral) ambivalence and tend to be suppressed in order to salvage and protect the communicative function of cultural codes – as in the case of resented and outlawed "blasphemy" (blurring the boundary between sacred and profane) and "profanity" (fogging the distinction between human and animal) analyzed by Edmund Leach, or more generally in the case of all "anomaly" (as Mary Douglas explained, anomaly is a "thing out of order" and therefore an inevitable by-product of all effort to impose purity and clarity upon the varied and confused experience of complex social reality with the help of mutually exclusive categories). Through the work of Douglas and Leach, Lévi-Strauss's insights have acquired direct relevance for the study of the political process and a growing significance in view of present-day neo-tribal urges and exclusionist tendencies.

Bibliography

Eribon, D. (1991) *Conversation with Claude Lévi-Strauss*. Chicago: University of Chicago Press.
Feket, J. (1984) "Descent into the New Maelstrom." In J. Feket (ed.) *The Structural Allegory: Reconstructive Encounters with the New French Thought*. Manchester: Manchester University Press.
Leach, E. (1973) *Claude Lévi-Strauss*. Chicago: University of Chicago Press.
Lévi-Strauss, C. (1971) *Totemism*. Boston: Beacon Press.
Lévi-Strauss, C. (1972) *The Savage Mind*. Chicago: University of Chicago Press.
Lévi-Strauss, C. (1974) *Structural Anthropology* vol. 1. New York: Basic Books.
Lévi-Strauss, C. (1983) *Structural Anthropology* vol. 2. Chicago: University of Chicago Press.
Lévi-Strauss, C. (1990) *The Elementary Structures of Kinship*. Boston: Beacon Press.
Lévi-Strauss, C. (1992) *Tristes Tropiques*. London: Penguin Books.
Lévi-Strauss, C. (1992) *The View from Afar*. Chicago: University of Chicago Press.
Lévi-Strauss, C. (1995) *Myth and Meaning*. New York: Shocken Books.
Lévi-Strauss, C. (1998) *Look, Listen Head*. New York: Basic Books.
Markus, G. "The Paradigm of Language: Wittgenstein, Lévi-Strauss, Gadamer." In *The Structural Allegory*.
Sonntag, S. (1963) Article in *The New York Review of Books*, 7: 6.

31 | **Niklas Luhmann**

Dieter Rucht

Ideas
Functionalism □ Systems theory □ Autopoiesis

Major books
Social Systems (1995)
Die Gesellschaft der Gesellschaft (1997)

Influences
Gehlen □ Husserl □ Malinowski □ Maturana □ Parsons □ Radcliffe-Brown □ Spencer-Brown

---

Biographical Details

Niklas Luhmann was born in Lüneburg, Germany in 1927 and studied law in Freiburg (1946–9). After his practical training and second-step examination in law, he worked for several years in public administration, including the ministry of education of Lower-Saxony (1956–62). In 1960–1 he was granted leave to study administrative sciences and sociology at Harvard University. There he met, and was deeply influenced by, Talcott Parsons. Back in Germany, Luhmann took a post-graduate degree at the School for Administration at Speyer (1962–5) and then became head of a unit at the Dortmund-based Social Science Institute of the University of Münster. In 1966 he did his Ph.D. and a post-Ph.D. (*Habilitation*), based on his already published work, under the mentorship of the sociologists Dieter Claessens and Helmut Schelsky. Two years later he became Professor of Sociology at the newly founded University of Bielefeld, where he spent his academic life until retirement in 1993. Luhmann died in 1998, after having published some 40 books and more than 250 articles.

Key Theoretical Contributions

Luhmann is one of the few sociologists in the second half of the twentieth century who aimed at the construction of a universal theory of society. By the end of the 1960s, after a series of publications focusing on administration, organization, and sociology of law, he concentrated all his energies on the elaboration of such a macro-sociological theory. The most important milestone for this work was the book *Social Systems*, first published in 1984. In 1997 his *magnum opus Die Gesellschaft der Gesellschaft* ("The Society of Society") concluded an impressive effort of theory building. As Luhmann recalls in the preface to this book, when he was asked in 1969 to list his current research projects: "My project was then as it is today: theory of society; duration: 30 years; costs: none" (Luhmann 1997: 11).

Luhmann distanced himself sharply from previous sociological thinking centered around concepts such as "person," "motivation," "means," "ends," etc. To him, it is strange and in fact wrong to view society as composed of people and of relationships between people. He argues that the prevalence of these ideas has blocked the understanding of complex societies and thereby progress in sociological theorizing. Instead, Luhmann deems it necessary to build a highly abstract theory of society based on a specific variant of systems theory. In contrast to Parsons's structural–functional theory, with its emphasis on structure and action, Luhmann promotes a functional–structural theory that stresses the aspects of function and communication. The starting point of this theory, which incorporates partial theories of communication, evolution, and differentiation, is the distinction between system and environment. Systems, such as an organic cell, an economic firm, or society as a whole, perform specific functions based on their structure. By developing and maintaining a structure, a system stabilizes boundaries with its environment. The latter is conceived of as a complex set of contingencies, "everything that is neither necessary nor impossible" (Luhmann 1998a). Systems make certain things happen and thereby exclude other possibilities. They reduce the endless complexity inherent in their environment by specializing on distinct functions. The operations of systems are triggered by environmental conditions and these operations, in turn, modify the environment.

All social systems are composed of communications rather than individuals. While the latter, including their bodies and their psyches, are part of the environment of social systems, the communicative acts of persons, e.g., their conversations, marriages, shopping tours, voting acts, etc., belong to social systems. Society is the most encompassing social system. It therefore has only non-social environments. Society is differentiated into specific social systems such as economy, politics, law, science, art, religion, and love, on each of which Luhmann has written a monograph.

Each societal subsystem is guided by a binary code that makes the crucial difference to the respective system. For example, the code of the economic system is payment/non-payment. What is not expressed in terms of a system's own code is essentially irrelevant information and hence just "noise." In order to orient communication in concrete settings, codes must be specified in the form of "programs." For example, in a very general sense, prizes are programs to tell people what they can (or want to) buy. Similarly, the criminal law is a program to inform people about the consequences of specific illegal actions.

Societal systems include systems at two more specific levels: organization and interaction. Organizations are mechanisms to secure action (in the sense of reducing risks related to the reproduction of the system) and to make binding decisions (in the sense of reducing contingency by excluding other possibilities). Besides explicit rules of entry and exit, organizations imply rules of communication based on programs and decisions. Membership has to be "known" and requires the acceptance of the organization's rules. The conditions of membership, not the performance of roles, are at the center of Luhmann's organizational analysis. Interactions are encounters of physically present actors. Although interaction is usually structured by membership in social systems and organizations, it is more volatile and hardly manifests itself in long-lasting systems. Examples of interaction are the chatting of people sitting around a dinner table and a lecture in a university which, in turn, is an organization belonging to both the social systems of science and education.

Up until the late 1970s Luhmann had emphasized the relationship between systems and their environment; however, in his subsequent writings he turned towards communication within systems. Complex social systems are characterized as "autopoietic." This term, borrowed from the biologists Humberto Maturana and Francisco Varela, means that systems are "operationally closed," "self-referential," and self-reproducing. They follow their own logic and functional imperatives. Their environment is only represented as a theme of communication in the system, and only when the environment is perceived as a problem or threat to the system does it become a theme.

Luhmann is essentially interested in modern societies. These, unlike their forerunners, are not hierarchically but functionally differentiated, without a center or a top. Moreover, they cannot be identified along territorial boundaries but have converged into a world society marked by aspects such as the "full discovery of the globe," the introduction of a common time system, and the differentiation of functional systems with a global communicative reach. In a broad historic perspective this implies a shift from past to future, from identity to difference, and from tradition to contingency. In a world society, identification of people with particular parts of society is of secondary importance only. Functionally differentiated systems such as science and politics are universal because they all observe world society. At the same time, however, they are specific because they all observe according to their specific code.

Besides communication, which Luhmann conceives as a synthesis of three selective acts, namely information, notification (*Mitteilung*), and understanding (*Verstehen*), another key operation of social systems is observation. In modern societies, observation becomes increasingly important and complex, resulting in observation of observations. For example, social sciences observe how another system, say the political system, observes itself by the use of opinion polls and press analyses. Observation of observation is just one of many reflexive mechanisms. Another is learning of learning. It allows systems to cope with different, difficult, and hardly predictable challenges – a mechanism superior to one specialized in dealing with very concrete challenges.

Following his own account of how systems effectively cope with complexity, Luhmann limits his role to offering observations about society. This has at least three implications. First, he specializes on theory building and renounces systematic empirical work. Second, his theory building is highly abstract. It is, as he warns his readers in the foreword of *Social Systems*, a flight "above the clouds, and we must reckon with a rather thick cloud cover" (Luhmann 1995: preface). Only occasionally, and then often in footnotes, does he illustrate his general ideas with very concrete examples, then talking about plum-cake, the role of pee breaks in political decision-making, and other mundane aspects of life. In addition to its high level of abstraction, his theory is also "polycentric" and therefore not easy to overview. It resembles, in Luhmann's own words, a "labyrinth more than a freeway off into the sunset" (ibid). Third, Luhmann, as a sociologist, deliberately abstains from such practical intervention as providing political and moral advice. To him, the search for a "good" or "just" society is part of an "old-European" enterprise and is not only naive because it underestimates the complexity of society, but also fruitless since it relies on the wrong idea of society as a unity that can be steered from a superior vantage point. There is no overarching viewpoint, value, or discourse, because every system is operationally closed. Hence the sociologist can talk only to sociologists. No wonder that Luhmann makes few concessions to popularize his ideas, although he has occasionally published articles in newspapers. He creates his own autopoietic system, using a specific language that is not easily accessible for the average sociologist. While some accept this approach as a logical consequence of differentiation and specialization in all spheres of life, others have criticized it for being closed-minded. This brings us to additional and probably more fundamental criticisms.

Major Criticisms

Luhmann's theorizing, so highly praised by some scholars (e.g., Richard Münch: "sociological enlightenment at its best"; Constans Seyfarth: "the most stimulating theorist in German sociology"), has also attracted a number of harsh criticisms. Three main aspects appear of particular importance.

First, some sociologists are of the opinion that Luhmann offers essentially formal if not empty categories which are not helpful to explain why social reality is as it is. Dirk Käsler, in his review of *Social Systems*, criticizes Luhmann for presenting trivial facts in the guise of a new language. "Hence, behind the facade of unbelievable difficulty and a complicated wheel mechanism of artistic categories there is just a handful of simple sentences" (Käsler 1984: 189–90).

A second criticism is that Luhmann misrepresents, or systematically ignores, important aspects of social reality. Jürgen Habermas, for example, argues that not all spheres of social life can be conceived as systems ruled by a binary code. Moreover, the identification of a system requires the demarcation of boundaries and conditions of survival, which, in some cases, may be an impossible task. Others have blamed Luhmann for neglecting the role of human agency, informal power, and social inequality, thereby providing a purified picture which has little to do with reality (see, for example, Kössler 1998).

Third, and partly related to the latter criticism, several scholars have criticized Luhmann for being inherently conservative or promoting an approach of "inhuman" social engineering in spite of his explicit denial that social science knowledge can be applied to social praxis.

A discussion on whether or not these criticisms are justified is beyond the scope of this short overview. However, there is little doubt that Luhmann presents "a provocation fed by knowledge" (Peter Fuchs, *Die Tageszeitung*, November, 1998) to conventional theorizing along the lines of structural functionalism, neo-Marxism, rational choice, symbolic interactionism, etc. Whereas most adherents of these competing approaches remain unconvinced of Luhmann's theory as *the* key to understanding contemporary societies, virtually all of those who have closely studied his work admire, or at least respect, Luhmann's originality and creativity, the immense breadth of his knowledge, and the systematicity of his approach which, in the eyes of some, represents a masterpiece of theoretical architecture. Even Habermas, who has engaged in the earliest and probably best-known dispute with Luhmann (see Habermas and Luhmann 1971), has adopted some of his opponent's concepts as adequate tools for analyzing certain elements of social reality. Already during his lifetime Luhmann has triggered a number of important debates, as well as books that introduce, interpret, elaborate, and apply his ideas. Although the resonance of his work in various parts of the world is still very uneven, there is a good chance that Luhmann will be counted among the "classics" of theoretical sociology.

Bibliography

Habermas, J. and Luhmann, N. (1971) *Theorie der Gesellschaft oder Sozialtechnologie*. Frankfurt am Main: Suhrkamp.

Käsler, D. (1984) "Soziologie: 'Flug über den Wolken'." *Der Spiegel,* December 10: 184–90.

Kössler, R. (1998) "Weltgesellschaft? Oder: Die Grenzen der Luhmannschen Gesellschaftstheorie." *Soziologische Revue,* 21, 2: 175–83.

Luhmann, N. (1964) *Funktionen und Folgen formaler Organisationen*. Berlin: Duncker and Humblot.

Luhmann, N. (ed.) (1970) *The Differentiation of Society*. New York: Columbia University Press.

Luhmann, N. (1977) *Funktion der Religion*. Frankfurt am Main: Suhrkamp.

Luhmann, N. (1979) *Trust and Power*. Chichester: Wiley.

Luhmann, N. (1985) *A Sociological Theory of Law*. London: Routledge and Kegan Paul.

Luhmann, N. (1988) *Die Wirtschaft der Gesellschaft*. Frankfurt am Main: Suhrkamp.

Luhmann, N. (1989) *Ecological Communication*. Chicago, IL: University of Chicago Press.

Luhmann, N. (1990) *Political Theory in the Welfare State*. Berlin: Walter de Gruyter.

Luhmann, N. (1991) *Wissenschaft der Gesellschaft*. Frankfurt am Main: Suhrkamp.

Luhmann, N. (1993) *Risk: A Sociological Theory*. Berlin: Walter de Gruyter.

Luhmann, N. (1995) *Social Systems*. Stanford, CA: Stanford University Press.

Luhmann, N. (1997) *Die Gesellschaft der Gesellschaft*. Frankfurt am Main: Suhrkamp.

Luhmann, N. (1998a) *Love as Passion: The Codification of Intimacy*. Stanford, CA: Stanford University Press.

Luhmann, N. (1998b) *Observations on Modernity*. Stanford, CA: Stanford University Press.

Luhmann, N. (2000a) *Art as a Social System*. Stanford, CA: Meridian.

Luhmann, N. (2000b) *Politik der Gesellschaft*. Frankfurt am Main: Suhrkamp.

Luhmann, N. (2000c) *The Reality of the Mass Media*. Cambridge: Polity Press.

32 | Jean-François Lyotard

James Williams

Ideas
Libidinal economy □ Postmodern □ Differend □ Sublime □
Inhuman

Major books
Discours, figure (1971)
Économie libidinale (1974)
La Condition postmoderne (1979)
Le Différend (1983)
L' Inhumain (1988)
Political Writings (1993)

Influences
Freud □ Kant □ Marx □ Nietzsche □ Wittgenstein

Biographical Details

Jean-François Lyotard (1924–98) contributed influential theoretical ideas across a wide set of subjects. His work continues to be important in politics, philosophy, sociology, literature, art, and cultural studies. It cannot be viewed as providing a full theory; rather, he provides us with a series of concepts and approaches to problems that allow for important positions to be articulated despite the fact that they are resistant to a final classification within theory. His philosophy seeks forms of expression for those who have been marginalized or silenced, but without having to compromise with the dominant structures or political positions that have failed to hear them. He attempts to explain how there can be claims to justice that defy any given understanding and how conflicts may arise that are completely resistant to just resolutions. Lyotard wrote for the French militant socialist group *Socialisme ou barbarie* from 1956 to 1963. He was an academic in France and the United States, as well as writing books on art and literature.

Key Theoretical Contributions

Lyotard's attempt to reflect upon unbridgeable differences, allied to the political desire to bear witness to that which has been excluded, informs the development of his most influential idea, the postmodern condition. The idea implies a radical fragmentation of society. This philosophy of radical and primary fragmentation is refined from its first definition in *The Postmodern Condition* (1979) to a definition in terms of absolute difference in *The Differend* (1983). The arguments for this radical heterogeneity are based on a basic mapping of society according to the concept of the language game adopted from Wittgenstein's philosophy of language. This is later refined following a rigorous reading of Kant.

The most important theoretical claim in *The Postmodern Condition* is Lyotard's disbelief in metanarratives. He argues against the possibility of justifying the narratives that bring together disparate disciplines and social practices (for example, science, history, and culture) into a single account associated with progress and the elimination of conflicts and differences. Instead, the language games whose rules determine correct moves for given pursuits are heterogeneous and the various genres of discourse that determine the stakes of these pursuits are incommensurable. There are no overarching rules or laws in the postmodern condition and there are no final stakes. So the narratives that we tell to justify a single set of laws and stakes are inherently unjust. Lyotard does not limit this disbelief to a given "postmodern" epoch. For him, all times are postmodern and metanarratives have never been justified. It is the task and capacity of postmodern works, in all times, to trigger our disbelief in given metanarratives.

Lyotard's concern with the marginalized and with people subjected to terror dates back to his earliest work. It finds its most powerful and poignant form in his early essays written for the journal of the *Socialisme ou barbarie*. These essays, reproduced in *Political Writings* (1983), describe and hope to encourage the Algerian fight for independence from France and an Algerian socialist revolution. Lyotard taught in Algeria (Constantine 1952–4) and the failure of mass revolutionary movements had a lasting negative effect on his belief in the possibility of modern socialist revolutions.

In order to combat the nihilism that followed from this failure and from the collapse of the student movements of May 1968 in his university of Nanterre and society at large, Lyotard developed his second philosophical phase: libidinal economics. This marks a further drift away from Marx and Freud, not in the sense of abandoning their works, but in the sense of finally breaking with Marxist and psychoanalytical theoretical and political positions. In addition to Marx and Freud, further influences inform Lyotard's *Libidinal Economy* (1974). These are his lifelong interest in modern art and art history, an innovative reading of Nietzsche, and a development of a philosophy of desire within a structuralist framework, but breaking with orthodox structuralism.

Libidinal Economy was poorly received in Marxist circles and by many other academics and commentators. Lyotard later distanced himself from the book and its incendiary style. Yet the book is perhaps his greatest achievement in attempting to live with modern nihilism through an undermining of the structures associated with subjectivity and teleology. This subversion works through a passivity to libidinal events. These events, the occurrence of intense feelings and desires, energize us and force us away from set patterns and structures. As is often the case in his thought, this passivity is learnt from a reading of key figures in modern art, most notably Cézanne.

The central theoretical term in *Libidinal Economy* is dissimulation. On the one hand, structures conceal or dissimulate libidinal intensities. These intense feelings and desires cannot be handled by the structure without it having to change. So all structures are open to intrinsic changes that they cannot avoid. It is the task of libidinal economists to exploit intensities to encourage such transformations and openness. On the other hand, despite the fact that libidinal intensities are the positive term in libidinal economics, they cannot give rise to a final set of positive goals and hence to a teleology, towards a "pure libidinal society" for instance. This is because the second claim of dissimulation is that there can be no intensities without structures. So the dream of escaping the repressive properties of structures is futile and the only proper aim of libidinal economics is to open structures to intensities with no other purpose or direction, in particular, with no illusions about the necessary return of structure.

Despite the fact that he moved away from *Libidinal Economy*, Lyotard never abandoned experimental and innovative styles in philosophy. Each of his works is not only rewarding for its ideas, but also for the way in which style and ideas are in harmony. This creative approach makes Lyotard's works difficult, but it also ensures that they retain a depth and sensitivity lacking in more prosaic works. For libidinal economics, this means that the style merges different genres and registers in a way that makes them interfere with one another so that no theory or genre comes to dominate. Instead, the point is that libidinal energy comes from this disruptive intervention of external events within structures that seek order and self-containment.

In *The Differend* style reflects heterogeneity and fragmentation through a series of disjointed aphorisms. The central thesis of the book on the importance of unbridgeable differences is defended on the basis of a controversial development of Kant's views on the separation of the faculties of Understanding, Reason, and Judgment. This development depends upon a well-defended inflation of the role of the feeling of the sublime in Kant. This feeling then becomes all-important in Lyotard's aesthetics, philosophy, and politics. It guides the style and content of the majority of the numerous essays written after *The Differend*.

The relation of the sublime to the differend is that the former allows us to testify to the latter despite its paradoxical status as something that can be felt but not understood. A differend is a conflict between two parties that cannot be resolved justly from both points of view. However, given that we can become aware of such conflicts, is that not already a way to their resolution? If we can understand the claims of both parties, then that understanding can act as a preliminary bridge between them. However, the feeling of the sublime is neither an understanding nor a simple feeling that could give rise to a system built upon it. Instead, it is the conjunction of two opposed feelings: attraction (pleasure) and repulsion (pain). In the case of a differend we feel that there is an injustice that demands a remedy, but at the same time we feel that there can be no such resolution. All that remains, then, is to testify to this disabling state against any unjust attempt at resolution.

The point of the later essays, in *The Inhuman* (1988), is to deploy the feeling of the sublime against rational ideas moving towards consensus. For example, the sublime intimation of the inhuman as something to fear, but also as something infinitely precious and to seek out, is deployed against cosmopolitan ideas of humanity. Even the idea of humanity involves exclusions and closure. It is the task of the philosopher to testify for the inhuman against the final dominance of the idea of humanity, not to eliminate the idea, but to temper it and open it to its other.

Major Criticisms

There are three major criticisms of Lyotard's work. Each coincides with a school of thought. Jacques Derrida and Jean-Luc Nancy have written deconstructions of Lyotard's work (Derrida 1992; Nancy 1985). They focus on Lyotard's postmodern work and on *The Differend* in particular. A differend depends upon a distinction drawn between groups that itself depends upon the heterogeneity of language games and genres of discourse. Why should these differences be privileged over an endless division and reconstitution of groups? In concentrating on specific differences, Lyotard's thought becomes overly dependent on differences between categories that are given as fixed and well defined. From the point of view of deconstruction, Lyotard's philosophy gives too much credit to illegitimate categories and groups. Underlying any differend there is a multiplicity of further differences; some of these will involve crossing the first divide, others will question the integrity of the groups that were originally separated.

Manfred Frank (1988) has put the Frankfurt School criticism best. It attacks Lyotard's search for division over consensus on the grounds that it involves a philosophical mistake with serious political and social repercussions. Lyotard has failed to notice that an underlying condition for consensus is also a condition for the successful communication of his own thought. It is a "performative contradiction" to give an account that appeals to our reason on behalf of a difference that is supposed to elude it. So, in putting forward a false argument against rational consensus, Lyotard plays into the hands of the irrational forces that often give rise to injustice and differends. Worse, he is then only in a position to testify to that injustice, rather than put forward a just and rational resolution.

From a Nietzschean and Deleuzian point of view (Williams 2000), Lyotard's postmodern philosophy returns to the destructive modern nihilism that his early work avoids. The differend and the sublime are negative terms that introduce a severe pessimism at the core of Lyotard's philosophy. Both terms draw lines that cannot be crossed and yet they mark the threshold of that which is most valuable for the philosophy, that which is to be testified to and its proper concern. It is not possible repetitively to lend an ear to the sublime without falling into despair due to its fleeting nature. Whenever we try to understand or even memorize the activity of testimony through the sublime, it can only be as something that has now dissipated and that we cannot capture.

Bibliography

Bennington, G. (1988) *Lyotard Writing the Event*. Manchester: Manchester University Press.

Derrida, J. (1992) "Before the Law." Trans. A. Ronell in D. Attridge (ed.) *Acts of Literature*. London: Routledge.

Frank, M. (1988) *Die Grenzen der Verständigung. Ein Geistesgespräch zwischen Lyotard und Habermas*. Frankfurt: Suhrkamp.

Lyotard J.-F. (1971) *Discours, figure*. Paris: Klincksiek.
Lyotard J.-F. (1974) *Économie libidinale*. Paris: Minuit. Trans. I. Grant, *Libidinal Economy*. London: Athlone Press, 1993.
Lyotard J.-F. (1979) *La Condition postmoderne*. Paris: Minuit. Trans. G. Bennington and B. Massumi, *The Postmodern Condition: A Report on Knowledge*. Manchester: Manchester University Press, 1984.
Lyotard J.-F. (1983) *Le Différend*. Paris: Minuit. Trans G. van Den Abeele, *The Differend: Phrases in Dispute*. Manchester: Manchester University Press, 1988.
Lyotard J.-F. (1988) *L'Inhumain: causeries sur le temps*. Paris: Galilée. Trans. G. Bennington and R. Bowlby, *The Inhuman: Reflections on Time*. Cambridge: Polity Press, 1991.
Lyotard J.-F. (1993) *Political Writings*, ed. B. Readings and P. Geiman. London: UCL.
Nancy, J.-L. (1985) "Dies Irae." In J. Derrida (ed.) *La Faculté de juger*. Paris: Minuit.
Readings, B. (1991) *Introducing Lyotard: Art and Politics*. London: Routledge.
Williams, J. (1998) *Lyotard: Towards a Postmodern Philosophy*. Cambridge: Polity Press.
Williams, J. (2000) *Lyotard and the Political*. London: Routledge .

33 | Herbert Marcuse

Jem Thomas

Ideas
Surplus repression □ Performance principle □ One dimensional
man □ Negation □ Repressive tolerance □ Totalitarian
democracy

Major books
Reason and Revolution (1941)
Eros and Civilization (1955)
Soviet Marxism (1958)
One Dimensional Man (1964)
Repressive Tolerance (1965)
Five Lectures (1969)
The Aesthetic Dimension (1978)

Influences
Freud □ Hegel □ Heidegger □ Marx □ Sartre

Biographical Details

Of all the critical theorists of the Frankfurt School, Herbert Marcuse
achieved the greatest fame, or notoriety. In the late 1960s and the 1970s
he became known as the preeminent theorist of the New Left and the
student movements of Germany, France, and the USA. In the media he
was associated, unfairly, with much of the political disruption and some
of the excesses of those years, leading to a reaction against his work that
has obscured many of his achievements until comparatively recently.

Herbert Marcuse was born in Berlin in 1898 and died in Starnberg,
Germany, in 1979, but from 1934 onwards he spent most of his life in
the United States. Just after World War I, Marcuse was a member of a

German Soldiers' Revolutionary Council, which he soon abandoned when officers were allowed to join. He was a member of the radical SPD, but soon left that too. During studies in the late 1920s he came under the influence of the philosopher Martin Heidegger, whose importance he never repudiated, though he broke with him personally after World War II.

Marcuse joined the Institut für Sozialforschung (Institute for Social Research), popularly known as the Frankfurt School, in 1932. He went almost at once into exile with them, first briefly in Geneva, then in the United States. Unlike some others, Marcuse did not return to Germany after the war, and when he visited Frankfurt in 1956, the young Jürgen Habermas was surprised to discover that he was a key member of the Institute.

Between 1943 and 1950 Marcuse worked in US Government Service, rising to the position of Bureau Chief in the State Department. These years gave him a command over empirical material about postwar European, Soviet, and American social developments that was occasionally lacking in other critical theorists and which helped form the basis of his book *Soviet Marxism* (1958).

Subsequently, Marcuse worked in Brandeis University from 1958 to 1965, then at the University of California until his retirement. It was during his time at Brandeis that he wrote his most famous work, *One Dimensional Man* (1964).

Key Theoretical Contributions

Two aspects of Marcuse's work are of particular importance; firstly, his use of a language more familiar from the critique of Soviet or Nazi regimes to characterize developments in the advanced industrial world; and secondly, his grounding of critical theory in a particular use of psychoanalytic thought. Both these features of his thinking have often been misunderstood and have given rise to critiques of his work that miss the point of his targets.

Marcuse's analysis of modernity

Marcuse's main works often seem to blur the boundaries between capitalist liberal democracies and the repressive regimes of Nazism and communism. Political liberalism is "repressive tolerance" (Marcuse 1965b), the social changes that brought more relaxed attitudes to sexuality and women's social position are a "repressive desublimation" (Marcuse 1964).

Democracy itself is "totalitarian democracy"; part of a "totalitarian technological society" (Marcuse 1968) and, moreover, it is a society "without opposition" (Marcuse 1964). In fact, Marcuse was well aware of the crucial differences between the Western democracies and the Nazism he had fled, or the Soviet system he had studied and whose distortions of the Marxist vision he had exposed in *Soviet Marxism*. He declared that bourgeois democracies were "infinitely better" (Marcuse 1978–9: 148) than authoritarian regimes and, even in his critique of tolerance, stated that censorship was invariably wrong and that democratic tolerance was always better than institutionalized intolerance (Marcuse 1965b: 89, 99). As early as 1947 he maintained that the Western democracies had a legitimacy that the Soviet Union lacked, precisely through the ability of the former to provide for their citizens, and the inability of the latter to build a social order that was freer or happier than the capitalist world.

How are we to understand this particular use of language? Marcuse was haunted, almost throughout his career, by the fear of fascism. In his 1947 theses on the postwar situation he thought that the contradictions within capitalism were tending towards fascism, not socialism (Marcuse 1998: 222) and that the Western states would progressively eliminate the achievements of bourgeois democracy. A second bourgeois revolution would be needed to defend the classic bourgeois rights (Marcuse 1978–9: 148). Although briefly a more optimistic note was to enter his work in the late 1960s and early 1970s in response to the student movement, the burgeoning women's movement, and the growth of civil rights protest in America, the dominant tone of his work remained haunted by the sense that social life under conditions of late modernity is in grave danger, is in an emergency situation. In 1954, in the epilogue to *Reason and Revolution*, he maintained that the tendency to totalitarianism had not been prevented by the retreat of Nazism and his unpublished writings from the early 1970s reveal that he continued to believe that a neofascist phase of capitalism might reemerge (Marcuse 2001).

The point is that, in spite of his continued and abiding recognition of the actual differences between capitalist and authoritarian regimes, he wanted his readers to understand the skull beneath the skin, the fundamentally distorted and damaging character of life in modern, liberal capitalism, and the huge difficulties that there are in conceptualizing those distortions and opposing them.

The difficulties in opposing them come about because the working classes can no longer be considered a revolutionary subject, capable of overthrowing capitalism. The proletariat in Marxist theory has an absolute need to overthrow capitalism in order to have anything approximating to a human existence. Its poverty and desperation means that it must visualize an end to the system – rendering it a potentially revolutionary class. But the working classes of late modernity are in nothing like this situation, they have undergone an embourgeoisement and are increasingly integrated into the productive system. Marcuse put this view forward as early as 1947 and it lies at the heart of his great work *One Dimensional Man*. The way of life is a "good way of life – much better than before" (Marcuse 1964: 12). There are really two points here: first, the working classes increasingly cooperate in their own exploitation precisely because the collaboration is generating an enormous wealth in which they have a stake; secondly, at the same time, it increasingly becomes identified culturally with the class of its exploiters. A working class of hard manual labor is a minority and has given way to a proletariat that includes a large middle class, whose tastes, income, education, and culture merge imperceptibly into that of the bourgeoisie. Any revolutionary forces are either hopelessly dispersed throughout society or else pushed to the margins. This identification with the ruling class means that the character of the proletariat becomes an affirmative, not a "negative" one.

These two tendencies mean that a modern society of organized capitalism works by generating and satisfying false needs. These needs are primarily those for the endless, glittering array of consumer goods paraded before a public whose greed is ever regenerated through advertising and the culture industry. But the false needs run deeper than that, because the world of consumption works on preformed identities. The agent in a modern administered society is no longer strictly speaking a subject, if by "subject" is meant a stable essence capable of entering a wide range of relationships. Instead, privacy, the crucial condition for forming a personality, fighting out conflicts, engaging with others, is hopelessly vitiated by the commodification of sexuality, the fracturing of families, and the insistent invasion of technologies of persuasion into all spheres of life. The selves that we all are as agents are in a sense very similar to the psychoanalyst Winnicott's (1986) false selves, adopted because the emotional space to develop a true self has never been made available.

These views were best dealt with in *One Dimensional Man* but were present in Marcuse's unpublished writings very much earlier. Modernity has become an organized capitalism, an administered society able to stabilize itself by this integration of the working classes and by a massive development of the technologies of destruction and of mass culture. The technologies of destruction play an important double role: an economic one of providing a focus of employment, technological development and investment, and a psychological one through the way that they encourage the perpetual play of aggressive instincts through our culture.

The hugely overdeveloped wealth and technology of the modern world make it theoretically possible to abolish most work, to reduce the labor time socially necessary to reproduce social existence and provide people with the genuine leisure and privacy to develop themselves as free, creative subjects. Instead, modern identity is dominated by the performance principle. It is an essentially alienated identity, geared to work, to productivity, to competitiveness and achievement, and to accumulation. In other words, just at the point at which society might reduce the repressive burdens of the work ethic, whose foundations in Protestantism have long been eroded, it instead intensifies what Marcuse calls surplus repression. All social life involves some form of repression, understood in the Freudian way as the renunciation of immediate gratification, but the modern world entails overcoming scarcity under circumstances of social domination, so that the demands on modern citizens to give up their aspirations to a fulfilling and authentically happy life are greater than in the past. In Freudian terms, the modern world works by continually activating and manipulating the fundamental drives, most notably the death instincts. Aggression, competitiveness, envy, and destructiveness are mobilized as the main engines of continued production and expansion – modernity, almost literally, plays with the Devil.

This account of modernity is vulnerable to the criticism, made most forcibly by Alisdair MacIntyre (1970), that these theories are self-referentially inconsistent. If the modern world deprives its citizens of full subjectivity, enslaves them to false needs, manipulates them into high competitiveness, while cutting off the possibility of their formulating a critique of their situation, then how can Marcuse know? How can he avoid himself being so caught up in modernity that he fails to see its inherently totalitarian character beneath the surface? The critique is overstated. Marcuse made it quite clear that he was "projecting these tendencies" (Marcuse 1964: xlix) not describing a completed process, and further that the aesthetic tradition of great art contained a potential space for a critical, negative perspective on the contemporary world that had not yet vanished (Marcuse 1978). Even so, the criticism is well made, and all the Frankfurt School are vulnerable to it, but in an important way Marcuse is the least so, because of his particular use of psychoanalytic theory.

Eros and critical theory

Although *One Dimensional Man* remains Marcuse's best-known work, perhaps his most important book was *Eros and Civilization* (1955). In it he laid the foundations for the critique of modernity present in his account of advanced industrial society and also outlined the basis from which critical theory works, and to which he was to return at the end of his life. Marcuse borrowed from Freud the idea that there are two fundamental drives underpinning all human action. One drive is the life instinct, Eros, the other is the death instinct, Thanatos. The two are in a dynamic relationship; if one is repressed or contracts, then the other expands to take its place. Eros is far more than sex. Sex, in conditions of late modernity, is in any event commodified and can be imbued with a deathly destructiveness, for example in sado-masochism. Instead, Eros is the drive to form relations with other people ("object relations" in the language of modern psychoanalysis); it is a drive towards intimacy, privacy, quiet, tenderness, peace and, to some extent, solidarity (Marcuse 2001). Of course it expresses itself through sexual desire and the sexual act, but it is present too, sublimated, in human cooperation, friendship, love, and in the sensuous desire to create and sustain a pleasant environment. Precisely what was ghastly in Nazism was that it substituted a solidarity built around the death instinct, Thanatos, for erotic solidarity. Its bonds were those of shared aggression and cruelty. As capitalism continues its remorseless expansion, one which Marcuse rightly predicted would eventually embrace Russia and China, so it, too, endlessly mobilizes aggressive tendencies, while also leaving them frustrated and unsatisfied.

Freud is in some ways the most important influence on Marcuse; his instinct theory had an "explosive content" Marcuse claimed towards the end of his life (Marcuse 1978–9: 127). It is this instinct theory that makes possible critical theory's "negative" approach to modernity, its insistence that the quantitative accounting present in the market's calculability is not to be confused with rationality *per se*. Human beings are material beings with definite needs. It is always possible, Marcuse says, to distinguish true from false needs; the key is simply that it is better to live than not to live, and it is better to live well than to live badly (ibid: 136–7; Marcuse 1964: 228). There is therefore in human beings an indestructible demand for happiness, grounded in their very physical organization; in the end, it is simply not possible rationally to will evil. Rationality, for Marcuse, precisely is those intellectual and social operations which expand the human capacity for happiness, for those lie at the core of human nature. At the very end of his life, Jürgen Habermas, representing the second generation of the Frankfurt School, suggested that rationality is based in the discursive formation of the will. Marcuse explicitly repudiated this position, insisting instead that reason is rooted in Eros, the life instincts, in the containment of destructiveness and the expansion of the scope for human connection.

Eros is repressed in modernity, aggression has expanded, and the failure of earlier attempts at social revolution lies in their failure to expand the capacity for sensuality and freedom in the very substratum of human character (Marcuse 2001). Nevertheless, although it is repressed, Eros survives, as it were underground. As a fundamental feature of human nature it is indestructible and continues as a cooperative, solidary sensuality, which can always form the nucleus of another environment (ibid). And it also forms the basis of critical theory itself, the point from which it is possible to formulate an alternative vision of the world and, negatively, a critique of this one; the point from which we can make "the great refusal." No matter how "one dimensional," we *all* can potentially sense the damage in the world, from the standpoint of those parts of our lives which contain the sublimated sensuality, and the longing, which Marcuse, following Freud, called "erotic." A keen gardener will endure scratched arms and an aching back, but enjoy the hours of work that allow her to create a rich, beautiful, and vibrant environment. What is practiced in miniature in a postage-stamp garden expresses the basic drive, which, rationalized and reflected on, exposes the essential inhumanity of advanced capitalism.

Major Criticisms

Looking back on Marcuse's work more than two decades after his death both his greatness and his limitations are becoming clearer. The publication of his previously unpublished papers (Marcuse 1998, 2001) is considerably facilitating a scholarly reappraisal of his achievements.

Marcuse's critique of affluence, as itself the very source of environmental and personal destructiveness and inauthenticity, led him to see social revolution as necessarily an economically backward step. In 1947 he saw the movement towards socialism as a "leap into a lower standard of living," one whose consequences would not all be benign: "in many instances, the technical machinery would remain unused. A backwards movement would begin, which ... would also bring poverty and affliction" (Marcuse 1998: 225). Later, he was to place more emphasis on the revolution as a long slow process of global disintegration, perhaps lasting a century or more (Marcuse 1978–9: 152; 2001: 159). And he also emphasized how much it was a matter of conceiving of new ways to live, rather than a superseding of what was already there. Nevertheless, it is difficult to see how a critique of superabundance can do anything but imply material loss. But that poses a problem: it is difficult to say that life can be poorer but better, in circumstances where "better" is widely understood to mean "richer." When, on his own admission, political and social legitimacy rests on the idea that the system delivers the goods, enormous difficulties are placed in the path of advocates of change. This sort of consideration has led some critics to caution against the utopian tendency in Marcuse's thinking. Jameson, for example, objects to Marcuse's vision of a world free from aggression, "that there is always the possibility that such a society is precisely impossible" (Jameson 1971: 115). Although well taken, criticism of Marcuse's utopian tendency can also underestimate the difficulty inherent in posing a critique of affluence as social and psychological limitation.

The role of psychoanalytic categories in Marcuse's thought has been sharply criticized. For instance, Chodorow (1989) believed his very use of drive theory, rather than object relations theory, committed him to seeing sociability as unnecessary. It resulted, she claims, in his theorizing liberation as freedom *from* relationships, rather than the development of liberated relations. While this partly underestimates the way Marcuse uses drive theory, nevertheless his handling of the notion of the instincts, especially the death instinct, is not always secure. He explicitly sees Eros as the formation of object relations, what the French psychoanalyst André Green (1999) has called "objectalisation." Sometimes Marcuse conceives the death instinct, logically, as the opposite, as what Green called "désobjectalisation," refusing, destroying, leaving personal relations. But for much of the time he thinks of the death instinct not as the opposite of the life instinct, but as a sort of ghastly perversion of it, or in fusion with it. That is, as aggression, destruction, and cruelty, around which social relations can form, as, indeed, they did in Nazism. Conceived this way, the death instinct can be controlled by Eros, Marcuse's very definition of rationality, but then it too could enjoy an underground existence, ready at all times to call to account the achievements of civilization. But thinking of the death instinct in the other way, as a withdrawal of emotional investment in relationships, implies a quite different pathology of capitalism, one of social isolation, apathy, and loss. In other words, if capitalist societies do indeed depend on the constant revocation of the death instincts, the price to be paid might not be in competition and conflict, but in loneliness and defeat.

Bibliography

Alford, C. (1985) *Science and the Revenge of Nature: Marcuse and Habermas.* Gainesville: University of Florida Press.

Bokina, J. and Lukes, T. (eds.) (1994) *Marcuse: New Perspectives.* Lawrence: University of Kansas Press.

Brunkhorst, H. and Koch, G. (1987) *Herbert Marcuse zur Einführung* [Herbert Marcuse: An Introduction]. Hamburg: Junius Verlag.

Chodorow, N. (1989) *Feminism and Psychoanalytic Theory.* New Haven, CT:

Yale University Press.
Geoghegan, V. (1981) *Reason and Eros: The Social Theory of Herbert Marcuse*. London: Pluto Press.
Green, A. (1999) *The Work of the Negative*. London: Free Association Books.
Jameson, F. (1971) *Marxism and Form: Twentieth-Century Dialectical Theories of Literature*. Princeton, NJ: Princeton University Press.
Katz, B. (1982) *Herbert Marcuse and the Art of Liberation*. London: New Left Books.
Kellner, D. (1984) *Herbert Marcuse and the Crisis of Marxism*. Berkeley: University of California Press.
Lind, P. (1985) *Marcuse and Freedom*. Beckenham: Croom Helm.
MacIntyre, A. (1970) *Marcuse*. London: Fontana/Collins.
Marcuse, H. (1932) *Hegels Ontologie und die Grundlegung einer Theorie der Geschichtlichkeit* [Hegel's Ontology and the Foundation of a Theory of Historicity]. Frankfurt am Main: Klostermann.
Marcuse, H. (1941) *Reason and Revolution: Hegel and the Rise of Social Theory*. New York: Oxford University Press.
Marcuse, H. (1955) *Eros and Civilization: A Philosophical Inquiry into Freud*. Boston: Beacon Press.
Marcuse, H. (1958) *Soviet Marxism: A Critical Analysis*. New York: Columbia University Press.
Marcuse, H. (1964) *One Dimensional Man: Studies in the Ideology of Advanced Industrial Society*. Boston: Beacon Press.
Marcuse, H. (1965a) *Kultur und Gesellschaft I and II* [Culture and Society, 2 vols.]. Frankfurt am Main: Suhrkamp.
Marcuse, H. (1965b) "Repressive Tolerance." In R. P. Wolff, B. Moore, and H. Marcuse, *A Critique of Pure Tolerance*. Boston: Beacon Press.
Marcuse, H. (1968a) *Negations: Essays in Critical Theory*. Boston: Beacon Press.
Marcuse, H. (1968b) *Psychoanalyse und Politik* [Psychoanalysis and Politics]. Frankfurt am Main: Europäische Verlagsanstalt.
Marcuse, H. (1969a) *An Essay on Liberation*. Boston: Beacon Press.
Marcuse, H. (1969b) *Five Lectures: Psychoanalysis, Politics and Utopia*. Boston: Beacon Press.
Marcuse, H. (1972) *Counterrevolution and Revolt*. Boston: Beacon Press.
Marcuse, H. (1973) *Studies in Critical Philosophy*. Boston: Beacon Press.
Marcuse, H. (1978) *The Aesthetic Dimension: Towards a Critique of Marxist Aesthetics*. Boston: Beacon Press.
Marcuse, H. (1979a) *Schriften Band 3: Aufsätze aus der "Zeitschrift für Sozialforschung"* [Writings Vol. 3: Essays from the "Journal for Social Research"]. Frankfurt am Main: Suhrkamp/KNO.
Marcuse, H. (1979b) *Schriften Band 5: Triebstruktur und Gesellschaft* [Writings Vol. 5: The Structure of the Drives and Society]. Frankfurt am Main: Suhrkamp/KNO.
Marcuse, H. (1984) *Schriften Band 8: Aufsätze und Vorlesungen 1948–1969. Versuch über die Befreiung* [Writings Vol. 8: Essays and Lectures 1948–1969: Considerations of Liberation]. Frankfurt am Main: Suhrkamp/KNO.
Marcuse, H. (1987) *Schriften Band 9: Konterrevolution und Revolte / Zeit-*

Messungen | Die Permanenz der Kunst [Writings Vol. 9: Counterrevolution and Revolt / Assessments of the Times / The Permanence of Art]. Frankfurt am Main: Suhrkamp/KNO.

Marcuse, H. (1989a) *Schriften Band 2: Hegels Ontologie und die Theorie der Geschichtlichkeit* [Writings Vol. 2: Hegel's Ontology and the Theory of Historicity]. Frankfurt am Main: Suhrkamp/KNO.

Marcuse, H. (1989b) *Schriften Band 4: Vernunft und Revolution. Hegel und die Entstehung der Gesellschaftstheorie* [Writings Vol. 4: Reason and Revolution: Hegel and the Emergence of Social Theory]. Frankfurt am Main: Suhrkamp/KNO.

Marcuse, H. (1989c) *Schriften Band 6: Die Gesellschaftslehre des sowjetischen Marxismus* [Writings Vol. 6: The Social Theory of Soviet Marxism]. Frankfurt am Main: Suhrkamp/KNO.

Marcuse, H. (1989d) *Schriften Band 7: Der eindimensionale Mensch Studien zur Ideologie der fortgeschrittenen Industriegesellschaft* [Writings Vol. 7: One Dimensional Man: Studies in the Ideology of Advanced Industrial Society]. Frankfurt am Main: Suhrkamp/KNO.

Marcuse, H. (1998) *Technology, War and Fascism: Collected Papers of Herbert Marcuse, Vol. 1,* ed. D. Kellner. London: Routledge.

Marcuse, H. (2001) *Towards a Critical Theory of Society: Collected Papers of Herbert Marcuse, Vol. 2,* ed. D. Kellner. London: Routledge.

Marcuse, H., Habermas, J., Lubasz, H., and Spengler, T. (1978–9) "Theory and Politics: A Discussion." *Telos,* 38: 124–53.

Martineau, A. (1986) *Herbert Marcuse's Utopia.* Montreal: Harvest House.

Pippin, R., Feenberg, A., and Webel, C. (eds.) (1987) *Marcuse: Critical Theory and the Promise of Utopia.* South Hadley, MA: Bergin and Garvey Press.

Schoolman, M. (1980) *The Imaginary Witness.* New York: Free Press.

Winnicott, D. (1986) *Home is Where We Start From.* Harmondsworth: Penguin Books.

34 | Claus Offe

John S. Dryzek

Ideas
Contradiction □ Crisis □ Decommodification □ Disorganization
□ New social movements □ Transition

Major books
Strukturprobleme des Kapitalistischen Staates (1972)
Contradictions of the Welfare State (1984)
Disorganized Capitalism (1985)
Modernity and the State: East, West (1996)
Varieties of Transition: The East European and East German Experience (1996)

Influences
Habermas □ Luhmann □ Marx

Biographical Details

As a student at the Free University of Berlin from 1960 to 1965, Claus Offe became steeped in leftist thinking, and much of his work, at least until the early 1980s, takes its bearings from Marxism. However, Offe was never a Marxist in any simple sense (especially when it came to his theory of the state), and the Marxist influence fades in his later writings. In 1965 Offe went to Frankfurt to work with Habermas, who shared an interest in the politics of higher education; this association lasted for a decade. Offe has held university positions at Frankfurt, the Max Planck Institute (Starnberg), Bielefeld, Bremen, and Humboldt (Berlin), though he is equally at home in the English-speaking world. Offe's work has often engaged empirical social science, as well as ranging widely across bodies of theory as diverse as rational choice and systems theory.

Key Theoretical Contributions

Claus Offe came to prominence – especially in the English-speaking world – as an analyst of the contradictions of the (Keynesian) welfare state, and is perhaps the most important theorist of the welfare state. His first book on these themes was *Strukturprobleme des Kapitalistischen Staates* (1972). More widely known and influential are the essays collected in *Contradictions of the Welfare State* (1984). The analysis of the contradictions of the welfare state was originally framed in a systems-theoretic vocabulary taken from Luhmann.

Offe developed his account of these contradictions in the 1970s, anticipating the various crises of, and attacks upon, the welfare state that would occur in the 1980s in many developed countries. Moving beyond simple Marxist theories that locate contradictions in the capitalist economy itself, and treat the state as the instrument of the ruling class, Offe argues that the welfare state – the primary device that was developed to defuse the contradictions of capitalism – is itself crisis-prone. Defining a contradiction as "the tendency inherent within a specific mode of production to destroy those very preconditions on which its survival depends" (Offe 1984: 132), Offe argues that the contradiction of the welfare state lies in its simultaneous drives toward commodification and decommodification. Decommodification involves management of the disruptive effects of capitalism through massive state interventions, especially in social policy. These interventions stabilize and legitimize; the contradiction arises because they also undermine incentives to work and business profitability.

Offe believes that contradiction produces only "crisis tendencies," such that there is little or no prospect of the demise of the welfare state, still less of capitalism. He is skeptical of the program of the New Right to roll back the state, because the welfare state remains essential to capitalism. However, the degree to which the New Right was subsequently able to "commodify" relationships within the welfare state (through devices such as internal markets) may have surprised him. More feasible than the program of the New Right was, he believed, the extension of corporatism to encompass peak-level management of contradictions by representatives of business, labor, and the executive branch of government. Again, however, he was in the end skeptical because corporatist bargains are necessarily skewed in favor of business against labor, tend to impose their costs on third parties (such as consumers), and bypass constitutional processes. As such, corporatism threatens to exacerbate the legitimation problems of the state.

The welfare state is part of the institutional complex whereby anarchical capitalism was transformed into organized capitalism. Offe's writings in the 1970s and early 1980s try to capture the ways these very institutions become disorganized. The essays collected in *Disorganized Capitalism* (1985a) emphasize how this disorganization is manifested in the labor market and in structures of interest representation. Offe believes that changes in the nature of work, its declining centrality to individuals' lives, rising unemployment, and increasing differentiation of workers' interests all mean that the labor market is finding it increasingly difficult to reconcile its dual functions of distributing income and allocating the resource of labor power. Moreover, the institutions that once intervened to compensate for capital's domination in the labor market (unions, interest intermediation, and government) are finding it increasingly difficult to maintain any balance.

For Offe, the advantage when it comes to both the labor market and the state is always held by capital. He is scathing about liberal social scientists who assume equality across different so-called interest groups. This assumption ignores the reality of social class, and the "two logics of collective action" (Offe and Wiesenthal 1980) that apply to each. While capital finds it easy to associate and act instrumentally, labor unions have to respond to and organize the entire range of their members' needs. This underscores the bias of both liberal social scientists and liberal institutions that treat capital and labor alike. Offe notes too that even such surface neutrality is not being sustained by the liberal state, which increasingly intervenes to try to shape "interest groups," corporatism being only the most extreme example in the way it disciplines labor. Once the institutions of the liberal state are seen to be unfair, their legitimacy is undermined.

Offe's critique of welfare capitalism initially neither proceeded from, nor really developed, any normative vantage point; nor does he search for any privileged historical subject such as the proletariat in Marxism. He states the central role of social science in terms of the need for critique, especially of those social relations that liberal social science wrongly treats as immutable. But Offe is not a critical theorist in the Habermasian sense, either in terms of the epistemological categories of the earlier Habermas, or the later critical theory of communications (though eventually Offe did contemplate the question of how Habermasian discourse ethics might be promoted in political practice).

The task of the critical social scientist ends, for Offe, at exposure. Yet he does have political commitments, and obviously cares about the program of European social democracy when it comes to the strategic choices of political parties and labor unions. By the beginning of the 1980s he was applauding the arrival of new social movements (such as feminism, environmentalism, peace and anti-nuclear struggles) and their role in the reconfiguration of a less statist progressive politics. Indeed, he was one of the most acute analysts of these movements, characterizing them in terms of the non-economic and non-negotiable character of their demands, the quite privileged (new middle class) location of many of their activists, the kind of spontaneous actions they engaged in, and their "selective radicalization of modern values" (Offe 1985b). Though these movements highlight the degree to which deradicalized social democratic parties have lost their capacity to facilitate the coexistence of capitalism and democracy, they are seen as contributing to the learning capacities of society as a whole, rather than presaging any kind of revolution.

New social movements might form an alliance, Offe hoped, with democratic socialism, constituting perhaps a "non-bureaucratic, decentralized, and egalitarian model of a self-reliant 'welfare society'" (Offe 1984 157), with a revitalized public sphere. Offe (1996b: 88) looks forward to multidimensional and paragovernmental "societal self-regulation" coexisting with the welfare state, helping to compensate for the state's loss of agency and declining capacity as the demands upon it increase. His normative theory of the state becomes quite pluralistic. Such developments would help ward off market liberal deregulation (though he regards individualization as an ineluctable structural force).

By the 1990s this work connected to themes of deliberative democracy and social capital in political theory. Declaring sympathy for a "left-liberal" or civic republican democratic theory in opposition to the "libertarian" (or liberalism proper) alternative, he asked what "supportive institutional conditions" might create competent citizens who could rise above selfish preferences (Offe 1997: 103).

His enthusiasm for social movements did not mean, then, that Offe turned his back on the state. In the 1980s and 1990s he continued to devote a great deal of effort to ways in which the welfare state and social policy could be reformed in order to cope with changing conditions, such as the declining importance of work – which in his view backed the need for the state to provide a guaranteed basic income (Offe 1996b). He continued to regard the welfare state as both necessary and desirable, but part of the argument for a basic income is that it would involve simplification, hence an unburdening of the welfare state.

Come the demise of the Soviet bloc, Offe quickly turned his attention to post-communist societies, arguing that they, too, would have to develop an effective welfare state and social policy to cope with the pain of transition. Though accepting that liberal democracy was now the universal political model, he never shared in any celebration of the "end of history" – indeed, his first major work on Eastern Europe bore the title of *Der Tunnel am Ende des Lichts* – the tunnel at the end of the light (much of which appeared in English in Offe 1996c). Offe's work on post-communist societies covers topics as varied as property restitution as the most defensible way to convert state socialism into capitalism, retrospective justice for communist-era crimes, the ills of ethnic politics, and the implications of the demise of the Soviet bloc for the program of the left in the West.

Offe was quick to point out that post-communism meant not a single transition, but a "triple transition": one of the economic system, one of the political system, and a third concerning the identity of the nation-state (in terms of territoriality and ethnicity). Each of these transitions could cause trouble for the other two. His later work on Eastern Europe emphasized how institutional redesign might cope with these sorts of difficulties. Offe brought to bear sophisticated conceptions of institutions and the need for transformations to be appropriate to political traditions of particular societies, because the meaning actors ascribe to institutions is crucial. He criticized the hyperrationalist approach to institutional redesign followed in some post-communist countries (see Offe 1996a). He also developed a sophisticated analysis of the various kinds of cleavages that arose in post-communist societies and their relationship to each other and to the prospects for (liberal) democratic consolidation. He notes that liberal democracies are much better at processing socioeconomic conflicts than differences concerning favored regime type (old versus new) or (ethnic) identity – and here any lingering Marxism has by now thoroughly disappeared from his analysis. Thus the kind of conflict that is easiest to process is the rarest in post-communist societies, because of the lack of clarity concerning socioeconomic interest that the communist era bequeathed (see Offe's chapter 7 in Elster. Offe and Preuss 1999).

Major Criticisms

Claus Offe is a moving target, having engaged many substantive topics and bodies of theory (indeed, one might question his eclecticism and willingness to abandon earlier commitments). Economists might criticize his sweeping formulations that deal with economic topics but are not grounded in economic theory. Market liberals would argue that experience in the Anglo-American countries since the 1980s shows that the welfare state can indeed be rolled back with no dire consequences. Offe's skepticism about corporatist solutions to the contradictions of the welfare state is called into question by the fact that corporatist states have done much more than any others when it comes to delivering social justice (and, at least until the late 1990s, economic prosperity).

Offe is perhaps better at discovering tunnels than in finding lights, in the West no less than in the East. His language of "crisis tendencies" seems to downgrade the degree to which crises might also involve opportunities for transformation. Critical theorists might be frustrated by the extent to which his work stops short at exposure of contradictions, and the associated lack of development of any intimation that enlightenment might lead to remedial action.

Bibliography

Elster, J., Offe, C., and Preuss, U. K. (1999) *Institutional Design in Post-Communist Societies: Rebuilding the Ship at Sea*. Cambridge: Cambridge University Press.

Offe, C. (1984) *Contradictions of the Welfare State*, ed. J. Keane. London: Hutchinson.

Offe, C. (1985a) *Disorganized Capitalism: Contemporary Transformations of Work and Politics*, ed. J. Keane. Cambridge: Polity Press.

Offe, C. (1985b) "New Social Movements: Challenging the Boundaries of Institutional Politics." *Social Research*, 52: 817–68.

Offe, C. (1996a) "Institutional Design in East Europe Transitions." in R. E. Goodin (ed.) *The Theory of Institutional Design*. Cambridge: Cambridge University Press.

Offe, C. (1996b) *Modernity and the State: East, West*. Cambridge: Polity Press.

Offe, C. (1996c) *Varieties of Transition: The East European and East German Experience*. Cambridge: Polity Press.

Offe, C. (1997) "Micro-Aspects of Democratic Theory: What Makes for the Deliberative Competence of Citizens?" In A. Hadenius (ed.) *Democracy's Victory and Crisis*. Cambridge: Cambridge University Press.

Offe, C. and Wiesenthal, H. (1980) "Two Logics of Collective Action." In M. Zetlin (ed.) *Political Power and Social Theory*.

35 | **Richard Rorty**

Matthew Festenstein

Ideas
Pragmatism □ Contingency □ Liberalism

Major books
The Linguistic Turn (ed.) (1967)
Philosophy and the Mirror of Nature (1979)
Consequences of Pragmatism (1982)
Contingency, Irony, and Solidarity (1989)
Objectivity, Relativism, and Truth (1991)
Essays on Heidegger and Others (1991)
Achieving Our Country (1998)
Truth and Progress (1998)

Influences
Dewey □ Kuhn □ Nietzsche

Biographical Details

Richard Rorty (b. 1929) is one of the most controversial and provocative of contemporary philosophers. With the arguable exception of Jacques Derrida, it is hard to think of a living philosopher who has had such a broad cultural impact and been the subject of such fierce and unremitting denunciation: at least in these respects, Rorty has come to resemble his guru, the American pragmatist John Dewey. Rorty was trained as an analytic philosopher, but as he grew more critical of this tradition, his work began to range more widely across literature and politics. In part, this reflected the interests of his upbringing as a "red diaper baby" who revered not only Trotsky but T. S. Eliot (Rorty 1998a; 1999: 3–20). But it also expresses a key tenet of his wide-ranging work: that inquiry should sacrifice the pursuit of objectivity for personal self-creation, on the one hand, and social improvement, on the other.

Key Theoretical Contributions

In a series of influential works beginning with *Philosophy and the Mirror of Nature* (1979), Rorty debunks what he takes to be the founding pretensions of philosophy, as the ultimate arbiter of what counts as knowledge. This is the view of the discipline he finds in Plato, Locke, Kant, Russell, and much modern analytic philosophy. The idea of this arbiter, he argues, is built upon the complementary illusions of nature, envisaged as wholly independent of the categories through which humans come to understand it, and of the human subject, whose own essential nature is to gain an increasingly complete and accurate view of nature. This vision encouraged the belief that in order to achieve knowledge of nature, and to know that we have achieved it, we require "a special privileged class of representations so compelling that their accuracy cannot be doubted" (Rorty 1979: 163). If only we can find a mode of access to reality which is absolutely certain, we can begin to sort out which of our beliefs is justified, and which unjustified. This suggests an immensely important cultural role for philosophy, as the supreme judge of claims to authority and rationality.

However, he argues, the picture on which this idea rests is fundamentally flawed. There is no single way of representing the world with absolute certainty. Rather, what gives a belief the power to justify other beliefs is its place in a social context of norms, expectations, and other beliefs. Nor is there a single essence of nature to be discovered. We should view our beliefs and discourse not as attempts accurately to mirror the world, but as attempts to forge tools for dealing with it. This may be successful for particular groups at particular times, but make no claim to represent the nature of the world as it truly is. Here Rorty suggests the influence not only of the American pragmatists such as Dewey and William James, but also Nietzsche, Heidegger, and Wittgenstein.

The justification of beliefs is instead viewed sociologically: rationality is not a privileged relationship between mind and nature, but a matter of "what our peers ... will let us get away with saying" (ibid: 176). Although it makes sense to hold that particular beliefs, embedded in particular "language games" or "vocabularies," can "correspond" to features of the world, this is because criteria to judge whether or not a belief corresponds to reality have been furnished by the language game. Vocabularies do not themselves correspond to the world; nor can there be reasons from outside all vocabularies for adopting the language of some particular vocabulary:

> We often let the world decide the competition between alternative sentences (e.g., between "Red wins" and "Black wins" or between "The butler did it" and "The doctor did it") ... But it is not so easy when we turn from individual sentences to vocabularies as wholes. When we consider examples of alternative language games – ancient Athenian politics versus Jefferson's, the moral vocabulary of Saint Paul versus Freud's, the jargon of Newton versus that of Aristotle, the idiom of Blake versus that of Dryden – it is difficult to think of the world as making one of these better than another, of the world as deciding between them. When the notion of "description of the world" is moved from the level of criterion-governed sentences within language games to language games as wholes, games which we do not choose between by reference to criteria, the idea that the world decides which descriptions are true can no longer be given a clear sense. (Rorty 1989: 5)

There is no view of the world *sub specie aeternitatis* against which particular human versions of that reality may be judged.

What are the implications of this for social and political theory? One answer is negative: our legal, political, economic, etc., practices continue as they are, but without the aspiration to philosophical support (if they ever had such an aspiration). Yet this would seem to suggest a blinkered faith in these practices. Rorty's own elaboration has been rather more nuanced, but it retains this skeptical core: philosophers, or theorists of any stripe, have no privileged standpoint from which to judge how societies should be run, what our true interests are, or whether or not history has come to an end. As well as lacking the authority often claimed for itself, "high" theory detracts from practical efforts at social improvement.

Rorty rejects the idea that social and political views, and specifically his own preferred liberalism, require philosophical foundations. Justificatory accounts of liberal (or other) political practice make the mistake of the epistemological tradition in trying to justify particular beliefs and practices by reference to a universally authoritative standard. By contrast, Rorty argues, we should reject the myth of such a standard: his belief in freedom of speech should be viewed as the product of his particular background, not as an insight into the underlying truth about all human beings. Yet Rorty holds on to the thought that someone who fails to have this belief is wrong, and not, as a relativist might argue, "right within the context of her culture or her system of beliefs." There is no neutral standpoint outside particular evaluative schemes or worldviews from which to assess those schemes. But it does not follow that it is impossible to appraise other worldviews; indeed, part of what it means to be a liberal is that one appraise other worldviews in particular ways. The question "Why be a liberal?" cannot be answered by constructing an "Archimedean point" from which everyone can be persuaded; it can only be treated as a particular sort of dialectical challenge, calling for the liberal to come up with enough concrete examples of the superiority of liberal proposals and practices to persuade her interlocutor. If the latter remains immune to such persuasion, in due course he is rather harshly written off as "mad" (Rorty 1991b: 187).

In rejecting the myth of the neutral standpoint for justification, Rorty also wants to preserve the idea that forms of human organization, including science, art, and politics, may progress, but does not want to view this as a process of "getting the world right" or of "more accurately expressing human nature." Instead progress occurs through a radical redescription of some subject matter until "a pattern of linguistic behavior [is created] which will tempt the rising generation to adopt it, thereby causing them to look for appropriate new forms of non-linguistic behavior, for example, the adoption of new scientific equipment or new social institutions ... Anything can be made to look good or bad, important or unimportant, useful or useless by being redescribed" (Rorty 1989: 9). Rorty's conception of progress is influenced by Thomas Kuhn's famous account of scientific revolutions. A vocabulary (say, that of democratic politics) congratulates itself as more progressive by its own standards (say, fairness). But the victory of this vocabulary is historically contingent, not a matter of a society shaping itself by standards which are valid outside any vocabulary.

Rorty acknowledges one kind of ethical problem which flows from his rejection of foundations: the theological and metaphysical belief in a common human nature served to glue together two competing sorts of motivation, self-interest and social obligation, in Platonic and Christian ethics, for example. If the idea of this nature is discarded, identity is at the mercy of what the changes in human vocabulary throw up. Accepting this contingency makes one an "ironist," that is, someone whose fundamental values and commitments (which Rorty calls "final vocabularies") become problematic in a particular way. An ironist's realization that anything can be made to look good or bad by being redescribed makes them "never quite able to take themselves seriously because always aware that the terms in which they describe themselves are subject to change, always aware of the contingency and fragility of their final vocabularies, and thus of their selves'(ibid: 73–4). For the ironist, this is a liberating revelation, unleashing powers of self-creation. Most people, however, are not ironists, and distrust the powers of redescription. For them, there is "something potentially very cruel" about the claim that their final vocabularies are "up for grabs"; for the "best way to cause people long-lasting pain is to humiliate them by making the things that seemed most important to them look futile, obsolete, and powerless" (ibid: 89). Fortunately, the liberal ironist's commitment *qua* liberal to eschew cruelty squares this circle: in public at least, she displays solidarity with her fellow citizens; in private, of course, she may describe them as she pleases.

Particularly in his recent writings Rorty has fleshed out his conception of solidarity or community. If we can create ourselves in any way that we wish through redescription, what becomes of our obligations to others? The absence of a common human essence and the license to redescribe ourselves freely means that we need not respect the needs and interests of others – or even to notice their humanity. Nor are we restrained from any actions on the grounds that they violate our essential nature: "our insistence on contingency, and our consequent opposition to ideas like 'essence,' 'nature,' and 'foundation,' makes it impossible for us to retain the notion that some actions and attitudes are naturally 'inhuman'" (ibid: 189).

To the extent that community is possible it is as an achievement not a presumption, and best promoted through detailed imaginative identification with the lives of others. In Rorty's opinion, the intensity of solidarity is stronger the more parochial the attachment is in scope. In the absence of any general grounds for identifying with the universal human community, we should acknowledge that the most potent identities are particular: fellow Americans, fellow Sikhs, or fellow Glaswegians constitute the groups whose lives we understand and with whom we may feel sympathy. Conscious that this argument may appear to endorse a complacent or vicious chauvinism, Rorty emphasizes that the burden of liberal political morality is to extend the sense of community in order to include hitherto neglected or despised social groups: it is "a form of life which is constantly extending psuedopods and adapting itself to what it encounters'(Rorty 1991b: 204). This too proceeds through radical redescription, the telling of stories which alter our self-understandings so that we come to see ourselves as sharing a common predicament with strangers. In the contemporary United States, he argues, increasing inequality and social fragmentation can at least in part be combated by a robust sense of patriotic solidarity (Rorty 1998a).

Major Criticisms

As noted at the outset, Rorty has enjoyed a wide cultural impact together with an extraordinary level of criticism. Rorty's occasional insouciance in stating his positions irritates critics, for many of whom he has become an icon of postmodern frivolity. His account of the philosophical tradition, and its pitfalls, has been called into doubt, and his readings of many thinkers important to him, such as Hegel, Dewey, and Heidegger, challenged as opportunistic and inaccurate. Others have sought to show that the errors which he wishes to diagnose are not errors at all, and that a (perhaps chastened) version of the philosophical tradition Rorty rejects is still fruitful (Malachowski 1990; Saatkamp 1995; Brandom 2000).

Rorty's account of the relationship between irony, liberalism, and cruelty has unsurprisingly been the subject of fierce opposition. Feminists accuse him of reinforcing the gendered and oppressive distinction between a political public sphere and the artificially depoliticized realm of personal relations. Liberals find his commitment to avoid cruelty is too bland a basis for their political morality, and contingency on the favorable dispositions of individuals too precarious a basis for it. The interest in self-creation and private redescription has been attacked as narcissistic, and the ironist's moral psychology as unstable. Finally, the decision to view solidarity in terms of the nation-state has been attacked as reinforcing a parochial nationalism. For more sympathetic commentators, he embodies at least an important challenge to the pretensions of social and political theory to a form of insight into human societies, grounded in a special perception of the requirements of reason or human nature (Festenstein and Thompson 2001).

Bibliography

Brandom, R. (2000) (ed.) *Rorty and His Critics*. Oxford: Blackwell.
Festenstein, M. (1997) *Pragmatism and Political Theory*. Cambridge: Polity Press.
Festenstein, M. and Thompson, S. (eds.) (2001) *Richard Rorty: Critical Dialogues*. Cambridge: Polity Press.
Geras, N. (1995) *Solidarity in the Conversation of Humankind: The Ungroundable Liberalism of Richard Rorty*. London: Verso.
Malachowski, A. (ed.) (1990) *Reading Rorty*. Oxford: Blackwell.
Rorty, R. (ed.) (1967) *The Linguistic Turn*. Chicago: University of Chicago Press.
Rorty, R. (1979) *Philosophy and the Mirror of Nature*. Princeton, NJ: Princeton University Press.
Rorty, R. (1982) *Consequences of Pragmatism*. Minneapolis: University of Minnesota Press.
Rorty, R. (1989) *Contingency, Irony, and Solidarity*. Cambridge: Cambridge University Press.
Rorty, R. (1991a) *Essays on Heidegger and Others*. Cambridge: Cambridge Uni-

versity Press.

Rorty, R. (1991b) *Objectivity, Relativism, and Truth: Philosophical Papers, vol. 1*. Cambridge: Cambridge University Press.

Rorty, R. (1998a) *Achieving Our Country: Leftist Thought in Twentieth Century America*. Cambridge, MA: Harvard University Press.

Rorty, R. (1998b) *Truth and Progress: Philosophical Papers, vol. 3*. Cambridge: Cambridge University Press.

Rorty, R. (1999) *Philosophy and Social Hope*. Harmondsworth: Penguin Books.

Saatkamp, H. (ed.) (1995) *Rorty and Pragmatism*. Nashville, TN: Vanderbilt University Press.

Eve Kosofsky Sedgwick

Annamarie Jagose

Ideas
Homosociality and homophobia □ Homosexual panic □ Closet
□ Queer

Major books
Between Men: English Literature and Male Homosocial Desire (1985)
Epistemology of the Closet (1990)
Tendencies (1993)
A Dialogue on Love (1999)

Influences
De Man □ Feminism □ Foucault □ Miller

Biographical Details

Eve Kosofsky Sedgwick (b. 1951) is one of the most prominent North American theorists of sexuality, her compelling and transformative works so foundational to gay studies and the subsequent and not-quite synonymous formation of queer theory that she is frequently described as their inventor. Given her undergraduate study "at the infamous Cornell of the infamous late sixties" (Sedgwick 1990: 54) and her graduate years at Yale (a place which, with the exception of Paul de Man's classes, she has characterized as "a hideously hostile and frigid environment for graduate students in general and for me very much in particular": see Williams 1993: 61), Sedgwick's work, perhaps predictably, is strongly marked by the muscular reading strategies of deconstruction and New Criticism. Less predictable is the way in which her work grafts to those interpretive protocols not simply a feminism attentive to the diacritical work of gender but a critical sensitivity to the disciplinary grammars – of which gender is one – that underwrite the reification of sexual categories, in particular heterosexuality and homosexuality.

In 1988, widely acclaimed for her ground-breaking study of the fraught relations between homosexuality, homosociality, and hetero-sexuality, *Between Men: English Literature and Male Homosocial Desire* (1985), Sedgwick moved from Amherst College to Duke University. Together with her colleagues Jonathan Goldberg and Michael Moon, Sedgwick consolidated what might be called the Duke School of queer studies, her next two books profoundly influencing the rapid development and institutionalization of the field. *Epistemology of the Closet* (1990) analyzes the founding incoherence of homosexual definition, foregrounding the closet to figure the dense relations of knowledge and ignorance animated by the subject of homosexuality, while *Tendencies* (1993), written concurrently with *Epistemology*, is a book of essays – including several of Sedgwick's most famous ("Jane Austen and the Masturbating Girl," for example, or the critical, autobiographical, and poetic "A Poem Is Being Written") – which address in various ways identification's ragged slice across the categorical neatness of classes of gender and sexuality. After an influential decade at Duke, in 1998 Sedgwick took up her position as Distinguished Professor of English at CUNY Graduate Center. Her latest book, *A Dialogue on Love* (1999), is marked by an emphatic turn to the autobiographical but continues her long-standing interrogation of twentieth-century sexual knowledges, the galvanizing fit or misfit between sexual identities and sexual identifications.

Key Theoretical Contributions

Sedgwick's work constitutes a strenuous reworking of received understandings of the ways in which homosexuality meshes with heterosexuality. While her work characteristically ropes together critical approaches which more usually have nothing to say to each other, effectively transforming the grounding assumptions as well as the future direction of gay studies, her signature gesture might rather be a refusal to foreclose on her own argument, an insistence that knowingness is not the measure of an argument's critical worth. This endlessly speculative, autocritical, and parenthetically qualifying character of her work, its free-wheeling energy, can be seen in her indomitable style of writing characterized as "Jamesian" by her admirers (Weeks 1992: 412) and her detractors alike (Van Leer 1995: 127).

In her early work Sedgwick theorizes the interface between homosexuality and heterosexuality through a consideration of the interworkings of the historical and cultural mechanisms of misogyny and homophobia. Her coupling of feminism with anti-homophobic analysis enables a sophistication of gender relations, more frequently assumed to take heterosexuality as their paradigmatic map, and considerably broadens an understanding of what might constitute an effect of gender. Amalgamating the critical insights of René Girard's literary analysis of erotic triangulation (Girard 1972) and Gayle Rubin's Lévi-Strauss-influenced discussion of the patriarchal traffic in women (Rubin 1975), Sedgwick argues in *Between Men* that, insofar as it negotiates and sanctions relations between men, male heterosexuality is importantly situated on a homosocial continuum, the elasticated reach of which also defines in crucial ways its opposite, male homosexuality. Consequently, Sedgwick's centralizing of male homosociality insists both "that the status of women, and the whole question of arrangements between genders, is deeply and inescapably inscribed in the structure even of relationships that seem to exclude women – even in male homosocial/homosexual relationships" (Sedgwick 1985: 25) and that there is a historically variable yet structurally consistent connection between the identity formations of male heterosexuality and male homosexuality.

Given the subsequent directions of Sedgwick's work, perhaps the most pertinent consequence of her description of the impacted knot of sexual and gendered identities concerns her understanding of homophobia's terroristic operation. For rather than figure homophobia as the consequence of distinct heterosexual and homosexual populations – or even as a strategy for distinguishing between them – Sedgwick's representation of the homosocial continuum argues instead that the tactical virulence of homophobia is an effect of the superimposition of the absolute imperative and the ultimate inability to tell the one from the other. Arguing that homosexuality and heterosexuality are permanently maintained in an unstable and unpredictable relation to each other, Sedgwick theorizes homophobia as "a mechanism for regulating the behavior of the many by the specific oppression of the few" (ibid: 88).

Sedgwick's next book, *Epistemology of the Closet*, furthers her investigation of heterosexual/ homosexual relations, raising to the second power her analysis of the structural incoherences of categories of sexual identification. While the overarching framework of *Epistemology* remains recognizably feminist, it no longer focuses on the ways in which the taxonomies of gender are underwritten by male homosociality, but puts its analytic energy into the project of demonstrating that "in twentieth-century Western culture gender and sexuality represent two analytic axes" (Sedgwick 1990: 30) that are distinct if inextricable. Indeed, the distance between this and her earlier work can be measured in her suggestion that "a damaging bias toward ... heterosexist assumptions inheres unavoidably in the very concept of gender" (ibid: 31).

Sedgwick argues that modern definitions of homosexuality, both homophobic and anti-homophobic, are irresolvably incoherent. She represents this incoherence as the effect of the mutually held but contradictory understandings of, on the one hand, minoritizing and universalizing definitions of homosexuality and, on the other hand, gender-liminal and gender-separatist definitions of homosexual identifications and desires. Minoritizing definitions of homosexuality understand that homosexuals constitute a small, delimitable population; universalizing definitions constitute homosexuality as potentially inflecting all sexual identity formations. Gender-liminal understandings of homosexual desire posit homosexuals as an intermediary gender category, neither wholly masculine nor feminine; gender-separatist understandings represent homosexuals as the very epitome, the defining heart of their gender. Although in her various writings it might be observed that Sedgwick favors the universalizing over the minoritizing trope, the liminal over the separatist, her most strenuous argument is that there is no possible adjudication between the oppositions. It is not, she argues, that one is more or less correct than its opposite but that, operating in tandem, they produce homosexuality as a profoundly incoherent category.

Sedgwick's insistence on the foundational incoherence of homosexual definition has a number of significant consequences. First, it contextualizes her privileging of the closet as a figure for "the relations of the known and the unknown, the explicit and the inexplicit around homo/heterosexual definition" (ibid: 3). Second, it energizes her theorizing of ignorance not as the absence of knowledge but rather as particular knowledge-effects, the strategies and outcomes of which are crucial to the networks of power that constitute the field of sexuality (Sedgwick 1993: 23–51). Third, it licenses her influential intervention in the historicizing of sexuality, enabling her caution that the necessary work of denaturalizing historical sexual knowledges and practices must not continue to reify as comparatively coherent and known the formation of contemporary homosexuality (Sedgwick 1990: 44–8).

The term "queer" and the associated resignification of regulatory sexual taxonomies that took place under its rubric inevitably proved productive for Sedgwick's later work. Its near-infinite potentiality is everywhere written across her collection of essays and their "attempt to find new ways to think about lesbian, gay, and other sexually dissident loves and identities in a complex social ecology where the presence of different genders, different identities and identifications will be taken as a given" (Sedgwick 1993: xiii).

Major Criticisms

Sedgwick's work – often enough, simply the provocation of Sedgwick herself – functioned as a particularly volatile flashpoint for the burgeoning anti-PC journalism of the early 1990s. Her gay-affirmative scholarship – in particular, her insistence that the literary canon already resonates with homosexual meanings – was spectacularly singled out as a symptom of that alleged disintegration of humanities scholarship diagnosed by the American intellectual right. Given Sedgwick's own critique of her scapegoating in the recent culture wars (ibid: 15–20), it is enough to note here that, whatever the avowed objections, the journalistic ridiculing of her work was everywhere animated by a homophobia complacent enough to figure as if indisputable "the flat inadmissibility of openly queer articulation" (ibid: 18).

Other criticisms can be recognized as more substantial to the degree that they are coterminous with Sedgwick's anti-homophobic project (although more than one critic, aggravated by Sedgwick's own play across categories of identity and identification, has described her work as homophobic: see Bergman 1991: 127; Van Leer 1995: 113–19). Sedgwick's relentless reading of homosexuality into tropes of unspeakability or silence has been critiqued as an oversimplification of the cluster of knowledges, abjected or not, that similarly secure their own representation through figures of indirection (Dean 1995: 118; Lane 1999: 233–7). Her analysis of the emergence of categories of homo/heterosexual definition, developed through her close reading of late nineteenth and early twentieth-century literary texts, has been characterized as inadequately historical (Kijinski 1994: 58–9; Lynch 1988: 130–1). A more sophisticated qualification of Sedgwick's historicity notes that her valuable insistence on the incoherence of modern homosexuality tends to elide the importance of "the historical problem of describing the differences between prehomosexual and homosexual formations" (Halperin 2000: 116–17, n. 7.) Tim Dean argues that Sedgwick's resistance, particularly in her later work, to psychoanalysis and what she characterizes as its inevitable transmission of heterocentric or homophobic paradigms leaves her without the most effective and developed means to theorize perverse desire (Dean 1995: 119–33).

A criticism frequently leveled by lesbian theorists is that Sedgwick's theoretical models privilege male homosexuality at the explicit expense of lesbianism. So, for instance, Sedgwick's framing of the significance of "the radically discontinuous relation of male homosocial and homosexual bonds" (Sedgwick 1985: 3) has been critiqued for its complementary and anodyne characterization of relations between female homosexuality and homosociality as relatively continuous, for its reluctance or inability to distinguish between a carnal lesbianism and an asexual feminism (Castle 1993: 68–72; De Lauretis 1994: 115–16; Vermeule 1991: 54–7). Similarly, Sedgwick's prioritization of sexuality over gender as an analytic category has been criticized for the ways in which it characterizes the former as dynamic and mobile (and more often than not associated with masculinity), the latter as fixed and unalterable (and more often than not associated with femininity) (Butler 1994: 23–4, n. 8; Martin 1996: 74–9).

Bibliography

Bergman, D. (1991) "Something About Eve: Eve Kosofsky Sedgwick's Closet Drama." *Raritan: A Quarterly Review*, 11: 115–31.

Butler, J. (1994) "Against Proper Objects." *Differences: A Journal of Feminist Cultural Studies*, 6: 1–26.

Castle, T. (1993) *The Apparitional Lesbian: Female Homosexuality and Modern Culture*. New York: Columbia University Press.

De Lauretis, T. (1994) *The Practice of Love: Lesbian Sexuality and Perverse Desire*. Bloomington: Indiana University Press.

Dean, T. (1995) "On the Eve of a Queer Future." *Raritan: A Quarterly Review*, 15: 116–34.

Girard, R. (1972) *Deceit, Desire, and the Novel: Self and Other in Literary Structure*. trans. Y. Freccero. Baltimore, MD: Johns Hopkins University Press.

Halperin, D. (2000) "How to Do the History of Male Homosexuality." *GLQ: A Journal of Lesbian and Gay Studies*, 6: 87–124.

Kijinski, J. L. (1994) "Gender Criticism, Aesthetics, and the Case of Oscar Wilde." *Review*, 16: 41–61.

Lane, C. (1999) *The Burdens of Intimacy: Psychoanalysis and Victorian Masculinity*. Chicago: University of Chicago Press.

Lynch, M. (1988) "Between Men." *Victorian Studies*, 32: 129–31.

Martin, B. (1996) *Femininity Played Straight: The Significance of Being Lesbian*. New York: Routledge.

Rubin, G. (1975) "The Traffic in Women: Notes Toward A Political Economy of Sex." *Toward An Anthropology of Women*, ed. R. Reiter. New York: Monthly Review Press.

Sedgwick, E. K. (1976) *The Coherence of Gothic Conventions*. New York: Methuen.

Sedgwick, E. K. (1985) *Between Men: English Literature and Male Homosocial Desire*. New York: Columbia University Press.

Sedgwick, E. K. (1990) *Epistemology of the Closet*. Berkeley: University of California Press.

Sedgwick, E. K. (1993) *Tendencies*. Durham, NC: Duke University Press.

Sedgwick, E. K. (1994) *Fat Art, Thin Art*. Durham, NC: Duke University Press.

Sedgwick, E. K. (ed.) (1996) *Gary in Your Pocket: Stories and Notebooks of*

Gary Fisher. Durham, NC: Duke University Press.

Sedgwick, E. K. (ed.) (1997) *Novel Gazing: Queer Readings in Fiction*. Durham, NC: Duke University Press.

Sedgwick, E. K. (1999) *A Dialogue on Love*. New York: Beacon Press.

Sedgwick, E. K. and Frank, A. (eds.) (1995) *Shame and Its Sisters: A Silvan Tomkins Reader*. Durham, NC: Duke University Press.

Sedgwick, E. K. and Parker, A. (eds.) (1995) *Performativity and Performance*. New York: Routledge.

Van Leer, D. (1995) *The Queening of America: Gay Culture in Straight Society*. New York: Routledge.

Vermeule, B. (1991) "Is There A Sedgwick School for Girls?" *Qui Parle*, 5: 53–72.

Weeks, J. (1992) "The Late-Victorian Stew of Sexualities." *Victorian Studies*, 35: 409–16.

Williams, J. (1993) "Sedgwick Unplugged." *The Minnesota Review*, 40: 52–64.

37 | Alain Touraine

Kevin McDonald

Ideas
Social movement □ Historicity □ Social relationship □ Action □ Subject

Major books
The Post-Industrial Society (1974)
The Self-Production of Society (1977)
The Voice and the Eye (1981)
Critique of Modernity (1995)
Can We Live Together? (2000)

Influences
Durkheim □ Friedmann □ Marx □ Weber

Biographical Details

Alain Touraine (b. 1925) is one of the most important twentieth-century French sociologists, shaping the discipline in both France and internationally. Born into a medical family, Touraine's early education followed the path of France's interwar elite to the École Normale Supérieure, where he studied history and philosophy (he was in the same preparatory class as Jean-François Lyotard). Touraine has likened these preparatory years to living as a seminarian, saying that "if I became a sociologist it was probably to reconnect with an outside world that I had been cut off from during those years of study" (Touraine 1977a: 27). In 1947 he dropped out of study and went to work in a coal mine in the north of France. There, during the general strikes of 1948, he encountered the struggle and culture of miners, and also read the work of Georges Friedmann (1961), who was working in the marginal discipline of sociology and exploring the social issues of industrial work systems. Touraine returned to study and in 1950 joined Friedmann's research team of sociologists, in a discipline at once looked down upon by the intellectual establishment while also opposed by the communist intellectuals as a "bourgeois science." From here we can trace Touraine's intellectual path, divided into three periods.

Key Theoretical Contributions

Touraine's first period of work began with exploring workers' involvement in labor conflicts at the Renault assembly plant (Touraine 1955). This established a pattern that Touraine would maintain throughout his career: building sociological theory on the basis of the encounter with social actors and their struggles.

This first period focused on exploring the social actors and conflicts of industrial society. The Marxist orthodoxy of the time underlined structural contradictions and the unfolding laws of history; Touraine was concerned with actors, social relationships, and class consciousness. This period of Touraine's industrial sociology was critical in producing core concepts that would remain central to his work. Of these, the idea of "historicity" and social relationship are the most important. Any society, Touraine argued, will have a form of social creativity that actors will attempt to shape in their image. In industrial society this creativity is expressed in the transformation of nature, or work. While the Marxist tradition affirmed a radical opposition between labor and capital, Touraine argued that workers and industrialists shared the same culture (confidence in progress, faith in science and rationality) while they are involved in a conflict around the social organization of shared cultural orientations. Actors and their conflicts produce society, Touraine (1965) argued in his first major theoretical book, not the laws of history – and this, he insisted, is what sociology should be exploring.

In 1967 Touraine became head of the new sociology department at Nanterre University, a new social science campus on the outskirts of Paris that was at the center of the birth of the May 1968 student movement. For Touraine, the movement pointed to the birth of a new type of society and was central to the second period in his work. Power, he argued, was shifting from control of the workplace to the production of culture as a whole. And while the student movement used the language of the proletariat and Marxism, Touraine believed that its practice pointed to a new field of conflict centered on culture and identity (Touraine 1971, 1974b). Over this period Touraine wrote his second major theoretical text (Touraine 1977b), where he placed social actors, their creativity and conflicts, at the center of what he called the production of society.

The optimism of May 1968 soon gave way to forms of extreme-left terrorism in France, Germany, Italy, and to an extent in the United States. This could only be understood as a sign of the weakness and crisis of social movements. Over this period Touraine wrote three books in the form of reflective essays (Touraine 1974a, 1977a, 1977c) in a period that he later called one of withdrawal. He was also deeply affected by the 1973 coup in Chile – not only for political and intellectual reasons (Touraine 1973), but also personally, as he had taught and researched there on several occasions and his wife was Chilean. Touraine's hopes for actors and renewal seemed to have given way to terror, the violence of dictatorships, and the dark pessimism of Foucauldianism and structural Marxism.

However, by 1976 there were signs of a renewal of social life in France: student mobilizations began to contest the restructuring of the university, and there were the beginnings of an ecology movement. Did these new forms of action contest the forms of power shaping an emerging postindustrial society? Touraine believed that increasingly social life was being organized around science and technology, and that these mobilizations contesting the social production of knowledge and technology may have within them a new social movement that would play the same role that the labor movement had played in industrial society.

From 1976 to 1985 Touraine undertook a decade of research to explore the extent to which emerging social conflicts were more than the expression of groups in crisis or interest groups, but were contesting central social orientations – what for Touraine represented a "social movement" (Touraine 1981). He and a team of researchers developed the "sociological intervention," a research method that reproduced social relationships in a research context, bringing together dominant and contesting social actors in the same research groups. The sociological intervention that was developed through this period is one of the most important innovations in qualitative research method of the past twenty-five years, in that it brings opposing social actors into a dialogue process, and asks movement activists to analyze this interaction in a process of self-analysis.

In the late 1980s Touraine's work moved into a third period centered on the "sociology of the subject." The research into new social movements had been premised on the idea of a rapid transition to a new postindustrial society, with its culture, resources, and conflicts. But it became clear that "society" as such was too integrated a concept to serve as a tool to explore social life. Globalization weakened the capacity of societies to generate norms, the economy was becoming increasingly independent of political constraints, while the ideas of role and institution, central concepts to sociology, were giving way to identity and community. Touraine analyzes this transformation in terms of "deinstitutionalization" and "desocialization" (Touraine 2000), underlining the weakening of institutions and norms in contemporary social life. This fragmentation of the social throughout the 1980s and 1990s was paralleled intellectually by the rise of postmodern theory, something Touraine sees as part of the decomposition of older images of cohesive society, but contributing little to the analysis of new social patterns and conflicts.

Touraine's work today focuses on the forms of domination and conflict present within contemporary social life, and on articulating possibilities of freedom (Touraine 1995, 2000). He underlines tensions rather than coherence, arguing that sociology's creativity lies in "constantly questioning the relations between social determinism and freedom, between structure and agency, between order and movement ... sociology ... is ... the body of thought and research concerned with this fundamental loss of unity in modern societies" (Touraine 1998: 128).

For Touraine, the decomposition of society involves the risk of an increasing distance between those who live in a world of global markets and those excluded from them. This fragmentation of society has parallels at the level of personal experience, where the individual's life runs the risk of becoming a series of events similar to zapping between television stations. In this context, throughout the 1990s, Touraine articulated what he calls a "sociology of the subject" (Touraine 2000). The subject, for Touraine, means the desire to be an actor. Contemporary conflicts are not centered on ownership of the means of production, but have shifted to the field of culture and meaning, increasingly around what individuality means in the emerging global social world.

For Touraine, the most critical political question confronting us today is the reconstitution of political control over economic activity. He rejects the idea of a return to the past, arguing that the post-1945 welfare state and nationally protected economy are finished. He argues that social life is shaped by the growing importance of intimacy, the private sphere, the rise of voluntary associations, and the entry of personal issues into the public sphere: sexuality, birth, death, collective memories. Human beings are no longer defined by social roles; a new set of questions is emerging. This emergence of new actors claiming new rights and identities must be the basis of a new form of democracy.

Major Criticisms

Several types of criticism have been directed at Touraine's project. The first concerns the scientific status of the sociological intervention. Michel Amiot (1982) argues that the intervention is an exercise in Touraine transferring his desire for movement action onto activists, more an exercise in prophecy than sociology. Touraine has responded that often the intervention has not revealed a social movement, but above all the difficulties that actors encounter in their attempt to produce a social relationship (for an overview of this debate, see Dubet and Wieviorka 1996; Hamel 1998).

In France, intellectual debates overlap with political debates. This is particularly the case in relation to the second major criticism, from the traditional left, centered in particular on the issue of globalization. Touraine argues that globalization must be critically embraced, while important currents within French intellectual life argue that globalization represents nothing more than Americanization and must be opposed. One of the most prominent examples of such critique comes from Pierre Bourdieu, who in the 1990s took on the role of a public spokesperson for the anti-globalization cause, and who attacked Touraine's school as an example of "Americanization," likening the sociological intervention to journalism, and rejecting the idea of actor-centered sociology (Bourdieu and Wacquant 1999). At stake here are intellectual issues (the opposition of a structurally determinist sociology to an actor-centered sociology) and debates about French political responses to globalization.

The third criticism addresses Touraine's claim that social life can be analyzed in terms of a core conflict, as opposed to a multiplicity of conflicts that do not necessarily converge. The most interesting statement of this theme is developed by Alberto Melucci (1989), who argues that it is it not possible to analyze social life in terms of a central conflict in the way that Touraine attempts. In a sense Touraine has accepted a dimension of this critique, and his shift from a sociology of social movements to a sociology of the subject involves an acceptance that there will not be a central social relationship in the way that the conflict between industrialists and the labor movement shaped industrial society. But Touraine resists the postmodern assertion that there is no unity to the forms of conflict and struggle in contemporary societies. Instead he is attempting to understand, often at a quite abstract or theoretical level, conflicts around the nature of individuality in a global social world. This informed Touraine's focus on theoretical questions over the 1990s (Touraine 1995, 2000). The critical question is the extent to which this permits an analysis of contemporary social life (McDonald 1999).

Bibliography

Amiot, M. (1982) "L'Intervention sociologique, la science et la prophétie." *Sociologie du travail*, 3: 415–24

Bourdieu, P. and Wacquant, L. (1999) "On the Cunning of Imperialist Reason." *Theory, Culture and Society*, 16, 1: 41–58.

Dubet, F. and Wieviorka, M. (1996) "Touraine and the Method of Sociological Intervention." In J. Clark and M. Diani (eds.) *Alain Touraine*. London: Falmer Press.

Friedmann, G. (1961) *The Anatomy of Work: Labor, Leisure, and the Implications of Automation*. Westport, CT: Greenwood Press.

Hamel, P. (1998) "The Positions of Pierre Bourdieu and Alain Touraine Respecting Qualitative Methods." *British Journal of Sociology*, 49, 1: 1–19.

McDonald, K. (1999) *Struggles for Subjectivity: Identity, Action and Youth Experience*. Melbourne: Cambridge University Press.

Melucci, A. (1989) *Nomads of the Present: Social Movements and Individual Needs in Contemporary Society*. London: Hutchinson .

Touraine, A. (1955) *L'Evolution du travail ouvrier aux usines Renault*. Paris: CNRS.

Touraine, A. (1965) *Sociologie de l'action*. Paris: Seuil.

Touraine, A. (1971) *The May Movement: Revolt and Reform*. New York: Random House.

Touraine, A. (1973) *Vie et mort au Chili populaire*. Paris: Seuil.

Touraine, A. (1974a) *Lettre à une étudiante*. Paris: Seuil.

Touraine, A (1974b) *The Post-Industrial Society: Tomorrow's Social History – Classes, Conflicts and Culture in the Programmed Society*. London: Wildwood House.

Touraine, A. (1977a) *Un Désir d'histoire*. Paris: Seuil.

Touraine, A. (1977b) *The Self-Production of Society*. Chicago: University of Chicago Press.

Touraine, A. (1977c) *La Société invisible: regards 1974–1976*. Paris: Seuil.

Touraine, A. (1981) *The Voice and the Eye*. New York: Cambridge University Press.

Touraine, A. (1995) *Critique of Modernity*. Oxford: Blackwell.

Touraine, A. (1998) "Sociology without Society." *Current Sociology*, 46, 2: 119–43.

Touraine, A. (2000) *Can We Live Together?: Equality and Difference*. Cambridge: Polity Press.

Touraine, A., Wieviorka, M., and Dubet, F. (1987) *The Workers' Movement*. New York: Cambridge University Press.

Touraine, A. et al. (1978) *Lutte étudiante*. Paris: Seuil.

Touraine, A. et al. (1981) *Le Pays contre l'Etat*. Paris: Seuil.

Touraine, A. et al. (1983a) *Anti-Nuclear Protest: The Opposition to Nuclear Energy in France*. New York: Cambridge University Press.

Touraine, A. et al. (1983b) *Solidarity: The Analysis of a Social Movement: Poland, 1980–1981*. New York: Cambridge University Press.

38 | Bryan S. Turner

Barry Smart

Ideas
Body □ Medical power □ Religion □ Citizenship □ Human rights

Major books
Weber and Islam (1974)
For Weber: Essays in the Sociology of Fate (1981)
The Body and Society (1984)
Citizenship and Capitalism (1986)
Medical Power and Social Knowledge (1987)

Influences
Foucault □ Nietzsche □ Weber

Biographical Details

The discourse of contemporary social theory continues to be reinvigorated by new translations, reinterpretations, and critical reflections on the works of the classical sociologists. However, while the agenda intrinsic to contemporary social theory continues to mirror in some important respects the central concerns of our intellectual forebears, that agenda has been reconstituted in order to take account of significant differences that exist between late nineteenth-century and early twenty-first century social conditions. Within contemporary social theory Bryan Turner is recognized as a leading interpreter of the classical tradition of sociological thought and as a prolific contributor to the reconstitution of social thought in general and the development of macro-sociological analysis, historical sociology, and comparative social research in particular.

Born in England in 1945, Bryan Turner's career in sociology began at

Leeds University, where he completed doctoral research on "The decline of Methodism." Subsequently Turner has proven that his style of
social theory really does travel well and he has held posts in universities
in England (Aberdeen, Lancaster, and Essex), Australia (Flinders and
Deakin), and the Netherlands (Utrecht). He is currently Professor of
Sociology at the University of Cambridge.

The scope and scholarly precision of Bryan Turner's work is consistently impressive and it is difficult to do proper justice to it in a brief
summary. Turner has made a substantial contribution to the discourse
of social theory, not only through sensitive reinterpretations and appraisals of the works of such key figures as Weber, Nietzsche, and Parsons, but also by providing original analyses of the body and the frailty
of embodiment, medical power and knowledge, and religion. In addition, Turner has produced influential texts on human rights, citizenship, and the modern/postmodern debate. Among social theorists of his
generation Turner has few if any peers.

Key Theoretical Contributions

Underlying the wide-ranging concerns addressed in Turner's work there
is an enduring critical analytical interest in the way in which modern
forms of embodied subjectivity have been constituted through religious,
medical, and legal institutional practices. It is an analytic interest that
reveals the dominant intellectual influence on his thinking of the work
of Weber, especially his writings on religion and his invitation to us to
think of Western culture in terms of variations in the relationship between "mind and body, spirit and flesh, culture and nature." The work
of Foucault, in particular his engagement with questions of the body
and medical knowledge and practice, has also played a significant part in
the development of Turner's theorizing. Given all this it is really no
surprise to find that, like Weber and Foucault before him, Turner's thinking has also been influenced by the philosophy of Nietzsche. In analyzing
the key institutional locations in and through which modern embodied
subjects have been constituted, Turner has drawn attention to a number
of closely articulated processes, including the emergence of dividing
practices which objectivize the subject in various ways, and an associated growth of legal and medical professions, itself a part of a wider-
ranging rationalization of social life manifest in the increasing
professionalization, secularization, and governmentalization of modern
society.

It might be argued that it is his series of sociological reflections on the
formerly neglected topic of the body that represents Turner's most

significant contribution to contemporary social theory; however, his work on the sociology of religion and his contributions to the debate over citizenship have also been very influential. His work on the "dominant ideology thesis" emphasized the facticity of everyday life and paved the way for a sustained analytic address of the body, conducted in the trilogy *Medical Power and Social Knowledge, Religion and Social Theory*, and *Body and Society*. Questions of historical and cultural differences as they bear on the condition of the body, our embodied experiences and informal and formally constituted understandings of the same, are now prominent features on the sociological agenda. In particular the social and cultural "nature" of the embodied realities and consequences associated with the phenomena of birth, aging, and death are, after Turner, matters sociologists can no longer ignore. Subsequent work, notably in the book *Regulating Bodies* and in other studies of human rights and citizenship, has continued to develop the concerns broached in the analytic trilogy on the body.

Turner has actively engaged with new developments in social thought and in particular he has sought to identify those features of poststructuralist and postmodern social thought that might be reconciled with the objectives of new social and political strategies that acknowledge and accommodate to "difference, pluralism and the incommensurability of values," while simultaneously seeking to nurture forms of solidarity. It is the radical potential of postmodernism that most interests Turner, in particular the possible respects in which the postmodern critique of "hierarchy, grand narratives, unitary notions of authority, or the bureaucratic imposition of official values" can simultaneously endorse the principle of tolerating differences and promote the possible development of a new style of politics while avoiding an "anything goes" relativism which treats all cultural positions as equally acceptable.

For Turner, questions of the body, citizenship, and human rights are closely connected concerns affecting all of us, concerns that demonstrate, notwithstanding acknowledgments of forms of cultural difference and pluralism, the existence of particular universal human conditions. It is clear from his work that he regards the nature of embodied citizenship and human rights in societies being transformed by a process of globalization as a vitally important focus for contemporary sociological theory, one that will continue to occupy analysts. The prominence assumed by such matters in his work exemplifies the practical moral–political interest that informs his social theorizing. As with the key figures in the classical tradition, Turner's theoretical work is profoundly concerned with the major problems encountered in modern society.

Bryan Turner has published major works on religion (Turner 1974,

1983, 1991b), the body (Turner 1984, 1996c), and medical sociology (Turner 1987, 1992, 1995). In addition he has provided significant analyses of the work of Weber (Turner 1974, 1991a, 1999a) and has co-authored influential volumes on the respective works of Parsons (Holton and Turner 1986) and Nietzsche (Stauth and Turner 1988). Other significant co-authored books include *The Dominant Ideology Thesis* and *Sovereign Individuals of Capitalism* (Abercrombie, Hill, and Turner 1980, 1986, respectively).

Turner's work ranges widely across concerns at the heart of social life and at the center of intellectual debate within sociology. While continuing to elaborate on his theoretical interests and build on his contribution to the field of historical sociology – the most succinct statement to date of his relationship to the classical tradition of social thought is to be found in his *Classical Sociology* (1999b) – Turner has added another dimension to his work by developing more empirically oriented projects on issues associated with citizenship, intimacy, and identity. The issue of citizenship has become an increasingly important focus of Turner's work, as current projects on the political sociology of citizenship, involving a historical investigation of citizenship rights, the welfare state, and the consequences of globalization effectively demonstrate. Projects on intimacy, health, and self-identity in older life and comparative studies of voluntary associations in a number of countries, including Australia (see Brown, Kenny, and Turner 2000), Sweden, Russia, Britain, and Argentina, will undoubtedly add to Turner's already well-established reputation as a leading figure within the discipline of sociology.

Turner's work has consistently addressed matters of prominent intellectual and sociopolitical concern and nowhere is this more evident than in his closely connected studies of the body, health, and citizenship. Reflecting on the issue of health, Turner remarked in the 1980s that in contemporary societies improvements in health standards increasingly have come to be regarded as an aspect of the expansion of citizenship rights. The difficulty, Turner argued, was how to reconcile the democratic pressure to enhance citizenship rights – for example, provide improvements in health standards and more equal access to healthcare – with the persistence of forms of social class inequality intrinsic to capitalist societies. Perceptively anticipating the problems that welfare states increasingly encounter, Turner predicted that healthcare systems were destined to become more politicized. The adoption within contemporary capitalist societies of neoliberal social and economic policies has ensured the persistence of economic inequalities and in such circumstances ever-rising expectations concerning health standards and healthcare are proving hard to meet, precisely as Turner anticipated would be the case. Indeed, rather than a continuing expansion of citizenship rights it might be argued that as far as health standards and healthcare are concerned, evidence of marked variations in the quality and quantity of services delivered by providers and increases in inequality of access to and outcomes of services for different categories of patient suggests that with the passage of time the rights of citizens might well become eroded.

Ultimately it is in the elaboration and development of a foundational sociology of the body that Bryan Turner's most profound contribution to the discipline currently lies. Critical of the analytic preoccupation with "decorative" forms of cultural representation of the body, Turner argues for a sociological analysis that engages with the inescapable corporeality of the body ("the phenomenal and experiential body of the everyday world of eating, sleeping, and working"), the complex forms of governmentalization to which the body is subject, and the range of ethical and moral concerns associated with socially and historically inflected processes of embodiment. Ultimately it is the issue of ontological frailty, the existing certainty of aging and dying, on which Turner places emphasis and it is the "frailty–precariousness–solidarity dynamic" that lies at the core of his work. Finally, the socially constructed self is compelled to confront the reality of its embodiment, literally its corpo*reality*. It is this common ontology, Turner argues, that binds us together and in turn provides a universal foundation for a sociological discourse of human rights able to make an effective contribution to moral evaluation and criticism of rights abuses.

Major Criticisms

It might be argued that to date there has been little or no attempt to develop a new theoretical synthesis or create a new theoretical system in Turner's work and for some analysts that might represent a critical weakness or limitation. While he has contributed significantly to the process of rethinking the object of sociological analysis, Turner has continued to demonstrate the significance and contemporary relevance of aspects of late nineteenth-century and early twentieth-century social thought for an understanding of present social conditions. His participation as a founding editor of the *Journal of Classical Sociology* demonstrates the significance he accords to the works of the late nineteenth-century and early twentieth-century social theorists. However, Turner is aware of the limits and limitations of the works of the classical sociologists, as indicated, for example, by his critical reflections on the theorizing of social class and ideology in the tradition of Marxist thought, and as signified by his support for and contribution to work on concerns that have been at best at the margins, if not entirely neglected, within classical sociology, for example studies of the body and citizenship.

It is premature to offer anything more than a provisional evaluation of Bryan Turner's work, as there is clearly much more to come. Existing research projects on modernization and postmodernization; cultural theory; citizenship; intimacy and identity; generations and cultural capital; and continuing work on the sociology of the body will undoubtedly contribute significantly to his standing and give rise to further reflections on his place within the discipline.

Bibliography

Abercrombie, N., Hill, S., and Turner, B. S. (1980) *The Dominant Ideology Thesis*. London: Allen and Unwin.

Abercrombie, N., Hill, S., and Turner, B. S. (1986) *Sovereign Individuals of Capitalism*. London: Allen and Unwin.

Brown, K. M., Kenny, S., and Turner, B. S. (2000) *Rhetorics of Welfare: Uncertainty, Choice and Voluntary Associations*. Basingstoke: Macmillan.

Featherstone, M., Hepworth, M., and Turner, B. S. (eds.) (1991) *The Body: Social Process and Cultural Theory*. London: Sage.

Holton, R. J. and Turner, B. S. (1986) *Talcott Parsons on Economy and Society*. London: Routledge and Kegan Paul.

Holton, R. J. and Turner, B. S. (1989) *Max Weber on Economy and Society*. London: Routledge.

Rojek, C. and Turner, B. S. (eds.) (1993) *Forget Baudrillard?* London: Routledge.

Rojek, C. and Turner, B. S. (eds.) (1998) *The Politics of J.-F. Lyotard*. London: Routledge.

Stauth, G. and Turner, B. S. (1988) *Nietzsche's Dance: Resentment, Reciprocity and Resistance in Social Life*. Oxford: Blackwell.

Turner, B. S. (1974) *Weber and Islam: A Critical Study*. London: Routledge and Kegan Paul. Reprinted with new introduction in 1998.

Turner, B. S. (1978) *Marx and the End of Orientalism*. London: Allen and Unwin.

Turner, B. S. (1981) *For Weber: Essays in the Sociology of Fate*. London: Routledge and Kegan Paul.

Turner, B. S. (1983) *Religion and Social Theory: A Materialist Perspective*. London: Heinemann.

Turner, B. S. (1984a) *The Body and Society: Explorations in Social Theory*. Oxford: Blackwell.

Turner, B. S. (1984b) *Capitalism and Class in the Middle East: Theories of Social Change and Economic Development*. London: Heinemann.

Turner, B. S. (1986a) *Citizenship and Capitalism: The Debate Over Reformism*. London: Allen and Unwin.

Turner, B. S. (1986b) *Equality*. Chichester: Ellis Horwood.

Turner, B. S. (1987) *Medical Power and Social Knowledge*. London: Sage.

Turner, B. S. (1988) *Status*. Milton Keynes: Open University Press.

Turner, B. S. (ed.) (1990) *Theories of Modernity and Postmodernity*. London: Sage.

Turner, B. S. (1991a) *Max Weber: From History to Modernity*. London: Routledge.

Turner, B. S. (1991b) *Religion and Social Theory*, 2nd edn. with a new introduction. London: Sage.

Turner, B. S. (1992) *Regulating Bodies: Essays in Medical Sociology*. London: Routledge.

Turner, B. S. (ed.) (1993) *Citizenship and Social Theory*. London: Sage.

Turner, B. S. (1994) *Orientalism, Postmodernism and Globalism*. London: Routledge.

Turner, B. S. (1995) *Medical Power and Social Knowledge*, 2nd revd. edn. London: Sage.

Turner, B. S. (1996a) *For Weber: Essays on the Sociology of Fate*, 2nd revd. edn. London: Sage.

Turner, B. S. (ed.) (1996b) *The Blackwell Companion to Social Theory*. Oxford: Blackwell. 2nd revd. edn. published in 2000.

Turner, B. S. (1996c) *The Body and Society: Explorations in Social Theory*, 2nd revd. edn. London: Sage.

Turner, B. S. (ed.) (1999a) *Max Weber: Critical Responses*, 3 vols. London: Routledge.

Turner, B. S. (1999b) *Classical Sociology*. London: Sage.

39 | Paul Virilio

Scott McQuire

Ideas
Dromology □ Logistics of perception □ Overexposed city □
Chronopolitics □ General accident

Major books
Speed and Politics (1986)
War and Cinema (1989)
The Lost Dimension (1991)
The Vision Machine (1994)
Open Sky (1997)
Polar Inertia (1999)

Influences
Einstein □ Husserl □ Merleau-Ponty

Biographical Details

Born in Paris in 1932, Paul Virilio is one of the most important and provocative contemporary theorists writing about the impact of technology on urban space and embodied subjectivity. Virilio has frequently acknowledged the traumatic childhood experience of the German blitzkrieg of World War II as a formative influence on his adult life and work, and also keeps a rock from Hiroshima on his desk. In his own words, "my work is a critical analysis of modernity, but through a perception of technology which is largely ... catastrophic" (Armitage 2000: 26).

As a teenager, Virilio converted to Christianity in 1950, joining the "worker-priest" movement of Abbé Pierre, and he remains a committed "anarcho-Christian." As a student he was strongly influenced by the phenomenology of Maurice Merleau-Ponty, with whom he studied at the Sorbonne in the 1950s. Other influences from this time include *gestalt* psychology, Einstein's and Heisenberg's relativity theory, and the philosophy of Bergson. At the same time, Virilio began a continuing involvement with the visual arts, working with renowned painters Henri Matisse and Georges Braque.

Following his participation in the "events" of May 1968, Virilio began a long association with the École Speciale d'Architecture in Paris, first as Professor (1969), then Director (1975), and finally becoming President in 1990. He has also continued to work as an activist on behalf of homeless people in Paris. While his published writings in French stretch back to the mid-1960s, it was only in the 1990s that Virilio became a major presence in the English-speaking world, with more than a dozen books translated since 1986.

Key Theoretical Contributions

Beginning with his explorations of the impact of military strategy on architecture and space (Virilio 1975), Virilio has become one of the most influential contemporary theorists of the relation between technological change, identity, and urban form. A continuous thread linking all his writings has been the insistence that modern technologies of transportation and communication have produced a continual acceleration of social life with decisive political effects.

In *Speed and Politics*, which was his first book translated into English, Virilio (1986c) argued that the political revolution of modernity could itself be understood in terms of the different velocities of circulation sustained by the interaction between new types of dynamic vehicles and urban forms. This "dromological" analysis (from the Greek *dromos* designating the science of the journey) characterizes modernity as the era in which speed becomes a primary social relation in its own right (Virilio 1986c: 153; 1997: 23). However, unlike earlier prophets extolling the virtues of speed, beginning with Marinetti's famous Futurist Manifesto of 1909, Virilio has never equated the increased potential for rapid movement with increased freedom. Instead he argues that the revolt against arbitrary constraints on movement in feudal society has become an "obligation to mobility" in modernity (Virilio 1986c: 29–30). For Virilio, this generates the fundamental tensions of "dromocratic" society in which increased social velocity is directly related to heightened social volatility. In this respect, his analysis shares key features of the modern dialectic explored by many other social theorists including Marx, Simmel, and Weber. Modern society has successfully developed technologies capable of moving people, products, and images further and faster, but this process of extension and acceleration has obliterated many of the reference points which previously secured the coordinates of personal identity and social solidarity.

Where Virilio's standpoint differs from those of many classical social theorists, particularly Marxists, is the extent to which he downplays the primacy of economic and class relations in order to emphasize the role of technology itself as an instrumental force in political, economic, and social change. In particular, Virilio has traced the historical shifts from "metabolic vehicles" (human bodies) to the new generations of mechanical vehicles with superior velocity and acceleration (trains, cars, aircraft), and finally to the current reign of what he has dubbed "the last vehicle" (Virilio 1989a): the audiovisual "vehicle" of electronic media.

In Virilio's terms, all these technologies of transport, communication, and information exchange are "motors" (Virilio 1995a) which manufacture speed, annihilating distance in favour of increasingly rapid interconnectivity. While his thesis can be compared with Marshall McLuhan's (1974), the two are poles apart in their reading of the effects of space-time compression. McLuhan presented an essentially optimistic picture of television, coining the phrase "the global village" to describe a utopian future in which electronic media would transcend the fragmenting effects of print technology to constitute new, potentially transnational communities. By contrast, Virilio argues that technological acceleration is itself tantamount to the wholesale militarization of society: "We have to face the facts: today, speed is war, the last war" (Virilio 1986c: 139).

In *War and Cinema* Virilio (1989b) explored the systematic use of cinematic techniques in modern military conflicts, highlighting a profound convergence between techniques of military observation and those associated with the "entertainment" industry. As he has since pointed out (Armitage 2000: 46–7), his theoretical elaboration of a military "sight machine" and an automated "logistics of perception" actualized through video and computerized imagery anticipated by some years the first "live" television war fought in the Persian Gulf in 1991. In other books, he extended his analyses of the effects of electronic media into the realm of everyday experiences of space, time, and subjectivity (Virilio 1991a, 1991b, 1994, 1997).

In particular, Virilio has developed original and highly influential analyses of the impact of electronic media and information technologies on urban form. He argues that the proliferation of screen technologies has created a condition of generalized "overexposure" in which the physical coordinates of the city are fundamentally destabilized (Virilio 1986b, 1991b). Dubbing the electronic screen "the third window" (Virilio et al.

1988) to distinguish it from the traditional architectural order of physical openings, Virilio argues that the ubiquitous electronic screen introduces a new "horizon" which is incessantly subject to abrupt shifts of perspective, point of view, and scale. Drawing on the invention of cinema, Virilio describes the emergence of a new "aesthetics of disappearance" (Virilio 1991a) in which the stability of the traditional painted image gives way to a transient order of ephemeral time-based images. The increasing influence of cinema, coupled with the spread of electronic media, produces a decisive interruption to traditional modes of occupying and inhabiting space by enhancing a collective sense of spatial discontinuity and fragmentation (Virilio 1991b: 13)

The ubiquity of the new electronic means for connecting physically discrete spaces transforms architecture by reorienting the traditional primacy of space along the axis of time (Virilio 1986b: 19). Extending this line of argument, Virilio's broader thesis is that the saturation of the world with techniques of instantaneous communication produces a profound leveling of space, causing geography to lose importance in strategic and political terms. For example, where colonization once demanded the direct physical occupation of territory, the "soft missiles" of the global media cross borders with impunity. Building on numerous examples, Virilio argues that the whole tradition of geopolitics, based around the physical occupation of space, is being overtaken by what he has dubbed "chronopolitics" (Virilio 1991b: 93). This term refers to the new primacy assumed by "technological time" in all aspects of life, from the high-speed data exchange of the global stockmarket to the constitution of "imagined communities" which gather, not in a shared space, but in the "real time" of a live television broadcast or an internet chat room.

For Virilio, the emergence of technologies which transmit images and information at "light speed" constitutes a profound threshold: "To have reached the light barrier, to have reached the speed of light, is a historical event which throws history into disarray and jumbles up the relation of the living being towards the world" (Virilio 1995b). One consequence of this is the potential reversal of the migratory tendencies of the modern age of transportation. Instead of the dynamism which characterized early modernity, what is now emerging is a "polar inertia" (Virilio 1999) such that, "From now on everything will happen without us moving, without us even having to set out" (Virilio 1989a: 112). Virilio forecasts that the integration of techno-science with virtually all aspects of daily life, from genetic engineering and the transplant revolution which promise to redesign the human body (Virilio 1997: 51), to the rule of the vision machines described above, brings us into the orbit of what he calls the general accident (ibid: 69–85). Building on his argument that each and every new technology implies its own accident (for example, the invention of the locomotive was simultaneously the invention of the train crash), Virilio contends that globalized interactivity means an accident affecting the network can no longer be localized. Instead, like the "love bug" virus released from the Philippines during 2000, it immediately appears everywhere, in all sectors. He has extended this apocalyptic scenario to its furthest scope, relating it to the prospect of global ecological breakdown as the cumulative effects of environmental destruction transcend local and national borders (ibid).

Major Criticisms

One of the most frequent criticisms leveled at Virilio concerns precisely the apocalyptic trajectory of his work. While he has recently protested his image as a doom-sayer (Virilio and Oliveira 1995), his protests seem rather hollow when matched to his biting rhetoric. However, his predominantly negative attitude to the trajectory of technological change is arguably where much of the power of his ideas and imagery is derived.

Virilio has also been criticized for his style of writing. His work certainly lacks sustained engagement with other thinkers, preferring isolated quotes to presenting an entire argument, a method Jonathan Crary describes as "aphoristic and epiphanic" (Crary 1988: 185). Virilio himself defends his strategy as modernist, describing his writing style as "cinematic" and comparing its rhythms to musical composition (Armitage 2000: 30–1).

Perhaps of more concern is a mounting degree of repetition in his work. The themes that were established in *Speed and Politics* are still prevalent two decades later. Admittedly, they are big themes and not easily exhausted. However, his basic frame of analysis, his way of resolving (or avoiding) certain questions, gives little sense that his work is still growing. Reading one or two of his books is extremely rewarding; reading a dozen risks tedium. There is a growing sense that he is simply confirming an analysis that he made long ago.

A more substantial criticism is his reliance on a model of the human subject, which presumes both its unity as a normative attribute, and its phenomenological "presence" as a grounding reference point. While this is a complex issue, his lack of engagement with poststructural "anti-humanism" is puzzling. For instance, his antipathy to Lacan (Virilio 1994: 24) ignores the fact that Merleau-Ponty was a mutual influence, albeit interpreted differently (see Lacan 1973). Even more surprising is his lack of engagement with Derrida (whom he describes as a close friend), given Derrida's development of a post-phenomenological approach to the metaphysics of "presence" via his readings of Husserl and Heidegger

(Derrida 1972, 1973, 1978). My concern (expressed more extensively in McQuire 1998, 1999) is that Virilio's refusal to problematize the authority of presence in the traditional phenomenological model tends to lead his analysis of screen technologies back into the historical impasse of a simple opposition between "image" and "reality."

Finally, it has often been noted that Virilio's work lacks effective political strategies to respond to the emerging "catastrophe" he describes. However, this seems less a reason to dismiss his work that to develop and extend it.

Bibliography

Armitage, J. (ed.) (2000) *Paul Virilio: From Modernism to Hypermodernism and Beyond*. London: Sage. Simultaneously published in *Theory, Culture and Society* (1999)16: 5–6.

Crary, J. (1988) Preface to "The Third Window: An Interview with Paul Virilio." In C. Schneider and B. Wallis (eds.) *Global Television*. New York: Wedge Press; Cambridge, MA: MIT Press.

Derrida, J. (1972) *Marges de la philosophie*. Paris. Trans. A. Bass, *Margins of Philosophy*. Brighton: Harvester Press, 1982.

Derrida, J. (1973) *Speech and Phenomena, and Other Essays on Husserl's Theory of Signs*, trans. D. B. Allison. Evanston, IL: Northwestern University Press.

Derrida, J. (1978) "Genesis, 'Structure' and Phenomenology." In *Writing and Difference*, trans. A. Bass. London: Routledge and Kegan Paul.

Lacan, J. (1973) *Le Séminaire de Jacques Lacan* Livre XI, "Les quatre concepts fondamentaux de la psychanlayse." Paris. Trans. A. Sheridan, *The Four Fundamentals of Psychoanalysis*. Harmondsworth: Penguin Books, 1979.

McLuhan, M. (1974) *Understanding Media: The Extensions of Man*. London: Routledge and Kegan Paul.

McQuire, S. (1998) *Visions of Modernity: Representation, Memory, Time and Space in the Age of the Camera*. London: Sage.

McQuire, S. (1999) "Blinded by the (Speed of) Light." *Theory, Culture and Society*, 16, 5–6: 143–59.

Virilio, P. (1975) *Bunker archéologie*. Paris. Trans. (of 2nd edn.) G. Collins, *Bunker Archeology*. Princeton, NJ: Princeton University Press, 1994.

Virilio, P. (1986a) *Negative Horizon*, trans. M. Polizotti. New York: Semiotext(e).

Virilio, P. (1986b) "The Overexposed City," trans. A. Hustvedt. *Zone*, 1–2: 14–31.

Virilio, P. (1986c) *Speed and Politics: An Essay on Dromology*, trans. M. Polizotti. New York: Semiotext(e).

Virilio, P. (1989a) "The Last Vehicle," trans. D. Antal. In D. Kamper and C. Wulf (eds.) *Looking Back on the End of the World*. New York: Semiotext(e).

Virilio, P. (1989b) *War and Cinema: The Logistics of Perception*, trans. P. Camiller. London: Verso.

Virilio, P. (1990a) "Cataract Surgery in the Year 2000," trans. A. Fatet and A. Kuhn. In A. Kuhn (ed.) *Alien Zone: Cultural Theory and Contemporary Science Fiction Cinema*. London: Verso.

Virilio, P. (1990b) *Popular Defense and Ecological Struggles*, trans. M. Polizotti. New York: Semiotext(e).

Virilio, P. (1991a) *The Aesthetics of Disappearance*, trans. P. Beitchman. New York: Semiotext(e).

Virilio, P. (1991b) *The Lost Dimension*, trans. D. Moshenberg. New York: Semiotext(e).

Virilio, P. (1992) "Aliens," trans. B. Massumi. *Incorporations: Zone*, 6: 446–9.

Virilio, P. (1993a) "The Law of Proximity," trans. L. E. Nesbitt. *Columbia Documents of Architecture and Theory*, 2: 123–37.

Virilio, P. (1993b) "Marginal Groups." *Daidalos*, 50 (December): 72–81.

Virilio, P. (1993c) "The Primal Accident," trans. B. Massumi. In B. Massumi (ed.) *The Politics of Everyday Fear*. Minneapolis: University of Minnesota Press.

Virilio, P. (1994) *The Vision Machine*, trans. J. Rose. Bloomington: Indiana University Press.

Virilio, P. (1995a) *The Art of the Motor*, trans. J. Rose. Minneapolis: University of Minnesota Press.

Virilio, P. (1995b) "Speed and Information: Cyberspace Alarm!" trans. P. Riemens. In *CTheory*: electronic journal at http://www.ctheory.com/a30–cyberspace_alarm.html

Virilio, P. (1997) *Open Sky*, trans. J. Rose. London: Verso.

Virilio, P. (1999) *Polar Inertia*, trans. P. Camiller. London: Sage.

Virilio, P. (2000) *The Information Bomb*, trans. C. Turner. London: Verso.

Virilio, P. and Defresne, D. (1999) "Cyberresistance Fighter: An Interview with Paul Virilio," trans. J. Houis. In *Apres-Coup*: electronic journal at http://www.apres–cou:org/archives/articles/virilio.html

Virilio, P. and Kittler, F. (1999) "The Information Bomb: Paul Virilio and Friedrich Kittler in Conversation," trans. P. Riemens. *Angelaki: Machinic Modulations* special issue, 4, 2.

Virilio, P. and Limon, E. (1996) "Paul Virilio and the Oblique." In S. Allen and K. Park (eds.) *Sites and Stations: Provisional Utopias: Architecture and Utopia in the Contemporary City*. New York: Lusitania Press.

Virilio, P. and Lotringer, S. (1983) *Pure War*, trans. M. Polizotti. New York: Semiotext(e). Revd. edn. (1997) with new postscript: "1997: Infowar."

Virilio, P. and Oliveira, C. (1995) "The Silence of the Lambs: Paul Virilio in Conversation," trans. P. Riemens. In *CTheory*: electronic journal at http://www.ctheory.com/ga1.7–silence.html

Virilio, P. and Philippe, P. (1999) *Politics of the Very Worst*, trans. M. Cavaliere. New York: Semiotext(e).

Virilio, P. and Wilson, L. K. (1994) "Cyberwar, God and Television: Interview with Paul Virilio," trans. L. Wilson, M. Fowler, and R. Stesan. In *CTheory*: electronic journal at http://www.ctheory.com/a–cyberwar_god.html

Virilio, P. and Zurburgg, N. (1995) "The Publicity Machine and Critical Theory," trans. N. Zurburgg. *Eyeline*, 27: 8–14. Reprinted as "'A Century of

Hyper-Violence': An Interview with Paul Virilio." *Economy and Society*, 25, 1: 111–26.
Virilio, P. et al. (1988) "The Third Window: An Interview with Paul Virilio," trans. Y. Shafir. In C. Schneider and B. Wallis (eds.) *Global Television*. New York: Wedge Press; Cambridge, MA: MIT Press.

40 | Raymond Williams

Andrew Milner

Ideas
Cultural materialism □ Selective tradition □ Structure of feeling

Major books
Culture and Society 1780–1950 (1958)
The Long Revolution (1961)
Modern Tragedy (1966)
Drama from Ibsen to Brecht (1968)
The English Novel (1970)
The Country and the City (1973)
Marxism and Literature (1977)
Towards 2000 (1983)
The Politics of Modernism (1989)

Influences
Gramsci □ Leavis □ Marx

Biographical Details

Raymond Williams (1921–88) was perhaps the most significant "left-wing" figure in late twentieth-century British intellectual life. *The Times* described him as an "equivalent to Sartre"; Cornel West called him "the last of the great European male revolutionary socialist intellectuals." Born into a Welsh working-class family in Pandy, Monmouthshire, he won a scholarship to Grammar School and eventually a place at Cambridge University, where he studied English. He served in the British army during World War II, returned to complete his degree, worked as an Oxford University adult education tutor, then as Lecturer in English and later Professor of Drama at Cambridge. He was an immensely

prolific writer, whose work ranged from the realist novel to science fiction; from pioneering studies of the mass media to literary criticism;
from historical philology to high cultural theory. In the mid-1950s he
emerged as one of the leading figures in the New Left. He was involved
in an array of radical causes, notably the Campaign for Nuclear Disar-
mament, the Vietnam Solidarity Campaign, and the Socialist Environment and Resources Association. Later in life he became increasingly
sympathetic to Welsh nationalism and was very active in solidarity work
with the Welsh NUM during the 1984–5 coalminers' strike. He died of
a heart attack at Saffron Walden, Essex, and is buried at Clodock in
Monmouthshire.

Key Theoretical Contributions

Trained in English, Williams derived much of his initial critical vocabulary from the Cambridge literary critic, F. R. Leavis. Formed by the
biographical experience of working-class life, he was a lifelong socialist,
with an enduring interest in Marxism. Williams coined the term "cultural materialism" to describe his own theoretical position, a coinage
intended to denote a simultaneous break from Marxism's *un*cultural
materialism, which reduced culture to the "superstructural" effect of an
economic "base"; and from Leavisism's cultural *im*materialism, which
idealized culture as the antithetical negation of material "civilization."
During the 1950s Williams addressed himself very directly to the definition of a third position, dependent upon but in contradictory relation
both to Leavisism and to Marxism.

His intellectual reputation was established by two early books, *Culture and Society 1780–1950* and *The Long Revolution*. The first was a
bold attempt to wrest the English "culture and society" tradition away
from the cultural conservatism of Leavis and T. S. Eliot. Rejecting
their view of the tradition as coextensive with "minority culture,"
Williams argued that culture was "not only a body of intellectual and
imaginative work; it is also and essentially a whole way of life" (Williams
1963: 311). Thus redefined, the literary-humanist ideal of a "common
culture" became supplemented, and importantly qualified, by that of a
plurality of class cultures. The common culture remained as a normative ideal, but in a characteristically leftist move Williams relocated it
from the idealized historical past to a still-to-be-made socialistic future. If culture was not yet fully common, it followed that tradition
was not so much the unfolding of a group mind, as in Eliot, but the
outcome of a set of interested selections made in the present. A "tradition is always selective," Williams wrote, adding that selection tends

to be "governed by the interests of the class that is dominant" (ibid: 307–8).

The Long Revolution was an equally bold attempt to chart the long history of the emergence of British cultural modernity, thereby establishing much of the initial subject matter for what would become cultural studies. In its opening theoretical chapters, the argument concerning selective tradition is repeated and significantly elaborated upon. Here, however, Williams also develops his first systematic theorization of the concept of structure of feeling, by which he means "the culture of a period . . . the particular living result of all the elements in the general organization" (Williams 1965: 64). Such structures are neither universal nor class specific. Nor are they formally learned, he stresses, whence follows their often peculiarly generational character. The concept was to prove extraordinarily fruitful, both in his own work, where it appeared in *The English Novel*, for example, and in *Drama from Ibsen to Brecht*, and in the work of such critics as Eagleton, Jameson, and Said.

During the 1960s and 1970s Williams's writing ranged widely across the whole field of literary and cultural studies. His work on the theater and on television exhibited a growing awareness of the social conventionality of form and of the interrelationship between technology and form, thereby clearly drawing attention to the materiality of what Marxism had viewed as "ideal" superstructures. This led him, in turn, to a rejection of technological determinism and of the notion of a determined technology (Williams 1974: 12–13) and thence to a more complex understanding of the notion of determination itself. The cumulative effect of this work is finally registered theoretically in *Marxism and Literature*. Hitherto, Williams had understood culture as transcendent of class and yet irredeemably marked by it. For all the eloquence with which this position had been argued, it remained fundamentally incoherent, a circle that stubbornly refused to be squared. From the late 1960s, however, his engagement with Western Marxism, and especially Gramsci's *Prison Notebooks*, made it possible to explain how structures of feeling could be common to different classes, yet nonetheless represent the interests of some particular class.

The first and last chapters of the first part of *Marxism and Literature* are devoted to two key concepts and two keywords, deriving respectively from Leavisism and Marxism: "Culture" and "Ideology." Williams argues for the theoretical superiority over both of the Gramscian notion of hegemony, on the grounds that it successfully combines a "culturalist" sense of the wholeness of culture with a Marxist sense of the interestedness of ideology: "Hegemony is . . . in the strongest sense a 'culture,' but a culture which has also to be seen as the lived dominance and subordination of particular classes" (Williams 1977: 110). Culture is therefore neither "superstructural" nor "ideological" but, rather, "among the basic processes of the formation" (ibid: 111). Tradition now becomes not only selective, but also decisively important in the effective operation of hegemony and dependent on identifiably material institutions and "formations" (ibid: 115: 117–20).

Like Gramsci, Williams was concerned with the problem of counter-hegemony. The alternatives to hegemony include both the "emergent" and the "residual," he argues, for unlike the merely archaic, the residual can itself be oppositional or at least alternative in character. Thus, Williams distinguishes organized religion and the idea of rural community, each predominantly residual, from monarchy, which is merely archaic. It is the properly "emergent," however, that most interests him, those genuinely new meanings, values, practices, and kinds of relationship that are substantially alternative or oppositional to the dominant culture (ibid: 123). For Williams, the primary source of an emergent culture is likely to be a new social class. But there is a second source: "alternative perceptions of others, in immediate relationships; new perceptions and practices of the material world" (ibid: 126). For Williams, the exemplary instance of a new social class is the development of the modern working class. At the second level, however, the situation is much less clear: "No analysis is more difficult than that which, faced by new forms, has to try to determine whether these are new forms of the dominant or are genuinely emergent" (Williams 1981: 205).

Marxism and Literature offers an unusually interesting formulation of the problem. An emergent culture, Williams argues, will require not only distinct kinds of immediate cultural practice, but also and crucially "new forms or adaptations of forms." Such innovation at the level of form, he continues, "is in effect a *pre-emergence* , active and pressing but not yet fully articulated" (Williams 1977: 126). The concept of structure of feeling is brought back into play at this point. Previously, Williams had used it to denote both the immediately experiential and the generationally specific aspects of artistic process. Both emphases are retained, but are now joined to a quite new stress on pre-emergence. So structures of feeling "can be defined as social experiences *in solution,* as distinct from other social semantic formations which have been *precipitated"* (ibid: 133–4). In short, they are quite specifically counter-hegemonic.

The substantive question of the precise interplay between the emergent or pre-emergent and novelty within the dominant became especially pressing in Williams's later work. The key texts here are *Towards 2000* and the sadly unfinished, posthumously published *The Politics of Modernism.* Both attempted to reformulate the earlier aspiration to community and to culture as a whole way of life by way of a critique of "postmodern" appropriations of modernism and the mass media. Williams now saw late capitalism as itself effectively collapsing the distinction between minority and mass arts. So modernism, which once threatened to destablize the certainties of bourgeois life, has been transformed into a new "'postmodernist' establishment," which "takes human inadequacy . . . as self-evident" (Williams 1983: 141). The deep structures of this postmodernism are present in popular culture, moreover, as "debased forms of an anguished sense of human debasement" (ibid: 141–2). The "pseudo-radicalism" of postmodern art is thus neither pre-emergent nor emergent, but rather a moment of novelty within the dominant. Hence, Williams's urgent insistence on the need for an art that will "break out of the non-historical fixity of *post*modernism" so as to address itself "to a modern *future* in which community may be imagined again" (Williams 1989: 35).

Major Criticisms

Theoretically, William's work is sometimes identified with that of Thompson and Hoggart as similarly "culturalist." Culturalism, it is argued, is both empiricist and lacking in any adequate sense of structural determinacy. This is clearly caricature: Williams's work is in many respects intensely theoretical; his notion of determination fully compatible with a strong sense of structure. At least one of his erstwhile critics has had the good grace to admit as much (Eagleton 1989). Politically, Williams's socialism and nationalism can be criticized as articulating a residual, rather than emergent, structure of feeling, a particularly telling charge when made from a feminist vantage point: clearly, working-class Welsh community was sustained by a patriarchal sexual division of labor. There is evidence in Williams of a real attempt at solidarity with the new women's movement, especially when he identifies it as one of the major "resources for a journey of hope" (Williams 1983: 249–50). Nonetheless, he seems unable to theorize such questions of sexual politics with any real adequacy.

Bibliography

Eagleton, T. (ed.) (1989) *Raymond Williams: Critical Perspectives*. Cambridge: Polity Press.
Higgins, J. (1999) *Raymond Williams: Literature, Marxism and Cultural Materialism*. London: Routledge

Higgins, J. (ed.) (2000) *The Raymond Williams Reader*. Oxford: Blackwell.

Inglis, F. (1995) *Raymond Williams*. London: Routledge.

Milner, A. (2002) *Re-imagining Cultural Studies: The Promise of Cultural Materialism*. London: Sage.

Williams, R. (1963) *Culture and Society 1780–1950*. Harmondsworth: Penguin Books. First published London: Chatto and Windus, 1958.

Williams, R. (1965) *The Long Revolution*. Harmondsworth: Penguin Books. First published London: Chatto and Windus, 1961.

Williams, R. (1966) *Modern Tragedy*. London: Chatto and Windus.

Williams, R. (1968) *Drama from Ibsen to Brecht*. London: Chatto and Windus.

Williams, R. (1970) *The English Novel from Dickens to Lawrence*. London: Chatto and Windus.

Williams, R. (1973) *The Country and the City*. London: Chatto and Windus.

Williams, R. (1974) *Television: Technology and Cultural Form*. Glasgow: Fontana.

Williams, R. (1977) *Marxism and Literature*. Oxford: Oxford University Press.

Williams, R. (1981) *Culture*. Glasgow: Fontana.

Williams, R. (1983) *Towards 2000*. London: Chatto and Windus.

Williams, R. (1989) *The Politics of Modernism: Against the New Conformists*, ed. T. Pinkney. London: Verso.

41 | Slavoj Žižek

Anthony Elliott

Ideas
Antagonism □ Enjoyment □ Kernel of desire □ Lack

Major books
The Sublime Object of Ideology (1989)
Looking Awry (1991)
The Metastases of Enjoyment (1994)
The Ticklish Subject (1999)

Influences
Althusser □ Freud □ Lacan □ Marx

Biographical Details

Slavoj Žižek (b. 1949) is one of the most outstanding and influential social and cultural theorists to have come of age in Europe in recent years. He has been described as "the most scandalous thinker in recent memory," "the Giant of Ljubljana," and "reinventor of what was genuinely exciting and revolutionary about the Lacanian school." A member of the Slovene Lacanian school, whose practitioners include Miram Bozovic, Renata Salecl, and Mladen Dolor, two debut works established Žižek as the world's foremost Lacanian cultural critic. *The Sublime Object of Ideology* (1989) was a provocative reconstruction of critical theory from Marx to Althusser, informed by a dialectical reading of Lacanian psychoanalysis. *Looking Awry* (1991) offered a complementary account of the political underpinnings of Lacan's "return to Freud," and was composed of a multiplicity of discourses (communitarianism, universalism, feminism, postmodernism) from which Žižek untangled secret libidinal investments at work in everything from ideology and liberal democracies to perverse sexual relationships and detective thrillers.

His work has been an intriguing mix of Hegel and Hitchcock, Spinoza and science fiction, Marx and the Marx Brothers. His productivity has been nothing short of astonishing, with a new work delivered every year or so, including *For They Know Not What They Do* (1991), *Everything You Always Wanted to Know about Lacan (but were Afraid to Ask Hitchcock)* (1992), *Enjoy Your Symptom!* (1992), *Tarrying with the Negative* (1993), *The Metastases of Enjoyment* (1994), *The Invisible Remainder* (1996), *The Plague of Fantasies* (1998), and *The Ticklish Subject* (1999).

Key Theoretical Contributions

The social theory of Žižek involves a complex theoretical attempt to situate the problem of decentered subjectivity into an account of the political field as thoroughly multidimensional, contingent, discontinuous. Following Lacan, Žižek is profoundly critical of philosophical traditions that see social and political identities as deriving from objective interests, needs, or desires. His position, by contrast, locates the emergence of identity as a contingent process of linguistic articulation. A discursive process of political hegemony at once creates social and cultural identities and, in so doing, covers over that insufficiency which is understood to lie at the heart of subjectivity.

While Žižek, like many poststructuralist thinkers, has sought to overthrow the notion of the unified subject, at the same time he criticizes the poststructuralist perspective, especially the notion that meaning derives from a play of absolute differences. The problem with this totalization of difference, Žižek argues, is that it has no conceptual means of tracing linguistic effects back to the self-identity of speaking subjects. In poststructuralist thought the human subject is reduced to an effect of a presubjective process, analyzed variously as the text (Derrida), power (Foucault), or desire (Deleuze and Guattari). Against poststructuralism, Žižek argues in favor of a Lacanian account of the split and decentered subject. For Žižek, the difference hinges on that lack, insufficiency, and loss which fundamentally marks the desire of the human subject. In Lacan's theory the first object of the imaginary order is only perceived as existing once it becomes lost to the human subject. This impossibility of recovering the longed-for object is then further distorted when the subject enters the domain of symbolic representation, as the subject dissolves into those differences of language which, for Lacan, constitutes the unconscious. In Žižek's view, the *subject of lack* exists prior to any mode of subjectivization. It is the "empty place" of individuality which different modes of subjectivization attempt to repress and fill out.

In contrast to authors who view the source of social antagonism at the level of the conflict between "subject positions" (see, for example, Laclau and Mouffe 1985), Žižek tries to show how the Lacanian real order disrupts subjectivity as well as all social relations. To illustrate the force of this constitutive antagonism he refers to class and sexual ideologies in modern society. In these ideological antagonisms, he argues, human subjects attempt to forge a social relationship which is "impossible." This impossibility, according to the Laclau/Mouffe position, is not a result of objective contradictions nor oppositions, but an outcome of a fundamental split structuring these relations. This split is a form of ideological misrecognition, such that subjects believe that once capitalist or patriarchal oppression is destroyed a new form of social organization can be established that will permit the full realization of self-identity. The radicalization of human potentials in such ideologies is tied to the destruction of the external enemy, in this case either the "capitalist" or "male chauvinist." It is this ideological interpellation – that it is the *other* which prevents individual subjects from realizing their true human capacities – which gives social antagonisms, such as class and gender, their enduring force (Laclau and Mouffe 1985). According to Žižek, however, while these ideologies are undeniably alienating, critical discourse must realize that the constitutive antagonism arises from the lack of the subject itself. On this view, it is the subject who is marked by a pure antagonism – alienated through self-blockage, insufficiency, internal traumatism – which is then displaced on to the symbolic field.

From this Lacanian vantage point we can now see why an ideological formation can never be closed on itself, structured entirely within discursive/symbolic supports, but is at its core always radically decentered, lacking, and insufficient. Such a standpoint carries some important implications for the analysis of ideology. First, the counterpart to the notion of the subject of lack is a conception of ideology as social fantasy, as an attempt to "suture" this lack. On this view, the function of ideology is to provide men and women with a fantasized scenario of the possibility of their own social condition. Ideology, in short, provides an idealized vision of a "society" which in reality cannot exist. "Fantasy," writes Žižek, "is basically a scenario filling out the empty space of a fundamental impossibility, a screen masking a void" (Zizek 1989: 125). Secondly, subverting this realm of social fantasy should consequently be a social and political aim; such deconstruction is a fundamental task of the criticism of ideology. Social criticism ought to theorize the subject's lack of plenitude, unearthing that antagonism which ideological fantasy masks – a method of ideology critique which Žižek calls "going through the social fantasy."

One example of the displacing of a fundamental antagonism which runs through a good deal of Žižek's work is the case of antisemitism. Antisemitism, Žižek argues, is constituted through a symbolic over-determination of floating signifiers into the figure of the Jew. Structured by unconscious displacement, the fundamental antagonism of the social is reconfigured around the supposed threat of the Jew, thereby masking the impossibility of "society" itself. This displacement of antagonism on to Jews is then further libidinally condensed. In Žižek's view, these condensations operate variously as economic antagonisms (Jews as profiteering parasites), political antagonisms (Jews having a secret plot for world domination), sexual antagonisms (Jewish sexual desire as being animalistic or corrupt), and so forth.

The figure of the Jew is important to Žižek as a special case of that suturing of antagonism which occurs in the ideological sphere. Jews are defined as something Other in modernity and are thereby constructed as the destructive force within an otherwise harmonious society. This argument is extended in Žižek's consideration of the reemergence of antisemitism in Eastern Europe in the 1990s. Here Žižek argues that the hatred of the Jews which has arisen in the nationalist populism of Eastern European states is experienced by subjects as an imaginary "theft of enjoyment." On Žižek's reckoning, this imagined theft of pleasure is painful and unbearable precisely for the reason that it acts as a reminder of the "impossibility" of one's own enjoyment. The hatred of the other is thus a hatred of the self, the inversion of which is an essential trick of all racist ideologies. The figure of the Jew is therefore a particular embodiment of a fundamental antagonism, a failed sense of selfhood, a compensation for that imagined theft which leaves subjects insufficient and lacking.

In his most recent philosophical work, Žižek has revisited the notion of Cartesian subjectivity in a curious way. Rejection of the Cartesian subject lies at the core, says Žižek, of contemporary "radical" philosophy. Poststructuralists, postmodernists, deconstructionists, feminists: all are united in their disowning of the Cartesian heritage. However, Zizek's argument is, in fact, that radical politics requires a "philosophical manifesto of Cartesian subjectivity itself." As he develops this at the outset of *The Ticklish Subject*: "The point is not to return to the *cogito* in the guise in which this notion has dominated modern thought (the self-transparent thinking subject), but to bring to light its forgotten obverse, the excessive, unacknowledged kernel of the *cogito*, which is far from the pacifying image of the transparent Self" (Zizek 1999).

Žižek's *The Ticklish Subject* examines the relationship between philosophy and emancipatory politics. It is a profound essay in intellectual history, one that offers a scintillating critique of contemporary notions of the human subject. From Heidegger's attempt to outflank subjectivity, through the post-Althusserian politics of Etienne Balibar, Alain Badiou, and Jacques Ranciere, to the thesis of the risk society proposed by Anthony Giddens and Ulrich Beck, this rigorous history of subjectivity is conceived and colored by the author's determination to dissect metatheory as psychoanalytic flashpoints, while simultaneously restoring the secretly libidinal hankerings of philosophy itself.

Žižek argues that, in conditions of postmodernity, we inhabit spaces of "post-politics." Post-politics doesn't mean that politics is dead. On the contrary, contemporary politics is ideological through and through. Žižek thinks that, notwithstanding the collapse of communism and the rhetoric of the advanced capitalist societies as non-ideological, globalization has unleashed an insidious inner colonization of human subjects, one that penetrates to our most intimate selves and deepest libidinal recesses. Postmodern culture, says Žižek, is jaded. Alongside changes in technology and communication, the functioning of self and society has undergone an implosion of signs, symbols, and significations. The self, for Žižek, has become structured around a fetish of political apathy: "I know what I'm doing is meaningless, but still I do it nonetheless."

Major Criticisms

Žižek shares with many post-Lacanian theorists a common major problem: the tendency to imagine that one particular mode of subjectivity, namely the constitution of an immutable gap between self and others, is intrinsic to the nature of the unconscious imaginary itself. Against this view, it has been argued (Elliott 1999) that to study ideological forms is not to analyze an imaginary "covering" or "papering" of a deeper, ontological lack, but is rather concerned with exploring the ways in which imaginary creations engender self-constitutions that are autonomous/ enabling or alienating/repressive. The unconscious imaginary should not be seen as just some derivative realm, an attempt to "suture" an original lack in the subject. Rather, the unconscious imaginary is the capacity to create and transform something; it is inseparable from fantasy, representation, and affect. It is therefore pointless to search for a wider baseline, such as the Lacanian category of lack, from which ideology and cultural forms can be derived.

Further, in my view the key thesis of Žižek's late work – that the culture of postmodernism is contaminated by a fetishistic logic of disavowal, symbolic destitution, and masochistic deception – is faulty. For not only does this approach reproduce some of the most questionable assumptions in Marxist epistemology (do we really want to return to the dead-ends of Althusserianism?), but many of Žižek's theoretical conclusions enter into an embarrassing contradiction with his stated political goals. Whether one is in the grip of identity politics, reading Hegel, or simply watching Oprah Winfrey, these are for Žižek all instances of ideological fantasy aimed at effacing the sour taste of ontological lack, gap, and antagonism. Social differentiation and cultural discrimination are lost in this approach, as Žižek simply passes over the complex, contradictory ways in which people come to challenge or resist political ideologies.

It is perhaps strange that, like many cultural theorists who have turned to psychoanalysis, Žižek thinks we live in an age in which an establishment culture destroys creative ways of living. Much like Herbert Marcuse's vision of the "one-dimensional culture" or Theodor Adorno's theory of the "totally administered society," Žižek believes we lack the necessary collective agency to confront the disorder of global capitalism.

Bibliography

Elliott, A. (1999) *Social Theory and Psychoanalysis in Transition: Self and Society from Freud to Kristeva*, 2nd edn. London: Free Association Books.
Laclau, E. and Mouffe, C. (1985) *Hegemony and Socialist Strategy*. London: Verso.
Torfling, J. (1999) *New Theories of Discourse: Laclau, Mouffe and Zizek*. Oxford: Blackwell.
Wright, E. and Wright, E. (eds.) (1999) *The Zizek Reader*. Oxford: Blackwell.
Žižek, S. (1989) *The Sublime Object of Ideology*. London: Verso.
Žižek, S. (1990a) "Beyond Discourse-Analysis." In E. Laclau (ed.) *New Reflections on the Revolution of our Time*. London: Verso.
Žižek, S. (1990b) "Eastern Europe's Republics of Gilead." *New Left Review*, 183.
Žižek, S. (1991a) *For They Know Not What They Do*. London: Verso.
Žižek, S. (1991b) *Looking Awry*. Cambridge, MA: MIT Press.
Žižek, S. (1992a) *Enjoy Your Symptom!* New York: Routledge.
Žižek, S. (1992b) *Everything You Always Wanted to Know about Lacan (but were Afraid to Ask Hitchcock)*. London: Verso.
Žižek, S. (1993) *Tarrying with the Negative*. Durham, NC: Duke University Press.
Žižek, S. (1994) *The Metastases of Enjoyment*. London: Verso.
Žižek, S. (1996) *The Invisible Remainder*. London: Verso.
Žižek, S. (1998) *The Plague of Fantasies*. London: Verso.
Žižek, S. (1999) *The Ticklish Subject*. London: Verso.

Index